FROM DELIVERANCE TO DESTRUCTION
Rebellion and Civil War in an English City

'From Deliverance to Destruction' is a study of the city of Exeter during the Great Civil War. It is not intended to supersede the excellent accounts of seventeenth-century Exeter's demography, economy and administration which already exist, but rather to offer a lively, immediate account of how one English city slid inexorably into chaos.

The book begins with a discussion of the relevant historiography, and a general introduction to Exeter. It goes on to examine the political and religious divisions which had existed within the city long before the national conflict broke out, paying particular attention to the tensions which were caused by the pre-war drive for moral reformation led by the puritan patriarch, Ignatius Jurdain. Chapter Four shows how, under the pressure of external events, the civic community split into two rival camps during the period 1637–42. The final chapters deal with the events of the war itself, and with the three major sieges which Exeter underwent between 1642 and 1646.

The book is accompanied by a large collection of transcripts from original seventeenth-century documents. These have been specially selected with the student and general reader in mind, and they draw on Exeter's experiences to illustrate the nature of the Civil War as a whole. The documents not only buttress the main text, but also provide a valuable teaching resource. They illuminate the conflict's effect on ordinary English men and women, and show just how closely engaged the people were with the national politico-religious debate.

EXETER STUDIES IN HISTORY
General Editors: Jonathan Barry, Tim Rees
and T.P. Wiseman

Also in the Exeter Studies in History series:

Security and Defence in South West England before 1800
edited by Robert Higham (1987)

Landscape and Townscape in the South West
edited by Robert Higham (1989)

Unity and Variety: A History of the Church in Devon and Cornwall
edited by Nicholas Orme (1991)

Maps and History in South-West England
edited by Katherine Barker and Roger Kain (1991)

Also by Mark Stoyle:

*Loyalty and Locality: Popular Allegiance in Devon
during the English Civil War* (1994)

FROM DELIVERANCE TO DESTRUCTION
Rebellion and Civil War in an English City

Mark Stoyle

UNIVERSITY
of
EXETER
PRESS

First published in 1996 by
University of Exeter Press
Reed Hall, Streatham Drive
Exeter, Devon EX4 4QR
UK
www.exeterpress.co.uk

Printed digitally since 2010

© Mark Stoyle 1996

The right of Mark Stoyle to be identified as author of this work has been asserted by him in accordance with the Copyright, Designs and Patents Act 1988.

British Library Cataloguing in Publication Data
A catalogue record for this book is
available from the British Library

ISBN 978 0 85989 478 4

Typeset in 10/12pt Monotype Plantin by
Kestrel Data, Exeter

To My Parents

Contents

List of documents	ix
List of illustrations and tables	xi
List of abbreviations	xiii
Acknowledgements	xv
Introduction	1
1: 'The Centre, Heart and Head of the West': Exeter before the Civil War	5
2: 'Zealous to Advance God's Glory': Ignatius Jurdain and the Puritan Dynamic	19
3: 'The Times Grow More Dangerous': The Descent into Civil War	38
4: 'Rebel City': Exeter under Parliamentarian Control	62
5: 'Reduced into the Power of His Sacred Majestie': Royalist Exeter, 1643–45	86
6: 'Close Begirt': The Final Siege	109
Conclusion	136
Notes	143
Documents	165
Tables	223
Index	227

List of Documents

1. Extracts from the chronicle of James White, 1640–41	165
2. The Parliament's Protestation	167
3. Extracts from a sermon by John Bond	168
4. Extracts from the chronicle of James White, 1641-42	170
5. Extract from an assize sermon	171
6. Extracts from the Chamber Act Book, 1642	173
7. Parliament intervenes in affairs at Exeter	176
8. Information given to the city sessions court, 1642	177
9. Extracts from the Chamber Act Book, 1642	178
10. The Exeter Covenant	180
11. Summons and response, 1642	182
12. Instructions for the city's defence	184
13. The 'Reformation' of the cathedral	187
14. Information presented to the city sessions court, 1643	188
15. Treatment of a suspected spy	189
16. The sufferings of Dr Whynell	192
17. Death of a bystander	194
18. Letter from one of the besieged	195
19. The siege of 1643: a Parliamentarian account	197
20. The siege of 1643: a Royalist account	198
21. Attack and surrender, 1643	199
22. Articles for the surrender of Exeter, 1643	201
23. Extract from a Parliamentarian news-book	203
24. List of the city ordnance	205
25. Information presented to the city sessions court, 1644	207
26. The Oath of Association	208
27. Petition of Honor Crutchett	209
28. The Exeter Oath	210
29. Summons and response, 1646	211
30. Treaty of surrender, 1646	214

31.	Description of Exeter's defences	219
32.	Provision for wounded Roundhead veterans	219
33.	Petition of Jeffrey Downing	220
34.	Petition of Christopher Boast	221
35.	Petition of Valentine Bishop	221

List of Illustrations and Tables

Maps

1. South West England	6
2. Exeter in the Early Seventeenth Century	13
3. Military Operations around Exeter, Summer 1643	79
4. Exeter's Royalist Fortifications	110
5. Parliamentary Dispositions near Exeter, late 1645	113
6. Military Operations around Exeter, early 1646	122

Plates

1. View of Exeter by Robert Sherwood, *c.* 1620–30	8
2. View of Exeter by Robert Sherwood, *c.* 1620–30	10

Tables

1. Attendance at Chamber Meetings, 1636–42	223
2. Attendance at Chamber Meetings, 1642–43	224
3. Attendance at Chamber Meetings, 1643–46	225

List of Abbreviations

BL	British Library, London
Bod.	Bodleian Library, Oxford
CAM	M.A.E. Green (ed.), *Calendar of the Committee for Advance of Money, 1643–56*, (three volumes, 1881)
CCC	M.A.E. Green (ed.), *Calendar of the Committee for Compounding, 1643–60*, (five volumes, 1882–92)
CJ	*Journal of the House of Commons*
CRO	Cornish Record Office, Truro
CSPD	*Calendar of State Papers Domestic*
CWA	Churchwardens' Accounts
D&C	Dean and Chapter
DCA	Dean and Chapter Archives, Exeter
DCNG	*Devon and Cornwall Notes and Gleanings*
DCNQ	*Devon and Cornwall Notes and Queries*
DCRS	Devon and Cornwall Record Society
DNB	*Dictionary of National Biography*
DRO	Devon Record Office, Exeter
E	Thomason Tracts, kept in the British Library
ECAB	Exeter Chamber Act Book, kept at the DRO
EHR	*English Historical Review*
ECL	Exeter Cathedral Library
EMAFU	Exeter Museums Archaeological Field Unit
EQSOB	Quarter Sessions Order Books for the City of Exeter, kept at the DRO
EQSR	Quarter Sessions Rolls for the City of Exeter, kept at the DRO
ERB	Exeter Receivers' Books, kept at the DRO
ERR	Exeter Receivers' Rolls, kept at the DRO
ERV	Exeter Receivers' Vouchers, kept at the DRO
HJ	*Historical Journal*

HMC	*Historical Manuscripts Commission*
JEH	*Journal of Ecclesiastical History*
KAO	Kent Archives Office
LJ	*Journal of the House of Lords*
Nd	No date of publication
P&P	*Past and Present*
PDAS	*Proceedings of the Devon Archaeological Society*
PRO	Public Record Office, London
QSB	Quarter Sessions Rolls for the County of Devon, kept at the DRO
QSOB	Quarter Sessions Order Books for the County of Devon, kept at the DRO
SP	State Papers
SRO	Somersetshire Record Office, Taunton
TDA	*Report and Transactions of the Devonshire Association.*
WCSL	West Country Studies Library, Exeter

Acknowledgements

Much of this book was written and researched under the auspices of Exeter Museums Archaeological Field Unit (now Exeter Archaeology). Nobody has contributed more to my work than Chris Henderson, the Director of Exeter Archaeology, and I am deeply grateful to him, not only for permission to reproduce sections of EMAFU reports 88.12 and 90.26, but also for his friendship, inspiration and advice over the course of the past decade. An only slightly smaller debt is owed to George Bernard, for his warm encouragement and wise counsel. Simon Baker, Jonathan Barry, Ian Roy and David Underdown all read and commented on earlier versions of the text and I have benefited greatly from their suggestions. Tom Dixon and Mike Rouillard drew the illustrations; the staff of the Devon Record Office, Exeter Cathedral Archives Office and Devon and Exeter Institution were efficent and helpful, as always. Among the many people who have supplied me with ideas and information, I should like to thank Gerald Aylmer, Stuart Blaylock, Alastair Duke, Todd Gray, Jannine Juddery, Susan Lawrence, John Morrill, Stephen Porter, Tim Reuter, Kevin Sharpe, Pam Wakeham and Peter Weddell. Most of all, I would like to thank my parents, my sister and my wife—last in this list, but highest in my affections.

Mark Stoyle,
University of Southampton, August 1995

Introduction

What was the response of the great provincial cities of England—Exeter, Bristol, Newcastle, Norwich and York—to the outbreak of the Civil War? Twenty years ago historians were confident that they knew the answer to this question. Taking Roger Howell's pioneering study of Newcastle as a model, they characterized the provincial urban response as essentially 'neutral', or 'localist': arguing that such communities, too remote and inward-looking to be interested in the quarrel between King and Parliament, had done their best to keep out of the national conflict until they were dragged into it as the result of 'an artificial injection of violence' from the centre.[1] This historiographical approach was enormously influential at the time, and has continued to affect the scholarly view of political attitudes in provincial cities ever since. In recent years, both Bristol—the second city of the kingdom—and York—the regional capital of the North—have been portrayed as communities in which there were 'no signs' of any partisan political movements before the Civil War, and in which 'the search for a safe neutrality persisted' until as late as possible.[2] More generally, it has been assumed that the conflict of the early 1640s was the cause, not the result, of local divisions: that it was only after the events of the Civil War had fractured the traditional culture of consensus in provincial English cities that the formation of political parties could begin.[3]

This localist viewpoint was itself grounded in the work of an earlier generation of scholars, who had emphasized the extent to which the provincial cities of early modern England retained a corporate, essentially medieval, outlook. Nowhere was the argument for a fundamental continuity in urban provincial attitudes more elegantly expressed than in W.T. MacCaffrey's classic study of Exeter, the regional capital of South

West England. In a seminal passage, MacCaffrey wrote that, at Exeter, 'the borough community . . . [had] embraced every important aspect of the townsman's life: political . . . religious and social . . . For him the city precincts were the limits of the world, and the greater world of England and Englishmen loomed hazily over its parapets. Primary social loyalties were still owed to the local community, and the individual reacted to the larger movements of society not as an Englishman but as a townsman of Exeter'.[4] These words—evoking as they did the image of a city which was close-knit, harmonious and above all a *community* —served as the perfect exposition of the localist viewpoint, while the effect of MacCaffrey's work as a whole was to convince scholars that Exeter itself had been a localist paradigm: the very model of the introspective English provincial city.

A re-examination of the situation in Exeter casts serious doubt on MacCaffrey's conclusions—and on the entire localist argument which his book helped to underpin. As the first part of this book will show, early Stuart Exeter was not a united community, but a city in which ideological consensus had already started to break down. By the 1620s and 1630s the inhabitants were taking an increasing interest in national affairs, and by the early 1640s nascent political parties had begun to form. The reaction of Exeter's ruling body to the national crisis of 1642 was not, moreover, one of neutralism or simple incomprehension. Rather, the city's governors sought to subdue the King's local supporters, while at the same time moving Exeter slowly but firmly into the Parliamentarian camp. In all these respects Exeter's experiences closely resembled those of Norwich: a provincial city which, as J.T. Evans has shown, was riven by ideological divisions throughout the immediate pre-war period.[5] Historians have tended to see Norwich as somewhat precocious and untypical.[6] Yet on the basis of the evidence from Exeter, of recent research on Bristol and of the trend of general studies elsewhere it is tempting to suggest that the 'partisan' response to the outbreak of the Civil War has at least as much right as the 'localist' one to be regarded as the typical reaction of provincial English cities.[7]

If the strength of localist sentiment during the pre-war period has been exaggerated, then so has the strength of neutralism during the war itself. In the 1970s it became fashionable to portray the English Civil War as a conflict in which the vast majority of the populace had been uninterested. This view was summed up perfectly by David Underdown when he spoke of the war having been waged 'between two minorities,

INTRODUCTION

struggling in a sea of apathy'.[8] Underdown has since modified his opinion, however, and has himself led an exhilarating charge against what is still the dominant orthodoxy: stressing that ordinary people could and did take sides, and that their choice was often informed by their own religious and political beliefs.[9] Once again the evidence from Exeter supports this view. I have demonstrated elsewhere that the city split apart into clearly defined camps during 1642-46, with different parishes supporting different sides.[10] This book further illustrates the extent of wartime division in Exeter and shows how pre-existent splits were exacerbated by the pressures of the war.

If scholars are still divided over the extent of popular commitment during the English Civil War, there is now general agreement that the conflict's physical and emotional impact was enormous. Over the last decade, the work of many historians—most notably Donald Pennington, Stephen Porter and Ian Roy—has revealed that the fighting impinged on almost every aspect of day-to-day life, and that the inhabitants of towns and cities were particularly badly affected.[11] Exeter was no exception and, as the final chapters of this book will demonstrate, the citizens had to contend with taxation, free-quarter, forced labour, impressment and disease—not to mention the destruction of many of their houses for defensive purposes. As the war took on a momentum of its own, the wishes of the civilian population were increasingly subordinated to those of the military commanders on both sides. Accustomed civic procedures began to break down in the face of this challenge and from 1643 onwards local records began to be less conscientiously kept than hitherto. From a historian's point of view, therefore, the situation in Exeter becomes increasingly obscured by the fog of war, and this is reflected in the structure of the book, which gradually, but necessarily, develops from an account of internal rivalries into a more purely military narrative.

The wide range of contemporary documents contained in the appendices to this book (each of which is introduced at the appropriate point in the text) are intended to add depth and human detail to the main narrative. They have been chosen partly to illustrate the partisan sense of commitment which motivated so many local people during the 1640s, and partly to give an impression of what it was like to live through the conflict. Together the documents provide a vivid collection of eyewitness accounts and individual testimonies, all of them serving to illuminate the grim, dark road which led from deliverance to destruction.

1

'The Centre, Heart and Head of the West'
Exeter before the Civil War

Hath the Lord placed this citty in the midst of our county, as a beacon upon a hill, yea, as the center, heart and head of the West, and shall this beacon not blaze . . . in every part, when there is holy, loyall, refining fire put into it by so great authority?[1]

This rhetorical question—put by John Bond, preacher of Exeter, to his listeners on the very eve of the Civil War—bears witness to a city which was in some ways remarkably similar to the Exeter of today, yet in other ways almost inconceivably different. Exeter is still the regional capital of South West England: still the 'centre, heart and head of the West' to use Bond's term (see map 1, p. 6). The city is still surrounded by the rich county of Devon, still embraced by the rolling green hills which provide such a vivid backdrop to Exeter's ancient red sandstone buildings. The sense of pride which Bond so clearly felt in his native city, moreover, is still shared by many present-day inhabitants of Exeter. But this apart, the links between the mental world of seventeenth-century Exonians and that of their late twentieth-century counterparts are few. The Exeter of the 1990s is a peaceful, rather sleepy, place, the Exeter of the early 1640s was a city in ferment. During 1641 men like Bond, emboldened by the 'great authority' of Parliament, lit a spiritual flame in Exeter, hoping that it would 'refine', or purify, the civic community. Instead that fire ran out of control over the next five years eventually transforming itself—through a tangled process of political turmoil, rebellion and civil war—into a

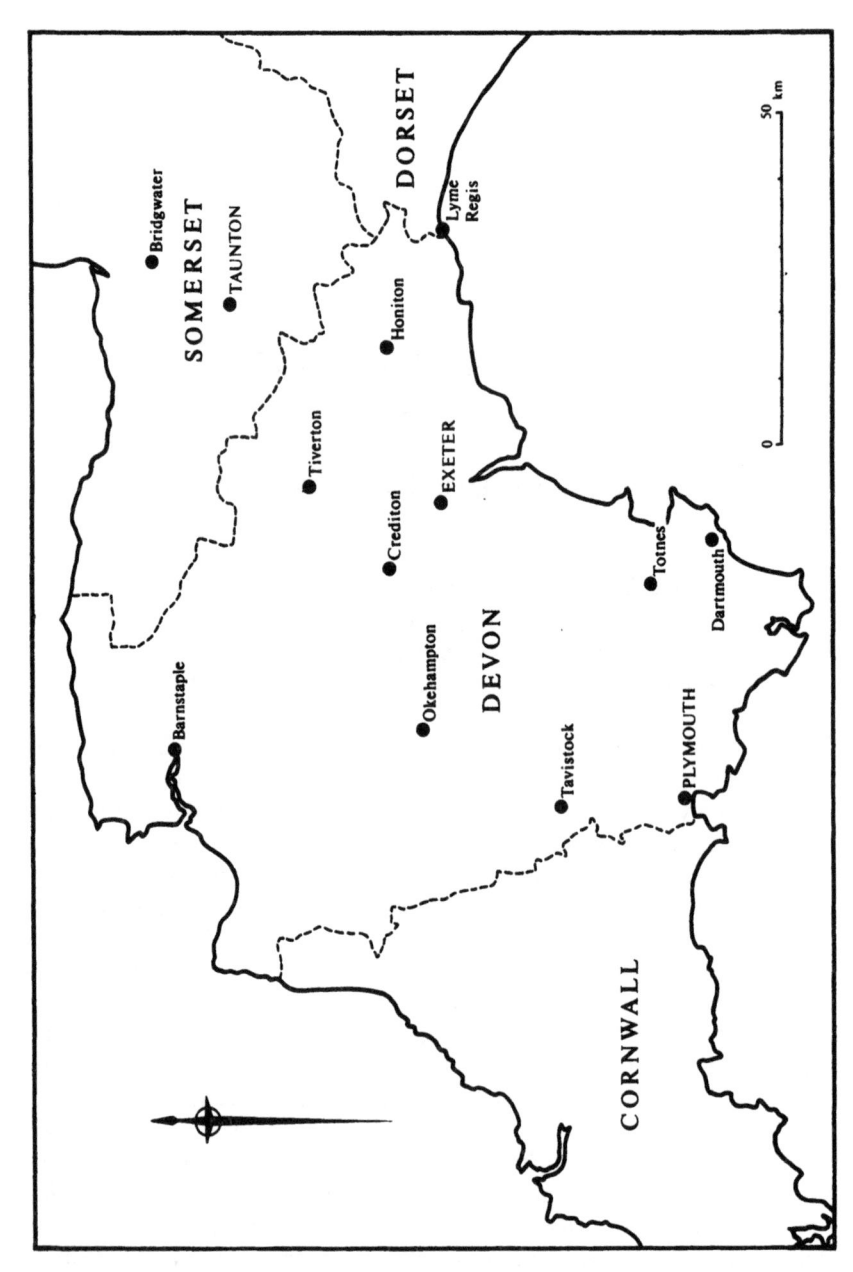

Map 1. South West England

physical conflagration which would reduce perhaps a third of the city to ashes. It is with the events of the period 1641-46—the most tumultuous in Exeter's recorded history—that this book is chiefly concerned. Yet before warming our hands at the bonfire of the 1640s, we should first consider the mixture of combustible materials from which that blaze was formed. The present chapter gives a portrait of Exeter as it was before the war began.

The Physical Background

During the early seventeenth century Exeter was the fifth largest city in the kingdom.[2] A vibrant, busy, bustling place, it contained a castle, a cathedral and nineteen parish churches: well over 10,000 people lived here in 1642.[3] A good idea of Exeter's general appearance at this time can be gained from the sketches which were made around 1620 by Robert Sherwood, the city surveyor. Sherwood eventually completed two full-scale drawings of Exeter, both of which are preserved in the civic archives (see plates 1 and 2).[4] Somewhat clumsy, even naive in style, these drawings have seldom been reproduced before, doubtless because the earlier map of Exeter engraved by Remegius Hogenberg in 1584-85 is so much sharper and so much more skilfully executed.[5] Yet idiosyncratic as they are, Robert Sherwood's forgotten plans provide a unique visual record of early Stuart Exeter.

What were the salient features of the city which Sherwood saw spread out before him over 350 years ago? The first thing which strikes one from the most detailed drawing (plate 1) is the remarkable compactness of early Stuart Exeter. As the sketch shows, much of the city was still contained within the medieval town wall. Over a mile long, and studded with towers and buttresses, this ancient defensive circuit was pierced by five major gateways: East Gate, South Gate, North Gate, West Gate and Quay Gate. Of these, Quay Gate—built in the south-west corner of the city during the 1560s in order to allow goods to be brought into Exeter from the quayside—was the most modest, consisting of little more than an archway cut through the wall. (The quay itself can be seen to the right of the gate on Sherwood's plan, together with the quay house and boats unloading cargo.) West Gate and North Gate were rather larger, but because the city was naturally well protected on these two sides—by the River Exe in the former case and by the Longbrook valley in the latter—little had been done to update them since the late medieval

7

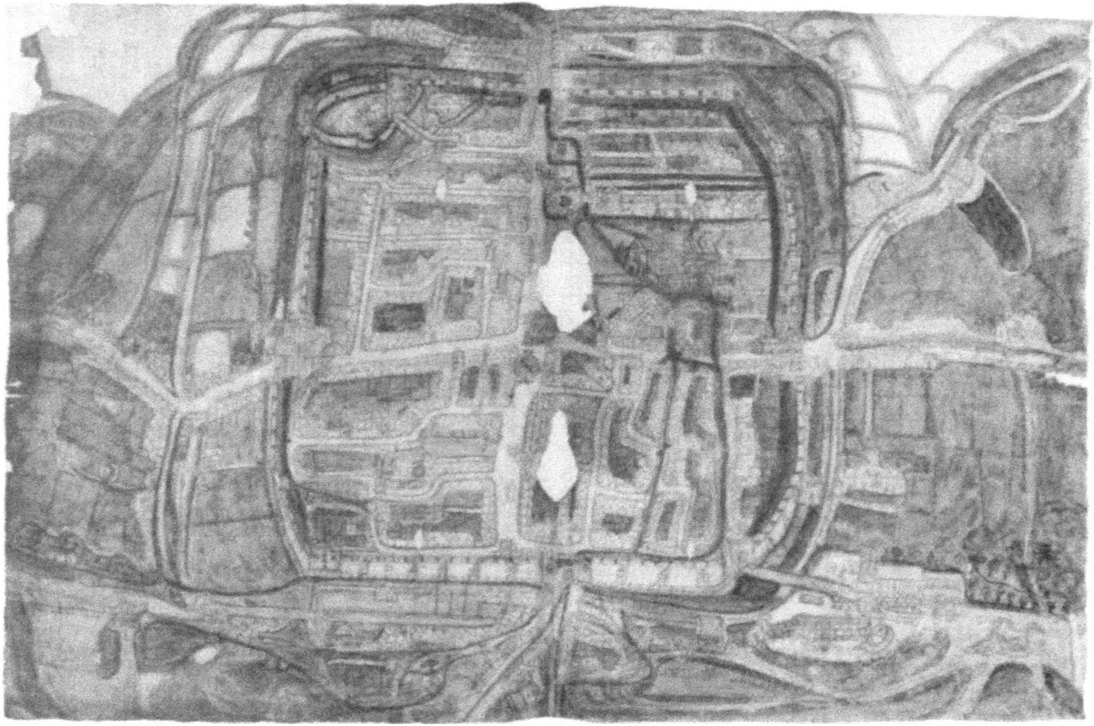

Plate 1. View of Exeter by Robert Sherwood, c. 1620–30

period. East Gate and South Gate were far more impressive. Both boasted huge defensive drum towers, while South Gate, the biggest gate of them all, incorporated the main civic prison within its forbidding walls.[6]

As Sherwood's plan reveals, Exeter's chief axis lay east to west, along the broad thoroughfare known as High Street. What would a traveller have seen if he had walked down this street in the years immediately before the Civil War? The first sight to greet him as he emerged from the dark arch of East Gate would have been the Little Conduit, the 'water fountain' which stood in the roadway some distance ahead. (Like Exeter's other conduits, this structure was supplied with water brought into the city from the suburban parish of St Sidwells, along a remarkable system of lead pipes and stone passageways buried deep underground.[7]) As the traveller strolled westwards, through the rich parishes of St Lawrence, St Stephen and All-Hallows Goldsmith Street, he would have seen much to catch his eye, either glittering on the baulks of the shops, or on the stalls which were erected in the High Street on market days.[8]

Having passed by All Hallows, the traveller might then have paused to admire the next major structure facing out onto the High Street: the Guildhall. This ancient building, the centre of civic government since the medieval period, had been refaced in the Italian style during the 1590s and its white facade—profusely decorated with columns and carvings—made an impressive sight.[9] A little below the Guildhall stood Broad Gate: the main entrance to the Cathedral Close from High Street. Gazing through this medieval gateway, the traveller would have been able to drink in the spectacle of Exeter's gothic cathedral, by far the largest and most imposing building in the city. From Broad Gate he could then have made his way further down High Street to Carfax (ie. Quatrefoix, or 'four ways'). This was the focal point of early Stuart Exeter, the place at which the city's three main thoroughfares—High Street, North Street and South Street—all met. Beside the road junction stood another 'fountain' known as the Great Conduit. Much bigger and grander than its counterpart at East Gate, the Great Conduit was a favourite meeting point for the citizens. Beneath the pinnacles of this imposing gothic structure, groups of women would queue for hours, chatting, chaffing and occasionally even fighting as they waited to fill their buckets.[10] The town authorities used the conduit as a backdrop for important civic occasions. Ministers were hired to preach here, and on the accession of a new monarch it was customary to proclaim the news

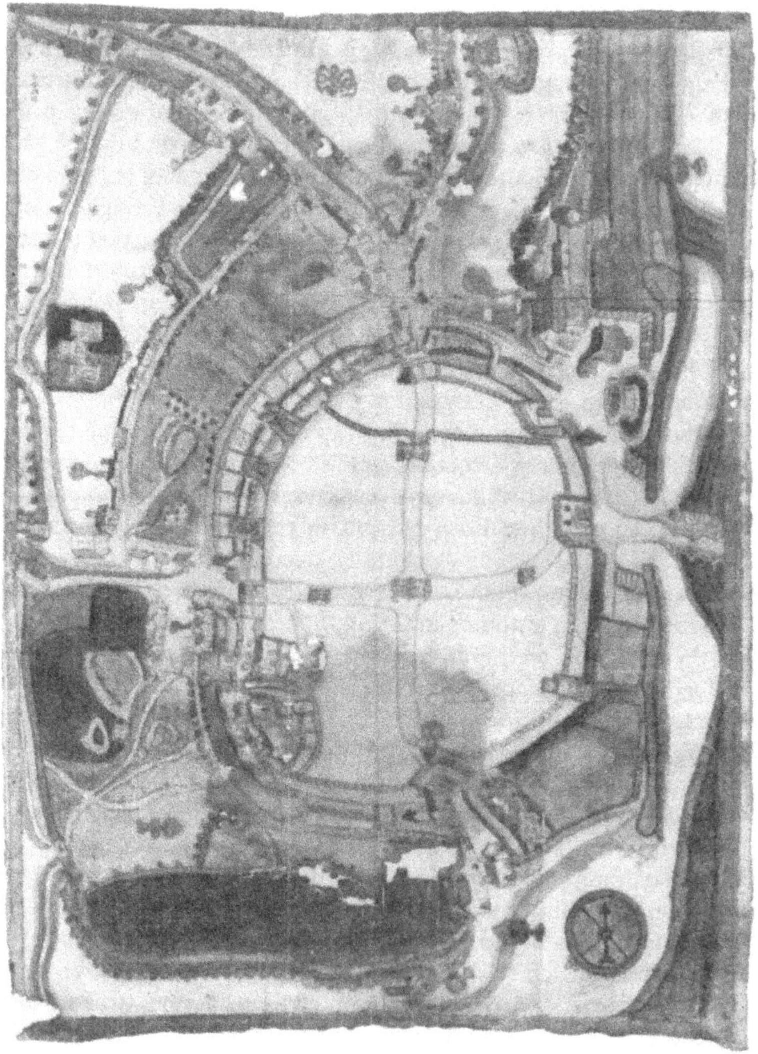

Plate 2. View of Exeter by Robert Sherwood, c. 1620–30

at Carfax.[11] A crowd of idlers, loafers and gossips could be found here at almost any time. If one wanted to find out what was going on in early Stuart Exeter, the Great Conduit was the place to come.

A little beyond Carfax, High Street starts to slope steeply downhill towards the river. In a city where sanitary facilities were rudimentary at best, it was unpleasant to live at the foot of a slope, and as the traveller strode through this less desirable part of High Street (now Fore Street) he would have noted the buildings around him becoming increasingly mean and shabby. Passing by St John's Bow he would finally have arrived at the church of All-Hallows on the Walls. This building—as its name suggests—stood immediately next to the city wall, and can be seen on plate 1 rising high above the battlements near West Gate. During the 1600s High Street proper came to an end here so, in order to reach West Gate, the traveller would have had to turn left and walk down a side road. Once arrived at the gate, he could have faced about and returned to Carfax again via Stepcote Hill. This cobbled street—the lower portion of which still survives—gives a good impression of what Exeter would have looked like during the 1600s (although today's pedestrians are spared the blood and guts which then flowed down the gutter from the butchers' shops in Butcher Row). Stepcote Hill was known as 'Strip-coat hill' in the seventeenth century, presumably because the ascent here is so steep.[12]

Stepcote Hill stands in the South Quarter of Exeter: the district between South Gate and West Gate. As Sherwood's map shows, this area was densely populated during the 1600s, with houses and gardens filling almost every available space. This was also true of the West Quarter: the area between West Gate and North Gate. The one large open space here was Friernhay, a rectangular plot of land in the north-west corner of the city, where the citizens stretched their cloth (the racks employed in this process can be clearly seen on plate 1. Only in the 1630s did a change come about, when the city authorities decided to convert Friernhay into a graveyard.[13] This decision caused alarm among local residents (presumably because they were afraid that the scheme might expose them to disease) and when workmen arrived to convert the site in 1636 a crowd of local women confronted the Mayor and 'oppose[d] that worke'.[14] Despite this initial opposition the scheme was quickly pushed through, and the new graveyard opened for business in 1637.

Many of the parishes in the South and West Quarters were poor, particularly those which lay closest to the river. It was in the middle of Exeter that the most prosperous parishes could be found: St Mary Arches and St Olaves in the West Quarter, St Kerrian and All-Hallows Goldsmith Street in the North Quarter (the district between North Gate and East Gate), and St Stephens, St Martins and St Petrocks in the East Quarter (the district between East Gate and South Gate) (see map 2, p. 13). Most of the wealth and power in early Stuart Exeter was concentrated in this 'golden heart'—almost all the members of the city's ruling élite lived in these parishes—and the further one moved away from Carfax, the meaner the houses tended to become. The intra-mural areas which lay next to the city walls were almost uniformly poor, and this was also true of the extensive city suburbs.[15]

Seventeenth-century Exeter possessed five main suburban areas. To the north lay the parish of St Davids, whose inhabitants mostly worked in the cloth trade, or in husbandry. To the east lay St Sidwells, the largest and most unruly of the suburban parishes; well over 1,500 people lived here in 1642.[16] Many of them were very poor, and the parish was notorious for riots and popular disturbances. To the south lay Holy Trinity parish. Unlike St Davids and St Sidwells, Trinity contained an intra-mural as well as an extra-mural area. Needless to say, it was in the former district that the most prosperous parishioners tended to dwell; Trinity parish without the walls was as poverty-stricken as St Sidwells.[17] The fourth suburban area lay on the west side of Exeter, between the city and the River Exe. Two crowded and populous little parishes stood here, St Edmonds and St Mary Steps. The West Quarter was heavily industrialized (the chief trade being that of cloth-making) and the area was considered to be rough and dangerous.

Across the River Exe lay St Thomas. Although outside the city boundaries and therefore not an Exeter parish in the strictest sense, St Thomas was integral to the local economy, and for all practical purposes can be classed as one of the city suburbs. Like the other suburban areas, St Thomas was densely populated; during the 1650s it was claimed that almost 2,000 people dwelt here.[18] All in all, there were probably around half as many people living in the suburbs of Exeter in 1642 as dwelt within the city walls.[19]

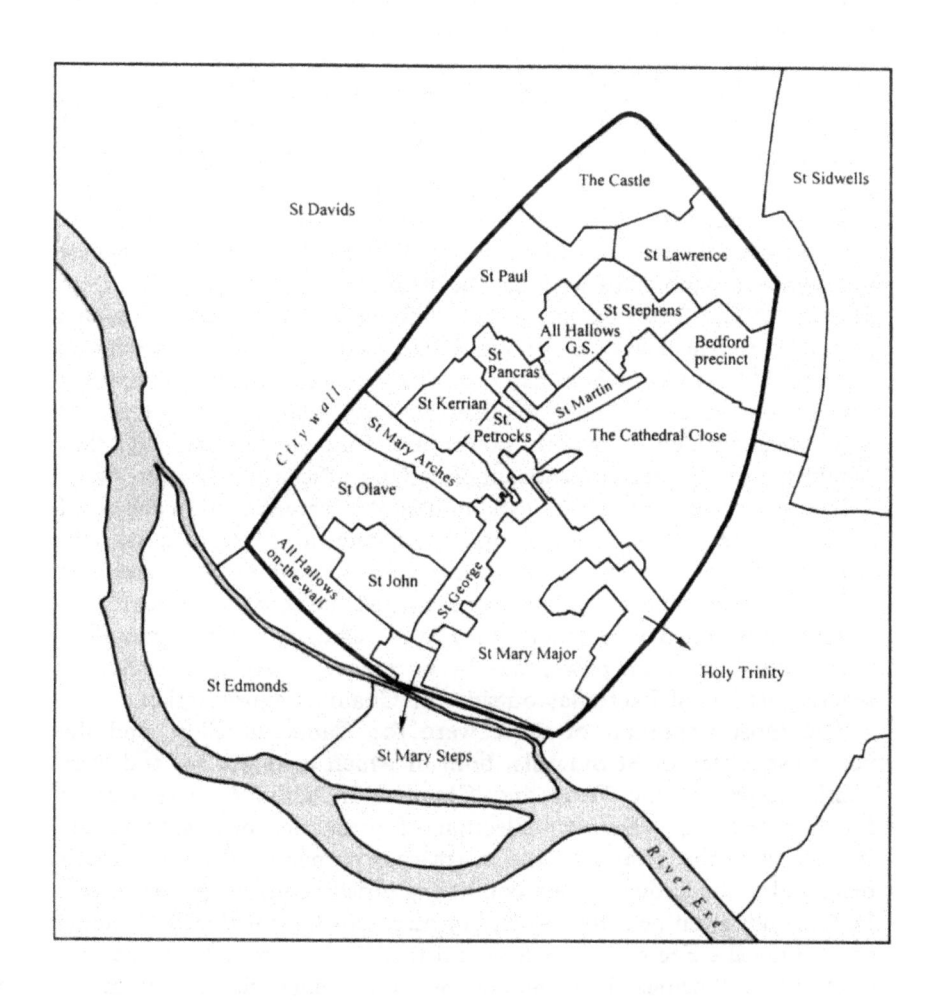

Map 2. Exeter in the Early Seventeenth Century

Civic Government

Responsibility for the governance of Exeter and its suburbs lay with the Chamber, or Council of Twenty Four: a body of twenty-four rich and influential men, who controlled the city's affairs from their headquarters at the Guildhall. The workings of the early Stuart Chamber have been admirably delineated by W.T. MacCaffrey and little more needs to be said about this complicated subject here. The chief point to stress is that the Chamber was not an elected body, but a self co-opting one; in the event of a sitting councillor dying or being dismissed, it was the surviving members who selected his replacement—usually from amongst the wealthy mercantile families who formed the civic elite. The Chamber's power was self-perpetuating, therefore, and the great mass of the inhabitants had little or no say in the Council's composition. Only at the annual mayoral elections—when the city freemen were entitled to decide between two candidates who had been selected by the Chamber from amongst themselves—was any outside influence in the Chamber's affairs permitted.[20] The mayor and the aldermen—the eight most prestigious city councillors, all of whom had previously served as mayors themselves—were the real governors of Exeter. They and their more junior colleagues wielded enormous power and influence in the city; they administered its finances and appointed its officials; they oversaw its defences and commanded the local militia; they served as MPs and acted as the government's local agents; they determined legal cases and regulated trade; they saw to the maintenance of civic property and kept an eye on charitable bequests; they managed the relief of the poor and expelled unwanted immigrants: they even regulated popular morals.[21] The councillors' local power was by no means absolute, however, for several districts of Exeter lay outside the Chamber's jurisdiction.

The most important of these were the Cathedral Close and the ecclesiastical fee of St Sidwells, both of which belonged to, and were administered by, the Dean and Chapter. In addition there was St Stephens Fee, a scattered collection of properties belonging to the Bishop, and the castle, in the north-east corner of the city, which belonged to the Crown. These conflicting jurisdictions caused problems. Few people dwelt near the castle, but hundreds lived within the bounds of St Sidwell's Fee and the Close and therefore lay outside the control of the city authorities. The Chamber actively resented this and, from the medieval period onwards, its officials made frequent attempts to arrest, fine and otherwise harass the Chapter's tenants. The clergymen fiercely resisted these attempts to encroach upon their jurisdiction, however, and enlisted powerful friends at Court to help them maintain their position.[22] Assisted by such backers, the Chapter usually managed to repel the Chamber's assaults and in 1600 they still maintained the vast majority of their ancient privileges. Exeter's civic leaders were constantly reminded of this galling fact by a series of stout wooden gateways which stood at the various entrances to the Close, and were locked by the cathedral porter every night.

Life in the City

Wherever one lived in early modern Exeter, life was hard and the future uncertain. Illness and disease stalked the city, and could strike at any time. Plague swept away literally thousands of Exonians in the 1620s and many more died as a result of a typhus epidemic during the Civil War.[23] Such major outbreaks were rare, but the city was an intrinsically unhealthy place and the citizens were constantly exposed to all sorts of dangerous infections. Even quite minor physical ailments were difficult to treat at this time and could cause excruciating pain. Toothache was especially feared, and Nicholas Vaughan received handsome payment for his services as a tooth-drawer during the 1640s.[24] Fatal accidents were commonplace, and people were regularly drowned in the River Exe.[25] Other luckless individuals were thrown from horses or flattened by falling trees.[26] As if this catalogue of accidental deaths and injuries were not enough, there was a high level of interpersonal violence too. Men fought each other with staves, swords and daggers, while both sexes were handy with their fists.[27]

Judicial violence added to the toll of suffering. Exeter women convicted of being 'scolds', or gossips, were placed in a contraption known as the Cucking-Stool and ducked in the Exe. Alternatively they might be dragged down the river behind a boat.[28] Men convicted of drunkenness or theft were locked in the stocks.[29] For 'idle livers' and fornicators the penalties were harsher still. Such persons were publicly whipped: either at the ring beneath the Guildhall or at the city workhouse. (Punishments of ten, fifteen or even twenty lashes were regularly meted out in both places.[30]) Those of whom the authorities wished to make a special example were roped behind a cart and paraded through the streets. One poor woman, convicted of sexual incontinence in 1619, was ordered to be whipped at the cart's tail 'as farr as Westgate, from thence upp thoroughe Rocklane [&] Southgate street and [thence] upp to the Guildhall'.[31] Those who suffered corporal punishment were the lucky ones. For murder, theft and all sorts of other crimes, the penalty was death, and every year the gaol yielded up its sad quota of prisoners to be executed on the gallows at Heavitree. Fear of these brutal punishments weighed heavily on many people's minds. John Coleman, who had already been punished by the city justices once, averred in 1627 that 'I will goe hange my selfe rather then I will come into their handes againe'.[32]

Injury, illness and the hazards of the law apart, the inhabitants of early modern Exeter had much else to worry about. In the days before property insurance, a house fire or a robbery could reduce a family from prosperity to penury in the twinkling of an eye, and even the richest merchants faced the threat of bankruptcy through losses at sea. The demands of the state could also bring ruin upon private individuals. During the troubled 1620s many Exeter men were impressed to fight as soldiers in Charles I's foreign wars. Two such unfortunates were Richard Jynkyns and Thomas Billinge, who were marched away from their homes to be 'billitted ... in the Countie of Sussex for 20 weekes togeather or more' in 1627. After the royal fleet had finally set sail for France, both men 'served his Majestie att the Isle of Ree, and in their retourne the said Billinge dyed and was cast overboarde'.[33] Jynkyns eventually managed to return to Exeter but it is hard to believe that his experiences can have left him unscarred. To add to the everyday burdens under which they laboured, the citizens believed themselves to be beset by supernatural dangers as well. Belief in witches was common, and one man who tripped over a stile and broke two of his ribs in 1620 attributed his misfortune to witchcraft, saying 'in his death bed that he did thinke verylie that the Wyddow Stone had bewitcht him'.[34]

In the midst of life, the inhabitants of early modern Exeter were indeed in death, and it is little wonder that many sought to blot out the hardship of their day-to-day lives by indulging in the pleasures of the flesh. The advice of Robert Herrick, parson of Dean Prior in South Devon, would have met with the hearty concurrence of many Exeter people:

> 'While the milder Fates consent,
> Lets enjoy our merriment,
> Drink, and dance and pipe and play,
> Kisse our [sweethearts] night and day,

> ... quaff [and] sing, for ere long,
> Death will come and mar the song.[35]

Herrick's choice of drink as the first in his list of pleasures would have been a popular one in early Stuart Exeter. People flocked to the city's many inns: to the Bear in Southgate Street, to the Anchor at St John's Bow, the Bell without West Gate and the King's Arms without Eastgate.[36] They packed the alehouses which stood on every street, consuming vast quantities of ale, beer and cider. Those who could afford it indulged in the pleasures of 'sack' (or sherry) and, then as now, the heady scent of alcohol was usually accompanied by the pungent reek of tobacco. Drink encouraged merriment, and many Exonians threw themselves wholeheartedly into 'dauncinge ... singinge and corowsinge'.[37] Following Herrick's injunction to 'pipe and play', they hired fiddlers to accompany them in their revels and indulged in a wide variety of games.[38] Sexual licence was widespread and Exeter contained several noted 'Houses of Bawderie'.[39]

If losing oneself in worldly pleasures was one way of coping with the unremitting harshness of day-to-day life, an alternative palliative was to concentrate upon the life of the world to come. Religion was of paramount importance in early Stuart Exeter and few were immune to its influence. As Sherwood's plan shows, the city was full of churches: their towers soared up towards heaven above the narrow, squalid streets, their doorways offered the prospect of an eventual escape from darkness into light. From pulpits all over Exeter clergymen constantly reiterated the message that, if only one had faith in God, one could yet exchange the misery of everyday existence for the bliss of eternal life. Church services were eagerly attended and many turned out to hear sermons every week. During the 1600s, as for centuries before, the citizens of Exeter owed their first allegiance to their parish, and it was the parish church which stood at the very heart of communal life.

Throughout the medieval period a shared religious faith had helped to bind the civic community of Exeter together, bridging the gap between rich and poor. During the sixteenth century this unity had been temporarily shattered when catholicism was replaced by protestantism as the official state religion, but the Elizabethan settlement of 1559 had gone a long way towards re-establishing the old consensus. By setting up a compromise system of Church government in England—one which, while essentially protestant, retained certain characteristics of the old faith—Elizabeth I and her ministers had succeeded in winning over the vast majority of ordinary men and women to their side. Some die-hard catholics refused to accept the new dispensation, of course, but as time passed away their numbers dwindled. The pattern of events in Exeter mirrored that which took place across England as a whole, and by 1600 the city was overwhelmingly protestant. Religious unity seemed to have been restored.

Yet the protestant consensus of 1600 was far less solid than the catholic consensus of 1500 had been. Deep divisions existed between the conservative/conformist majority, those who regarded the Elizabethan settlement as an end in itself, and the more zealous protestants, or 'puritans', those who felt that the Reformation had not gone far enough. This is, of course, a very simple description of what was an immensely complicated state of affairs; the early Stuart Church contained many subtly different shades of religious opinion.[40] Even so, an essential left/right polarity was always there and during the late sixteenth century disputes between the 'hotter sort' of protestants and their more conservative neighbours surfaced in many English towns and cities.

From around 1580 onwards 'the godly' (as zealous protestants often liked to term themselves) became increasingly influential in Exeter, and by the end of Queen Elizabeth's reign, puritanism was entrenched at the very highest levels of civic government. This was made crystal clear in 1599, when the Chamber appointed Edmund Snape, a well-known radical, as Exeter's hired preacher.[41] After frantic opposition from the Bishop of Exeter, Snape was dismissed. This stymied the Chamber's plans for well over a decade, but following the establishment of a permanent lectureship in Exeter in 1616, the Chamber was able to nominate a steady stream of puritan ministers to act as civic preachers: John Hazard in 1616, William Forde in 1617 and, most importantly of all, Henry Painter in 1627.[42] Meanwhile, other puritan clergymen were being appointed to the various city benefices: John Mico to St Petrocks, for example, John Bartlet to St Thomas and Thomas Manton to St Mary Arches.[43] As many of Exeter's tiny intra-mural parishes had no permanent minister at this time, the influence of the puritan clergymen was out of all proportion to their numbers. It was their ideas which were to be at the very centre of the city's political and religious life during the first half of the seventeenth century—and their ideas which were eventually to tear the civic community apart.

2

'Zealous to Advance God's Glory'
Ignatius Jurdain and the Puritan Dynamic

To give a fully detailed account of the rise of puritanism in Exeter would be impossible in a work of this scope.[1] Fortunately, much of the story is comprised within the career of one extraordinary individual, a man who—while much less famous than Sir Walter Raleigh and Sir Francis Drake—was undoubtedly one of the most remarkable figures that the Elizabethan west country ever produced. This man was Ignatius Jurdain, twice mayor of Exeter, four times MP for the city and commonly reputed the 'Arch-puritan' of the West.[2] Although Jurdain was later to achieve national fame, the circumstances of his birth showed few signs of future greatness. He was born at Lyme in Dorset in 1561, the son of a local merchant. The Jurdain family was a relatively prosperous one, but Lyme was a small place and it seems to have been decided that Ignatius would find it easier to make a career for himself in Exeter. Accordingly, while still a boy, Ignatius was packed off to Exeter to lodge with relations there. He may well have attended the city grammar school; certainly, he later showed signs of a good education. Nothing further is definitely known of him until 1576, when he was sent by his employer on a trading trip to Guernsey. Over the next few years Ignatius continued to learn the trade of a merchant and by the 1580s he had begun to prosper. In 1593 he married Elizabeth Baskerville, the daughter of a rich local physician.[3]

By this time Ignatius was already well established in St Mary Arches parish, one of Stuart Exeter's most desirable addresses, and over the following years his business went from strength to strength. He bought his own ships, to carry his own merchandise, and set up his own shop in the High Street.[4] Meanwhile, Jurdain's success in the commercial

19

arena had led him to become involved in local politics and administration. By the end of the 1590s Ignatius was ascending the *cursus honorum*, the ladder of civic offices which ambitious men had to climb if they were to reach the heights of local influence and prestige. In 1599 he was made one of the city bailiffs, and in 1608 he was appointed to the Chamber. In 1617 Ignatius finally reached the pinnacle of civic eminence when he was elected as mayor.[5]

So far, one might be forgiven for regarding Ignatius Jurdain as nothing more than a successful Jacobean businessman. Yet if the career-path which Jurdain followed was a relatively typical one, the inner fire which drove him on was not. A fierce protestant zeal burnt in Jurdain's breast, a zeal which was to direct the whole course of his adult life. It is possible that this intense religiosity owed something to the place of his birth, for Lyme was a town with an old radical tradition.[6] Yet even if childhood influences had predisposed him towards puritanism, it was not until the trip to Guernsey in 1576 that Jurdain experienced a real religious awakening, or 'new birth' as he afterwards termed it.[7] The precise circumstances of this spiritual rebirth are unknown, but Jurdain must surely have been influenced by the group of radical preachers who were then engaged in setting up a reformed church in the Channel Islands.[8] From 1576 onwards Jurdain renounced the sins of the world and set out to live a new life, wholly in accordance with the commandments of God.[9] It was a typical puritan story. But what exactly did this 'new life' involve?

Jurdain's extreme protestant belief manifested itself in a number of different ways. First there was his virulent hatred of catholicism. To Jurdain, as to most puritans, the Pope was only one step removed from the Devil himself. Second there was Jurdain's intense desire to obtain a spiritual union with God. Jurdain would rise, it is recorded,

> between two and three of the clock in the morning, and that in the coldest season of the year, and then ... meditate and pray in secret until sixe o'clock, the appointed time for the morning sacrifice in the family, when he was called from secret devotions to the exercise of religious family duties ... and if at any time he had overslept himself, and did not rise until four o'clock, he would much bemoan himself for that he had lost so much of his time of sweet and comfortable communion with God.[10]

Nor did Jurdain rely on private devotion alone, for he took advantage of every possible line of communication with the divine being. He was an assiduous attender at church services and sermons, and he loved the company of 'faithful ministers' or clergymen. Jurdain's intense desire to receive the word also led him to become a voracious devourer of 'godly books'. According to his biographer, he read the scriptures 'more then twenty times over' and Fox's Book of Martyrs seven times.[11]

Jurdain's zeal for religion was reflected in the pattern of his daily life. He gave generously to the city poor, scrupulously observed Sunday as a day of rest and was 'a very strict and conscientious observer' of the sabbath. He constantly talked of religion and 'heavenly things' with those whom he met in the course of his business and, like many other strict protestants, he was careful to avoid those who behaved in a dissolute or ungodly way. Swearing in particular, 'was most odious to him'.[12] On one occasion, while returning from London with a nobleman, Jurdain was invited to spend the next day, a Sunday, at his companion's house. Ignatius refused to do so until the man had promised that he, his wife and servants should 'refrain from profane swearing and behave decorously on the Lord's Day'.[13] That the nobleman agreed to abide by these conditions tells us much about the force of Jurdain's personality.

Suiting the Action to the Word

In a private citizen, such intense religiosity might have had little effect outside the immediate household. But Ignatius Jurdain was a man with a mission; he did not simply want to be godly himself, he wanted to make other people godly too. As his biographer observed, Ignatius 'was zealous to advance God's glory', and if this meant turning the old world upside down, then Ignatius was the man to do it.[14] Between 1610 and 1617 Jurdain used his increasing influence on the Exeter Chamber to push forward a strongly puritan programme. He was assisted in this by many other like-minded individuals—ministers, merchants, tradesmen and their wives—all of whom saw the world through the same zealously protestant spectacles as he did. Jurdain and his allies literally wanted to change the world. Like puritans all over England, they believed in the concept of a New Jerusalem, of a 'godly city upon a hill'. By purging their own community of ignorance and vice, by ensuring instead that it was run along strictly Christian lines, they believed that they could create what amounted to a little heaven upon earth.[15] During the thirty years which preceded the Civil War Jurdain and his supporters strained every nerve to transform Exeter into just such a godly commonwealth. And although their vision seems impossibly Utopian today, it came close to being achieved.

That this was so owed much to the efficient use which the godly made of Exeter's ancient administrative and judicial bodies, especially the city sessions court. This court was empowered to deal with almost all criminal cases, and was staffed by ten judges: the city recorder, the current mayor, and the eight city aldermen, all of whom had previously served as mayor themselves.[16] The full complement of justices rarely met, as it was only the serving mayor who was bound to appear at every single court sitting. Many criminal cases in Exeter were tried by the mayor alone, therefore, or by the mayor acting in concert with one or two of the more assiduous aldermen.[17] The mayor's powers were thus very great and during his mayoralty, he could hand out punishments for all sorts of offences, punishments which could do a great deal to influence the pattern of public behaviour in the city. Jurdain seized on the opportunities which the mayor's office afforded and once he himself became mayor in 1617–18 he caused a new minute book to be bought for the sessions court. This book still survives today.[18] It is a huge, weighty volume, quite different from anything which had preceded it, and it records every petty offence committed in Exeter during the second half of Jurdain's mayoralty. By its sheer bulk, and by the nature of the cases which it records, this book stands as an impressive monument to the determination with which Jurdain attempted to achieve his 'Godly Reformation' in Exeter.

It is recorded in other sources that Jurdain had a great horror of 'those evils whereby God was most highly dishonoured, [such] as swearing and sabbath breaking' and the minute book amply confirms this.[19] Under Jurdain's direction a full-scale assault was launched against such practices. Sabbath breaking was rigorously clamped down on, and even the most minor breaches of the ban on Sunday trading were punished. In June 1618 Jurdain ordered the city constables (the men who had the unenviable task of policing Exeter) 'to bring before him those that solde radishes on the sabbath's daie'.[20] A month later the constables were sent out again, this time with instructions to go and take the names of 'such as were playing at cudgells'.[21] As this last order suggests, Jurdain was particularly keen to punish those who participated in rowdy public sports on the sabbath day. Many elements of the 'festive culture' of Stuart England (such as church ales and maypole dancing) had their roots in the pre-Reformation era and were therefore regarded with peculiar horror by puritans. Nor were profaners of the sabbath the only moral offenders to suffer at Jurdain's hands: 'gamesters' were punished, while those who indulged in illicit games of shove ha'penny were fined.[22]

Jurdain's period of office came to an end in October 1618, but this did little to reduce his influence. Although he was no longer mayor, he was still rich, he was still a member of the all-powerful Council of Twenty Four, and he still possessed many younger allies who could hold the office of mayor in their turn. In early 1619, moreover, Jurdain was made an alderman. He now possessed the right to sit on the sessions bench whenever he chose and—unlike many previous aldermen—Jurdain exercised this right to the full. Between 1617 and 1638 he was one of the most assiduous attenders on the Bench.[23] All in all, Jurdain probably retained almost as much influence *after* 1618 as he had possessed during his mayoralty.

Throughout the rest of the 1610s and the early 1620s, Jurdain—more or less ably assisted by the city officials and other puritan members of the local élite—continued his campaign for a total reformation of manners in Exeter. Sabbath breaking continued to be discouraged and a man found 'animating of boyes to play att unlawfull games upon the sabbath daye' was promptly committed to prison.[24] Gamesters and swearers continued to be hounded, and there were many more convictions for playing cards, 'trap ball' (a bat-and-ball game) and shove ha'penny.[25] 'Undesirables' of all sorts were informed against and hunted down. One such was Jane Hall, a homeless woman, who in 1619 was reported to the sessions court '[for that she] dranke ale out of a halfe pecke and . . . did daunce in mans apparell and also . . . tosseth the pots much, and doth daunce much, and in her dauncing useth uncivill geastures'. The justices at once ordered that this 'Roaring Girl' should be ejected from the city.[26]

The concerted efforts of Jurdain and his allies gradually began to bear fruit, and by the early 1620s major public festivities at Exeter were in steep decline. Yet in the end it was thanks to something which we might call chance, but which Jurdain undoubtedly saw as divine intervention, that the old festive pastimes were finally abandoned. In 1625 Exeter was afflicted by a dreadful outbreak of the plague. Thousands of people died and most of the civic élite fled from the city, abandoning those who had been placed in their charge.[27] Ignatius Jurdain, however, was not the man to flee. Alone of all the magistrates, he remained at his post in the plague-stricken city, directing the constables, requesting help from other local communities, and making what arrangements he could for the care of the sick and the relief of the poor.[28]

An eye-witness later recalled that he had seen

> morning after morning coming to . . . [Jurdain's] door, sometimes 30, sometimes 40, sometimes 50, or three score or more [people]; some wringing their hands and crying that their husbands were dead, others that their children were dead, and that they had not anything to bury them, some again that their families were sick, and they had not wherewithal to relieve them; others that they had divers children, but they had no bread, nor money to buy it for them. Some cryed for bread, others for physic, some for shrouds. And . . . [Jurdain] not only gave them the hearing; but . . . his hands were stretched out for their relief. For standing within his shop, with his own hands, he gave supplies unto them all, and sent them to their homes for the present; and then the next morning there was a renewing of the sad complaints of the poore, and his renewing of his charitable care of them, and so [on], morning after morning, for near three moneths.[29]

The people of the surrounding countryside marvelled at Jurdain's courage, but he himself claimed that courage did not enter into it. 'What', said he, 'afraid of God's visitation? Let us fear rather the plague-sore of our owne hearts'.[30] This statement offers a crucial insight into Jurdain's mentality, showing that he did not regard the plague as an unlucky accident, but as God's punishment upon a sinful people. Many others shared this point of view, and once the sickness had finally passed away still greater efforts were made to purge the city of sin.[31] Fear of divine punishment combined with godly zeal to make the campaign for moral reformation more fervent than ever, and after 1626 that campaign achieved a remarkable degree of success. Major public festivities all but disappeared, public drunkenness diminished and even swearing went underground. It was later recalled 'by some that lived then in the city, and near the place of the greatest concourse of people, the corn market . . . that they did not hear an oath sworne for many years together'.[32] There could be no more striking evidence of Jurdain's success: in public at least, the 'godly commonwealth' of his dreams was close to becoming a reality.

Jurdain's behaviour during 'the plague year' won him many admirers and in late 1625 he was elected as MP for Exeter on a wave of popular support. 'Choose Jurdain', the voters cried, 'he will be right for the Common-Wealth and do the city service'.[33] This was not the first time that Jurdain had been elected as an Exeter MP, nor was it to be the last. Between 1621 and 1629 he served in this capacity on four separate occasions and his presence in Parliament permitted him to push his religious agenda on the national stage as well as the local one.[34] During the Parliamentary session of 1621, for example, he made speeches against 'scandalous' (or immoral) clergymen, while in 1625 he spoke out against swearing and prostitution.[35] Jurdain also introduced a bill prescribing the death penalty for adultery.[36] The bill was rejected, but this was not for want of trying on Jurdain's part.[37]

Much of our knowledge of Ignatius Jurdain comes from the biography which was written about him by Ferdinando Nichols, rector of St Mary Arches. Nichols was himself a puritan, and a friend of Jurdain's, so it comes as little suprise to find that the portrait which he paints is a very flattering one. The same is true of the other main study of Jurdain's life, the article written by Frances Rose-Troup in 1897.[38] To a writer of the Victorian era, Jurdain's rise to wealth and prosperity through sheer hard work, his devotion to civic duties and above all his intense religious commitment made him an extremely attractive figure. To Rose-Troup, as to Nichols, Jurdain was a warrior for the Christian faith, 'a pattern of piety and charity to succeeding generations'.[39] Yet the heroes of the past have a habit of turning into the villains of today, and—while Jurdain may have been venerated by the puritans of his own day, and by the stern Christian moralists of the Victorian era—from the perspective of the 1990s it is easy to appreciate that, to many Exeter people, the activities of Jurdain and his followers must have been anathema.

The Enemies of God

The records of the sessions court show that, although the godly held the upper hand in Exeter, many local people hated and despised them. Agnes Porter complained to the justices in 1618 that a neighbour had 'bid her go looke in her dissembling bible' and had 'called her puritan hoore'.[40] This was a stock term of abuse for godly women; when Rebecca Robertes tried to stop a group of men playing dice in the middle of the night, she too was rewarded with cries of 'puritant whore'.[41] The city constables were abused in similar terms, frequently being reviled as 'puritan rogues', 'puritant knaves' and 'dissemblers' (this last term meaning hypocrites, a vice of which the godly were constantly accused).[42] And equally bitter complaints were made against the city's 'puritan justice[s]'.[43]

Jurdain himself, of course, as 'the Arch-puritan', came in for more abuse than anyone else. Even Nicolls admitted that he was 'vilified and defamed and loaden with reproaches'.[44] Sometimes this abuse was relatively good humoured and amounted to little more than poking fun at Jurdain behind his back. Take the incident which occurred in 1620 when Elizabeth Brownscombe, a feltmaker's wife, was awakened at midnight by a strange noise. Creeping downstairs, she saw a shadowy figure crawling in through her shop window. As Elizabeth watched in amazement, the intruder—who was obviously very much the worse for drink—'came into her shop wyndowe, and in comminge in fell upon a coffer and brake the cover thereof, and from there fell into a tubbe of water, and there remained a good while without any speech', finally announcing 'Yt is I'. Recognizing the voice of Margaret Burnell, a neighbour, Elizabeth rushed over to pull her out. As she dragged Burnell from the tub, Elizabeth asked her what on earth she had been doing, to which her intoxicated guest replied, presumably with a drunken snigger, 'that Mr Jurdain had sent her thither to see if one Mr Peck of Taunton were in bed with the said Elizabeth'.[45] The jibe against Jurdain and his snooping ways was rather a good one.

Most of the comments made about Jurdain were far less amusing, however. In 1621 a city roofer was told by a friend that 'Mr Jurdayne is gone for London, whereupon . . . [he] made answer the Devill take him by the waye'.[46] These bitter words show just how much some people hated Jurdain. Like puritans everywhere, he was constantly accused of hypocrisy and deceit. Many claimed that he abused his power as a magistrate, embezzling the profits of justice. Jurdain only handed out fines, they said, so that he could pocket the money for himself. Typical was the man who claimed that 'he was bound over by Mr Jurdain . . . for love of only halfe a crowne'.[47] Those whose livelihoods depended on drinking and merriment, of course, were particularly hostile to Jurdain and many of his bitterest enemies were innkeepers. One such man, whose premises Ignatius had just raided, swore that 'if Mr Jurdain come againe . . . I will make his guts garter his heeles'.[48] Many similar cases could be cited: hostility towards Jurdain was clearly very widespread in Exeter.

This hostility was by no means socially specific, moreover. It was not just the ungodly poor who disliked Ignatius. A similar distaste for the

'Arch-puritan' was felt by religious conservatives at all levels of local society. Such people disliked and distrusted Jurdain's fiery brand of protestantism, and suspected him and his followers of being disaffected to the established church. These conservative elements were keen to resist the puritans and they did what they could to block their reforming programme. As a result, innkeepers, gamesters and other plebeian defenders of the festive culture found themselves receiving tacit support against the puritans from high-ranking clergymen in the Cathedral Close and even from certain members of the city council itself. In 1618 a man who had composed lewd songs against Jurdain boasted that Mr John Prowse, one of the most important of the city councillors, was 'hys frend'.[49] Six years later, a witness in a Star Chamber case deposed that he

> 'hath hearde ... Mr [Thomas] Walker, Mr John Prouse and Mr [John] Muddyforde, being 3 of the chief aldermen & justices of the peace of the said Cittie, to complain very much of ... Mr Jurdain for his unjust and cruell carriage'.[50]

The scrupulous care which the Chamber took to suppress any evidence of discord among its members means that little is known about these internal divisions.[51] Yet it is quite evident that they existed, and that the puritan drive for moral reformation had split the civic community at Exeter.

Conflict with the Crown

Is there any evidence of a similar split emerging between the city authorities and the Crown between 1603 and 1625? During the early years of James I's reign, the answer would appear to be no. James had arrived in England with good protestant credentials and although, as he repeatedly made clear, he was no favourer of radical sectaries (i.e. those puritan extremists who wished to separate themselves from the English church altogether), he could scarcely be suspected of concealing a contrary inclination towards the Pope. Had not catholic conspirators tried to blow him sky-high in 1605? For the majority of James's subjects, the Gunpowder Plot served as happy confirmation of their King's opposition to the machinations of Rome, and the appointment of the Calvinist George Abbot as Archbishop of Canterbury in 1611 still further reinforced the view of James as a staunchly protestant monarch. For much of the period 1603–15, Jurdain and his allies probably felt able to regard the King with relative equanimity.

Yet even during these years of outward calm Jurdain was already patronizing very radical puritan ministers, men who spoke out openly against the established forms of church government and thus, by implication, against the Crown itself.[52] That Jurdain should have consorted with such men makes it clear that obedience to the state was hardly his prime concern. In 1618, moreover, evidence appeared to suggest that Jurdain was not only dissatisfied with the established Church, but with its Supreme Head, with James I himself. On 26 June an Exeter man was arrested by one of the constables for having said that there were 'some' in Exeter who 'didd not love the King and did not care yf he were dead or hanged'. This comment was followed by a ringing denunciation of those who 'carryed the word of God in their mouthes & the Divill in their hart'.[53] The man clearly had Jurdain in mind, and his outburst is a remarkable one, suggesting that, by this time, it was commonly supposed in Exeter that Ignatius was hostile to the King. Why should such rumours have begun to circulate?

The answer, it seems, is connected with the vexed question of popular recreations on Sundays. As has been seen, Jurdain loathed church ales and other ungodly festivities and had embarked on a determined campaign to drive such pastimes out of Exeter. James I did not share the puritan view and during a tour of the North in 1617, he specifically ordered the Lancashire JPs to permit such 'lawful games'. Lancashire is a long way from Devon and it may be that the full implications of James's decree took a while to sink in. But next year similar orders were published across the whole kingdom. On 24 June 1618 James issued a declaration stating:

> that after the end of divine service [on Sundays], our good people . . . [shall not be] letted, or discouraged, from any lawful recreation, such as dancing . . . nor from having of May-games, Whitson ales and Morrice Dances . . . [nor from] the setting up of Maypoles, & other sports therewith used.[54]

A storm of controversy immediately broke out across the realm.

To the godly 'the King's Book of Sports' was an affront. By issuing such a directive they felt James had given his backing to the most dissolute elements in society, to those who spent 'God's day' in drinking and debauchery rather than in prayer and preaching. Not only this, he had condoned a set of activities which were inextricably rooted in a popish, anti-protestant past. Was this the action of a godly King, wondered the puritans? How could they have confidence in a monarch who behaved like this? James's declaration had practical implications as well, moreover. By ordering that recreations be officially permitted, the King had placed a powerful weapon in the hands of those who opposed the godly campaign for moral reform. Such people could now claim that their pastimes had full royal authority, and it did not take them long to do so. When one of the Exeter constables tried to stop two men playing at trap-ball in 1622 they openly defied him, retorting that 'they played att noe unlawfull game and that the King [himself] did allowe it'.[55] It was a statement which undermined the legitimacy of the entire puritan campaign.

Bearing all this in mind, it seems unlikely to be coincidence that the accusation that Jurdain hated the King was made only two days after the publication of the Book of Sports. Almost certainly Jurdain had made his distaste for the King's Book clear, and this in turn had set tongues wagging throughout the city. There can be little doubt that Jurdain's enemies hoped to bring him down by impugning his loyalty. Whispers that all was not well in Exeter clearly reached the ears of the King himself, for in 1623 he brusquely told a civic delegation 'that he understood that the citizens were puritans'.[56] Already signs of distrust between the Exeter Chamber and the Crown were emerging, each regarding the other as unsound in matters of religion.

The accession of Charles I in 1625 can only have made matters worse. Whereas James had had a record of opposition to catholicism, in the early part of his reign at least, his son possessed no such comforting associations. On the contrary, Charles was already suspected by some to be a secret *supporter* of Rome. The new King's past history was ominous. In 1623 he had travelled to Spain, that bulwark of European catholicism, in order to seek the hand of the Spanish Infanta. It had been widely rumoured at this time that Charles was about to convert to Rome himself, and although these gloomy prognostications had not, in the end, been fulfilled, some of the mud clearly stuck.[57] In 1624 rumours were circulating in Cornwall that the Prince of Wales was a secret 'papist', and such stories presumably reached Exeter, too.[58] Towards the end of that same year it became clear that Charles had again determined on a catholic bride, this time Henrietta Maria of France. In November 1624 a marriage treaty was agreed upon, and as part of the deal between the two countries, the English recusancy laws were suspended. In December an order was issued, directing that all catholics imprisoned for religious offences should be released at once.[59] Three months later James I died and was succeeded by his son.

What the rabidly anti-catholic Jurdain thought of these developments can only be surmised. What is certain is that the royal orders of December 1624 did not lead to a slackening of anti-catholic vigilance in Exeter. Rather, they saw a new determination to root out papists. Within three months of Charles's accession, a group of catholics was arrested in Exeter, including Alexander Baker, a seminary priest, and Nicholas Helliar, a local gentleman. Both refused to swear allegiance to the King, and were therefore committed to prison.[60] Yet even as the city authorities did their best to combat popery at the local level, catholicism was openly entering in at the very heart of state. In June 1625 Henrietta Maria arrived in England and wedded King Charles. Less than a month later, orders arrived in Exeter that Baker and Helliar should be set free.[61] Bitter protests about the order were made in the House of Commons, but to no avail.[62] Three months after the city authorities had reluctantly released the catholics, the worst plague in living memory broke out in Exeter.

To Jurdain and his allies, the fact that 'God's visitation' followed so hard on the heels of the catholics' release can hardly have appeared coincidental. The city was being punished by God, it seemed, not only for its own sinfulness, but also for its failure to apprehend the servants of Anti-Christ, the scheming papists who acted as moral pollutants and devourers of souls. Nor was it Exeter alone which was suffering. London too experienced 'a great sickness' within months of Charles I's accession, as one Exeter citizen recorded in his journal.[63] Was it not possible that the whole realm was being punished as a result of the King's affection to the catholics?

While the plague was at its height Exeter people were more anxious than ever for divine assistance, but they did not rush to the city churches. This was partly because most of the local clergymen had fled to escape the plague. Yet it was also because the puritan citizens had 'no very good affection' to the established church, 'nor fervent desire to attend it'.[64] Instead they flocked to the sermons of godly preachers, who—with the departure of the ecclesiastical authorities—found themselves able to flourish in Exeter as never before. Valentine Carey, the Bishop of Exeter (and a noted anti-puritan), was most unhappy with this situation and sent orders into the plague-stricken city that sermons were to cease at once.[65] Henceforth, people were either to attend the service established by law, or not to attend religious exercises at all.

To Jurdain, the bishop's order must have seemed monstrous. What right had this cowardly prelate, snug in a village well away from the infection, to stop up the mouths of those few brave ministers who had dared to remain in Exeter? How could he respond to God's visitation by blocking off the people's access to God? Was this the counsel of a caring spiritual pastor? Was it not more like the counsel of the devil himself? The bishop's order can only have strengthened puritan dislike of the ecclesiastical authorities. Many must have felt, moreover, that on this occasion, as on so many others, the bishop was simply acting as the mouthpiece of monarchy, as the trumpet through which the King himself spoke. Yet why should Charles have wished to keep God's word from his suffering people in Exeter? Those who already doubted the King's commitment to protestantism must have drawn their own grim conclusions, and Charles's subsequent behaviour was scarcely calculated to allay local fears. Between 1626 and 1629 catholics were arrested at Exeter on four separate occasions, but each time the King sent down orders that they should be released.[66]

By 1629 Jurdain and his allies had been given ample reason to suspect that Charles I possessed popish sympathies. Nor was it in Exeter alone that such anxieties were felt. Across the country as a whole, zealous protestants were becoming increasingly worried by an apparent change in religious direction, by Charles I's apparent desire to promote quasi-catholic practices in the English Church. William Laud, the new bishop of London, was suspected, along with many other churchmen, of being an 'Arminian', a member of a sinister faction which favoured elaborate ceremonies and exalted the power of the bishops. The Arminians, it was feared, were softening up the Church of England for a catholic takeover. Fears of a change in religion were accompanied by fears of a change in government, for popery and tyranny were regarded as inextricably linked. Stuart Englishmen looked across the Channel to France to see a catholic king ruling a slavish, subject people, devoid of rights (or 'liberties' as contemporaries termed them), and subject to enormous taxes. Would not the establishment of catholicism in England bring about similar social conditions here, people wondered? And, conversely, might not attacks on constitutional liberties in England be part of a grand plot to bring in popery?

At Exeter, as elsewhere, there is evidence of a growing distrust of the royal regime during the late 1620s. Just how deep this distrust went is shown by a letter sent to Jurdain by Mr Giles Carpenter in 1627, informing him of 'a daungerous plot intended agaynste the city'. Having first told Jurdain that the matter was so sensitive 'as I dare not comit it to writing', Carpenter went on to describe a scheme to establish a royal garrison in Exeter Castle. According to Carpenter the plotters—all 'Londoners and decayed courtiers'—planned first to repair the castle, next to station a garrison of one hundred soldiers in it 'at the King's charge' and finally to establish fairs and markets there, which would, of necessity, undermine the city's trade.[67]

Financially such a scheme would have been very damaging for Exeter. Yet Carpenter's words suggest that it was not only the *economic* implications of the plot which concerned him. He dwelt on the gun platforms which were to be built at the castle, platforms which would command the city itself, and elsewhere in his letter he grimly observed that 'the city of Antwarpe was sacked by such a meanes of a Castell within the walls of it within the memory of man'.[68] This was a remarkable comment. Together with the observation about the gun platforms, it suggests that, even as early as 1627, some *fifteen years* before the Civil War, there were people in Jurdain's circle who suspected that Charles I, or at least those around him, were capable of assaulting an English town. Moreover Carpenter's comparison with Antwerp would have possessed a special resonance for zealous protestants. The sack of this Dutch city by Spanish troops in 1576 was the classic example of a protestant citadel being assailed by the black forces of the popish Anti-Christ—and it is easy to imagine how Jurdain might have drawn parallels with the situation at Exeter.

Two years after Jurdain received this letter, Charles I dissolved his third Parliament, thus beginning the era known as 'the Personal Rule'. During this period Charles and his counsellors governed England alone and no parliaments were called. There has been much debate as to exactly what the country at large thought about this state of affairs. Some scholars have claimed that the vast majority of people were perfectly content during the 1630s, quite unconcerned by the King's decision to do without parliaments. Others have claimed that England was seething with discontent and, in Jurdain's case at least, it is the second picture which seems more plausible. The cessation of parliaments had prevented him from speaking out against his *bête noire*—catholicism—on the national stage. Not only this but Charles's dismissal of Parliament had halted *local* action against the catholics too. Between 1629 and 1640 not a single papist was arrested in Exeter, almost certainly because, with Charles I ruling England alone, the city authorities had concluded that it would be pointless, if not dangerous, to apprehend such people.[69] The King would simply order them to be released and, in the absence of a Parliament, there was no one who could protest. The cessation of parliaments brought an end to anti-catholic activity in Exeter, therefore, and this was reason enough for Ignatius Jurdain to hate the Personal Rule.

In 1633 he made an explicit attack upon royal policy. As in 1618, the issue which brought him into conflict with the Crown was that of Sunday recreations. In October 1633 Charles I had reissued his father's Book of Sports, ordering 'that no man do trouble or molest [our] people in . . . their lawful recreations'. The King's declaration specifically commanded '*all* . . . [justices] as well within liberties as without . . . to take notice of [these orders] and to see [them] observed', so there was no way that Exeter could wriggle out of the orders by virtue of its privileged county status.[70] In the absence of Parliament there was no way of voicing opposition at a national level either, and it seemed that the only hope of stopping the Book was to argue the point with Charles himself. Jurdain did not shrink from the challenge. In November he wrote a letter 'to moove the King for the calling in of his booke' and had it presented at Court.[71] The King's reaction was predictable. According to one source he was much 'offended with [t]his letter because it seemed to call his prerogative into question', while according to another, the King 'when he had read it, in a great anger said he would hang [Jurdain]'.[72]

Perhaps as a result of the royal outrage which this letter had provoked, Jurdain and his allies remained quiet between 1633 and 1637. There was little sign of overt opposition to Crown policy in Exeter during these years. It seems unlikely that this quiescent attitude reflected any genuine change of heart, however. This same period saw an upsurge in tension between the Chamber and the cathedral authorities, and it is tempting to suggest that Jurdain and his allies were now trying to carry on the fight against royal religious policies through other means.

Conflict with the Dean and Chapter

That Jurdain should have come into conflict with the cathedral establishment is hardly surprising. The ancient rivalry between the Chamber and Chapter has already been touched upon, and jurisdictional disputes between the two bodies were frequent during the early 1600s.[73] As a prominent member of the Chamber, Jurdain was bound to have become involved in these disputes, while he had his own reasons for disliking certain individual clerics. William Cotton and Valentine Carey—successively Bishops of Exeter between 1600 and 1627—were both opposed to the zealous strain of protestantism favoured by Jurdain; indeed Carey was regarded as an out-and-out Arminian.[74] Yet it is important to stress that Jurdain was not opposed to the cathedral clergy *per se*. Carey's successor as bishop, Joseph Hall, was a man with whom Ignatius had much in common. One of the few Calvinists to be appointed to the episcopal bench under Charles I, Hall had attacked the Arminians in print, while Laud 'suspected him as a favourer of the puritans'.[75] Hall and Jurdain were men who could, and sometimes did, act in concert.

Real power in the Close did not lie with the Bishop, moreover, it lay with the Dean—and Matthew Sutcliffe, Dean of Exeter between 1588 and 1629, was a man whose religious opinions strikingly paralleled Jurdain's own. Sutcliffe was the author of many rabidly anti-catholic pamphlets, for example, *A Challenge Concerning the Romish Church* and *De Turco-Papismo* (a work helpfully subtitled *The Resemblance between Mahometanism and Popery*). He was also a furious opponent of the Arminians, attacking them in polemical works and even in his will. Like Jurdain, Sutcliffe was a patron of nonconformist ministers and, like him, he came up against the Crown as a result of his religious beliefs, being 'sent for' by the Privy Council in 1621 'for speaking against the Spanish match'.[76] It is hard to doubt that Sutcliffe and Jurdain were allies. The two men were of a similar age, and they both owned houses in St Mary Arches parish.[77] Most important of all, they both adhered to the same zealously protestant world view. The significance of this last point cannot be overemphasized. By the time that Charles I came to the throne in 1625, both the secular and ecclesiastical government of Exeter had been dominated for many years by two individuals whose most salient characteristic was a fanatical hatred of catholicism. This must have had a powerful influence upon religious life in the city as a whole throughout the early seventeenth century.

IGNATIUS JURDAIN AND THE PURITAN DYNAMIC

As long as Sutcliffe remained Dean, Arminian doctrines had little chance of infiltrating the Close. But in 1629 Sutcliffe died, and godly hegemony in Exeter was immediately challenged. Sutcliffe was succeeded as Dean by William Peterson, one of the King's own chaplains.[78] Peterson may not have been an Arminian but he was certainly no puritan, and from this moment onwards the religious atmosphere in the Close began to change. Symptomatic of this was the fact that, soon after Sutcliffe's death, the Communion Table in the Cathedral Church of St Peter was railed in—a practice which the puritans regarded with intense distaste.[79] Over the next few years the whole panoply of Laudian church decoration was introduced into the cathedral. That this revolution in local ecclesiastical affairs should have begun in 1629—the very same year that Charles was reported to have 'done' with parliaments—can scarcely have seemed coincidental to Jurdain.

Following Sutcliffe's death, it became increasingly easy for the godly party in Exeter to see the cathedral clergy as a dangerous fifth column within the city walls, as a group of doctrinal revolutionaries intent on promoting the great catholic design against England. Whatever the town councillors did to effect a godly reformation in Exeter, it seemed, the cathedral clergy worked to counteract. Whatever measures were taken to enforce a better standard of moral behaviour in Exeter had to stop short at the cathedral gates. Within the walled-off precincts of the Close, Arminianism was preached with impunity, and gaming and drinking openly indulged in—or so the godly felt. In the minds of the more zealous Exeter puritans, indeed, the Close must have come to seem a 'sink of iniquity', a centre of spiritual pollution which threatened to infect the city itself. Resentment against the cathedral clergy was intensified by the fact that they themselves—confident in the King's favour—became increasingly assertive after 1629. This infuriated the godly, of course, but also alienated many conservative/conformist members of the civic élite, men whose religious beliefs might otherwise have led them to sympathize with the clergy. As a result city/cathedral tensions mounted steadily during the 1630s, finally coming to a head in 1636.[80]

The trouble was apparently initiated by one of the city constables, who, in January 1636, attempted to search a house in St Sidwells for stolen goods. St Sidwells lay within the Chapter's jurisdiction, and the constable was promptly confronted by a certain John Hoppyn, who told him 'he should meddle no more with the business he was about, until ... Hoppyn had acquainted the Dean ... therewithall, and willed ...

[the constable] to acquaint the Maior . . . with so much'. Later that day one of the Dean's servants came to the sessions court and informed the city JPs 'that he is now sent by his master to acquaint . . . [them] that they doe intrench and intrude upon the liberties of the Dean and Chapter, in fetching out of any felons, or felons goods, in . . . St Sidwells'.[81] This was an extremely blunt message. Even so the Chamber chose to ignore it, and in March 1636 two more constables became involved in 'a great affraye in St Sidwells'.[82] Infuriated, the Dean petitioned the King for redress.

In June 1636 a copy of the Dean's petition was read by the Chamber. The councillors were dismayed to see that Bishop Hall had joined with the Dean in petitioning against them, and they sent him a conciliatory message, promising 'that if the cittie have done them [i.e. the cathedral clergy] any wrong, they will make them satisfaccon'. Hall returned a brusque answer, making it clear that he and the Dean were united in their determination to protect the 'liberties' of the cathedral.[83] The city councillors now had a real fight on their hands, and it was one which they were unlikely to win. In mid-1636 the Personal Rule was at its height and the King stood unchallenged as the supreme arbiter of the realm. In any conflict between the conformist clergy of the Cathedral Close, and the puritan-dominated Chamber, it was clear where his sympathies would lie. The clergymen's petition appeared to have opened the way for the ancient jurisdictional battle between the Chapter and the Chamber to be decided once and for all—in the former's favour. This was a dreadful prospect for the city councillors, and they did what they could to avert it. Legal advisers were hired, and attempts made to demonstrate the councillors' own loyalty and religious conformity. In August 1636 the Chamber agreed that 'Mr Maior and his brethren should come to St Peters church att the publicke service there on the Coronation day'.[84] Such gestures did not improve the citizens' prospects, however, and next year they begged the clergymen to settle the dispute out of court, assuring them that 'if they wilbe pleased to sett downe . . . [their complaints] in writing, the cittie will make them a faire aunsweare'. It was all to no avail: the citizens' plea 'that these differences may be composed here without further trouble' was ignored.[85] Both sides were soon preparing to present their case in London, before the royal justices.

For the godly in Exeter, 1636 was a bleak, depressing year. Across the whole kingdom, puritanism was under attack and Laudianism gaining ground. The Personal Rule seemed as strong as ever, with little prospect of a Parliament. In Exeter itself the Chapter seemed about to triumph over the Chamber, bringing all hopes of a total reformation of manners in the city to an end. Even Ignatius Jurdain, for so long the driving force of Exeter puritanism, had begun to falter. In March 1636 he drew up his will and a few months later he failed to attend several council meetings, almost certainly because of ill-health.[86] Troubles crowded in upon the godly—but deliverance was at hand.

3

'The Times Grow More Dangerous'
The Descent into Civil War

> *When things are brought about by contrariety . . . that is the wonder. For . . . summer to come after spring is . . . naturall: but when high-noone shall spring out of deepe midnight, and mid-somer out of mid-winter, this must needs be done by a divine power.*[1]

As the year 1637 began, amid snow and ice, Jurdain and his allies had little reason to believe that the 'mid-winter' of the Personal Rule would not last for ever. But in Charles I's northern kingdom of Scotland a politico-religious thaw had begun, one which would eventually sweep southwards across the border and release the English puritans from the icy grip under which they had shivered for so long. During the summer of 1637 the King's attempts to introduce a new form of Prayer Book in Scotland broke down in humiliating failure. The strongly protestant inhabitants of that country rose up in arms to resist what they regarded as a dangerous, even popish innovation. Furthermore, they called for the trial of the Scottish bishops, who were seen as being responsible for the new Prayer Book. The disturbances grew worse, until the protesters had seized control of the entire country. By the beginning of 1638 the very existence of the established Church in Scotland seemed under threat.[2]

In England, public interest in the Scottish troubles was intense. Religious conservatives were sympathetic to the King, of course. How dare the Scots refuse to accept the doctrines of the established Church? Those whose religious beliefs were more zealously protestant, however, saw matters in a very different light. Men like Jurdain had long suspected that, under Charles I, the English Church was moving in the wrong direction. Now they saw that the Scots shared their suspicions. As a result English puritans began to feel an increasingly close identification with the Scots and their aims. Moreover, the Scots' determined resistance to the new Prayer Book created anxiety in the hearts of many English people who had previously been relatively content with the religious situation in their own country. All this fuss in the north could hardly be over nothing, they reasoned, and belief in the existence of a 'Popish Plot' began to spread. Under the influence of events in Scotland, in fact, unease about the whole direction of royal policy became much more apparent in England.[3]

Charles I remonstrated with the Scots, but they utterly refused to accept the new Prayer Book and were soon demanding the complete abolition of episcopacy as well. For a few weeks in early 1638 it seemed possible that Charles might decide to back down—and the spirits of the godly in England rose accordingly. If the King was forced to make such important concessions in Scotland, they hoped, he would find it difficult, if not impossible, to maintain his religious policies at home. Hopes of such a policy reversal were premature, however, for Charles was determined not to give in. In June 1638 the King asked his ministers to estimate the cost of raising an army.[4] War against the Scots began to seem increasingly likely, and as expectations of conflict rose, so did the confidence of religious conservatives. England would obviously win the war, they reasoned, and with the Scots crushed, the King would be free to crack down on religious dissent at home. Puritans would be chastened, radicals suppressed and the power of the bishops confirmed. The Personal Rule would continue as before, in other words, but with the King immeasurably strengthened. It was a tempting prospect and these high hopes surely help to explain why the inhabitants of the Cathedral Close at Exeter now started to behave with a confidence, indeed an arrogance, that was altogether new. During the summer of 1638 they went out of their way to bait and provoke the city authorities.

On 20 August the JPs were informed that Richard Comyns, the porter of Broadgate (the most important of the gates which surrounded the Close) had sworn at the city watchmen.[5] Comyns was summoned to appear before Ignatius Jurdain, who reprimanded him for his behaviour. The cathedral porter was then fined five shillings and released. However, Comyns stubbornly refused to pay his fine. He was probably encouraged in his intransigence by the drift of national events. During August and early September it had become increasingly clear that the King was preparing to intervene in Scotland. Indeed, on 17 September Charles had taken the decisive step of ordering that the royal armoury should be transferred from London to Hull.[6] War, it seemed, was only a matter of months away, and to the episcopal party in Exeter—those who upheld the cathedral clergy in their battle with the godly town councillors—the King's adoption of a hardline policy was a matter for jubilation.

Two weeks later this jubilation found expression in riot and disorder. The trouble was again provoked by Richard Comyns, whose continued refusal to pay his fine had angered the city authorities. On 27 September Jurdain ordered one of the town constables to collect the money from Comyns in person. The constable duly went to Broadgate and asked the porter to hand over the money, but Comyns refused to pay. Not only this, he insolently asked the constable 'whither he were come for his pursse and further said that he had noe monie for Jurdaine to boyle his pott', a remark which implied that Jurdain planned to keep the fine for himself.[7] Unable to make any headway the constable returned to the Guildhall. Much annoyed, Jurdain now ordered two *more* of the city constables to go to Comyns's house and forcibly remove property to the value of the unpaid fine.[8]

When the constables arrived at Broadgate, Comyns was nowhere to be seen, so they presented their warrant to his wife Elizabeth instead. Elizabeth proved no more accommodating than her husband had been. She utterly refused to hand over any of her household goods to the constables. Moreover, she questioned their right to interfere on her premises at all, pointing out that Broadgate lay within the Chapter's jurisdiction. Only the Bishop's bailiff had the authority to take a distraint in her house, she argued, the city officials had no business there. The constables were in no mood to quibble over technicalities and, brushing the angry woman aside, they marched straight into the house. Yet as soon as the men came in, Elizabeth dashed out, locking the door behind her, and shouting that 'she would acquaint the Lord Bishoppe therewith'. The constables took no notice, assuming that Elizabeth would soon return. They were wrong, Elizabeth did not come back 'until two howers or thereabouts' had passed. Meanwhile, news of the constables' predicament had begun to spread around the Close.[9]

Realizing that something unusual was afoot, people dropped what they were doing and hurried across to Broadgate. Within minutes of

Elizabeth's departure, a noisy crowd was assembled in front of Comyns' door, pointing and laughing at the imprisoned city constables. Some of the bolder spirits soon began to taunt them. George Smyth 'did ... severall times knocke att ... Comyns his dore and [said] with a lowde voice "where are you nowe, Peepe yee constables, I would give somewhat to see them peepe", with many other uncivill speeches'. Meanwhile Henry Pafford, 'a servant unto Mr Archdeacon Cotton', marched up to the house and 'in a peremptorie manner demaunded of ... [the constables] to what purpose they were come ... and likewise gave them many other unfitting speeches'.[10]

By this time a crowd of well over one hundred people had gathered before the Comyns' house. It is obvious that the inhabitants of the Cathedral Close were hugely enjoying the discomfiture of the city constables; George Smyth, who had clearly appointed himself master of ceremonies, now dashed 'out att the Broadgate [and] retourned hastilie again with something in his coate which ... were apples to throwe amongst the boyes and others in the foresaid assembly'. A witness later recalled that Smyth had 'two severall times ... cast apples amonge divers boyes before ... Comyns his dore, bidding them to showte and make a noyce'.[11] Smyth's action was by no means as pointless as it now seems. It was a long-established custom at Exeter that, following the annual election of the mayor, apples and pears would be thrown from the Guildhall balcony to the local boys.[12] Smyth's action was thus a gleeful parody of established civic procedure; by throwing apples among the boys who were jeering at the imprisoned constables, he heaped scorn upon the head of the city authorities.

Eventually the city magistrates got wind of the tumult and sent two more constables to Broadgate to reinforce their colleagues. Constable John Mortimore later reported that, on arriving at the Close, he 'did there see divers persons assembled togeather'. Among them was Elizabeth Comyns, who had by now returned to Broadgate to see the fun. Mortimore at once approached her 'and by vertue of his warrant required her to goe before ... Mr Jurdaine'. Elizabeth stoutly refused, telling Mortimore 'that he was under the authoritie of the Lord Bishoppe'. She then cast doubt on the validity of Mortimore's warrant, and asked the Bishop's clerk, Francis Gilbert, who was standing nearby, to examine it. Nothing loath, Gilbert came forward, seized the warrant —and refused to give it back. An unseemly tussle ensued, as Gilbert danced about the constable, waving the stolen warrant in his face and telling him that he would be summoned before the Bishop. A nearby citizen tried to intervene, remonstrating with Gilbert and telling him to be quiet, but to no avail.[13]

At this moment the Sherrif of Exeter, Richard Saunders, arrived upon the scene. Saunders—a puritan in the same stern mould as Jurdain himself—at once strode into the fray, 'askeing . . . Gilbert whither he did not knowe that he was the High Sheriffe of the Cittie and therefore willed him to keepe the peace'. Gilbert replied 'that he did not care a farte for the said Sheriffe'.[14] Spotting a friend, a fencing master, in the crowd, Gilbert then 'called . . . unto him and said that if he would stand by him, there should [be] noe sheriffe of them all [would] dare lay hands on him'. After this show of bravado Gilbert was eventually forced to give up the warrant. But the Bishop's clerk was not yet finished. Cursing and swearing and 'pressinge in amongst the . . . [crowd], Gilbert [next made] to strike . . . [one of the citizens] upon the head, saying this is the fellowe would set me by the heeles'. At this point Gilbert was 'reprooved' by John Darke, a bystander, for swearing. Irritated beyond measure by this pious intervention, Gilbert 'in a threatning manner . . . stretch[ed] out his arme towards the said John Darke, [and] swore by God's wounds and harte, he woulde meete with him, or find him againe'.[15]

The constables eventually managed to pacify the crowd and free their imprisoned colleagues. Two days later Gilbert was summoned before the city court and fined (although only after he had compounded his offence by swearing at the magistrates) and Mrs Comyns was punished too.[16] For the rest of 1638 Exeter remained quiet. Yet the riot in the Close had demonstrated that there were already two sides in Exeter: that of the Dean and Chapter, supported by those, like Gilbert, who were prepared to curse and swear, and that of the puritan city councillors, supported by men like John Darke, who considered swearing a mortal sin. The old conflicts over jurisdiction and local control had been intensified and made worse by new conflicts, conflicts which centred on religious belief and cultural identity. It is clear, moreover, that the behaviour of the two competing factions at Exeter was becoming increasingly 'locked-in' to events at the political centre, with the conservative Chapter party supporting Charles I's attempts to maintain the Personal Rule and the puritan Chamber party opposing them. Already the divisions which were to result in Civil War were widening. And from 1639 onwards, the pattern of events at Exeter was to reflect the ebb and flow of national politics ever more closely.

THE DESCENT INTO CIVIL WAR

In February 1639 Charles I issued orders for his troops to march to the north. This critical step triggered protest in Exeter, showing just how much national politics had begun to influence local affairs. When a royal proclamation against the Scots was read out in the cathedral, three of the city aldermen—Jurdain, James Tucker and Thomas Crossing—ostentatiously put on their hats, thus demonstrating their opposition to the King's proceedings.[17] A few days later the offenders were ordered to appear before the royal court of Star Chamber. When they made no move to obey this order they were commanded to appear before the Privy Council itself. Jurdain was bold enough to ignore this summons, too, pleading that ill-health made it impossible for him to travel. Tucker and Crossing rode up to London in May 1639, however, and made their submission to the Privy Council, claiming they had left their hats on merely 'in respect of the coldness of the season'. Apparently satisfied with this excuse, the Council discharged the two men, who promptly returned home.[18]

Opposition to the Scots War was widespread in Exeter, but few dared to express it. The puritan preacher John Bond later recalled that 'the godly . . . inferiour subjects [in the city] . . . could only mourne in secret . . . [for] what else had they power to doe in the depth of these commotions?'.[19] On the other hand, there were many in Exeter who 'would not stop those evils [and] would not quench the fier . . . but were subtill incendiaries, . . . all for pressures and severity'.[20] One such was Archdeacon William Helyer, who in April 1639 had the King's arms in the cathedral repainted, even though they had been 'very fair' before. Perhaps worried that this public demonstration of support for the war might elicit a hostile response from the citizens, the other members of the Chapter censured Helyer for his action.[21] However, that very same day they sent off £100 as 'a contribution . . . unto his ma[jes]ty from the Chapter'.[22] This substantial cash gift can only have been intended to boost the royal war chest, and again demonstrates very clearly where the Chapter's sympathies lay.

More than ever, all eyes were now turned to the north. Would it be the King who would win the field or the Scots? In the end, the answer was to be neither. A series of indecisive skirmishes took place between the two armies during May 1639 and in June a cessation was agreed on, with battle never having been joined. This was a humiliating result for the King, whose failure to inflict a decisive defeat on the Scots did nothing to bolster his authority at home. Emboldened by the Crown's obvious weakness, increasing numbers of Englishmen began to complain about alleged royal assaults upon their own liberties.[23]

This hardening of attitudes was clearly visible at Exeter. In July the Chamber not only took steps to defend the city's power of commission of peace and gaol delivery—which had recently been 'impugned' by the royal judges—but also determined to resist the encroachments of the Stannary Bailiffs.[24] Over the past few years these minor officials, servants of the royal courts which governed the tin-mining areas of Devon, had begun to trespass openly on the city's privileged jurisdiction. Now the town councillors decided that they would no longer brook such affronts. On 23 July it was noted in the Chamber Act Book that:

> whereas the Tin Bailiffs do of late intrude upon the liberties of this city by serving of process here, it is desired that the magistrates will take the same into their considerations, and to inflict such punishments upon such lewd persons as they shall deserve.[25]

At least two Stannary bailiffs were subsequently arrested.[26] As the city councillors knew full well, the Stannary organization lay under the direct protection of the Crown and an attack on its servants was bound to arouse royal indignation. Yet the citizens were determined to uphold their decision, specifically agreeing 'that defence shall be made of the same' if necessary.[27]

The swelling tide of opposition at Exeter was temporarily stemmed in September, when the puritan James Tucker was replaced as mayor by Robert Walker.[28] Walker was later to be a keen supporter of the King and his election suggests that conservative elements on the city council had managed to stage a fightback. They were, perhaps, encouraged by the rumours of a new royal offensive in the north which had begun to circulate in autumn 1639, again raising the prospect of a triumph for the King and an indefinite continuation of the Personal Rule.[29] Yet within weeks of Walker's election, the political situation changed once again. On 5 December the King, despairing of financing a new war against the Scots through extraordinary means, decided he had no choice but to summon a Parliament.[30] Hard-line supporters of the royal regime cannot have been pleased by this news. Indeed, it may well have been the rumours of a forthcoming Parliament which decided the Exeter Chapter to build up a war-chest of ready money. On 7 December they entered into an arrangement with Mayor Walker, by which he agreed to pay them the enormous sum of 8,000 for a local manor which they owned.[31] With Walker's money stowed away under their belts, the Chapter could at least hope to engage powerful backers if, as seemed all too likely, an assault was launched on them in the coming Parliament. Nor was this the only service which Walker performed for the cathedral clergy at this time. On 21 December it was noted that Walker, in his capacity as mayor, had 'commanded the [city] poor to forbear the Dean and Chapter's doors whereby they are freed from a great molestation'. The grateful clergymen agreed that £4 10s should therefore be given to Walker 'to be distributed amongst the poor this Christmas'.[32]

How should this incident be interpreted? What were these menacing crowds of people doing? The Chapter's decision to hand out money to the poor suggests that it was a desire for alms which had prompted so many to flock to the cathedral gates, and no doubt this was partly true. There was genuine economic hardship in Exeter at this time. The cloth trade—the mainstay of the local economy—had long been depressed and many workers had been laid off, so there was bound to be a clamour for charity.[33] Yet the sudden appearances of these crowds may also have been linked to the political situation. It was during this very month that the decision to summon a Parliament had been made, after a gap of nearly eleven years. To those (probably the vast majority) who saw Parliament as the ultimate guarantor of England's rights and liberties, this news came as an immense relief. And to that increasing minority who believed in the existence of a popish plot the relief must have been overwhelming. The King's decision to summon a Parliament was an admission that the Personal Rule could no longer be sustained. Now, zealous protestants hoped, the policies of the last eleven years could be reversed. Now, the drift to the right in religious matters could be halted. And, now, accounts could be settled with the 'Arminian' bishops who had promoted 'innovations' in religion and brought the country into war with the Scots. It seems possible, then, that some of those who appeared before the cathedral gates at Exeter in December 1639 had come to jeer at, or even to threaten, the discomforted clergymen and, certainly, the spectre of the mob was increasingly to haunt the Dean and Chapter over the next few months.

On 18 January 1640 the Chapter sent £500 to the central authorities in London, ostensibly as 'a free gift towards the repairing of the Church of St Pauls'.[34] Quite possibly this money really *was* intended for the rebuilding of St Paul's Cathedral; Charles I had been gathering money for such a project throughout the 1630s.[35] Yet it is also possible that the Chapter hoped that the money would be put to other uses, that—assisted by financial contributions such as this—the King might somehow manage to wriggle out of summoning a Parliament. If this was indeed their hope, it was doomed to disappointment. In March 1640 official writs reached the city for the election of MPs.[36]

Little is known about the election contest which took place in Exeter over the next few days, but the two candidates who eventually emerged victorious (on 17 March) made an interesting pair; they were Alderman James Tucker and Mayor Robert Walker.[37] That two such very different men should have been chosen is significant, for it suggests that political opinion among the city freemen (the body of around 1,000 respectable citizens who elected Exeter's MPs) was sharply divided.[38] Walker's election demonstrated once again that he and his conservative supporters possessed a powerful constituency across the city as a whole. Yet in the Chamber they remained badly outnumbered, a fact of which they were soon to be forcibly reminded.

The summoning of Parliament had acted as a green light to the forces of opposition in Exeter, and within two weeks of the writs' arrival an attack had been launched on the position of the conservative mayor. On 24 March the Chamber passed what was described as 'an act for matters for the public good to be viewed and acted though the Mayor will not consent'. The import of this unprecedented act was that the mayor would no longer be allowed to set the agenda of Chamber business, as he had always done in the past, but that any councillor should be permitted to suggest matters for discussion. As long as a majority of the councillors considered the subject worthy of attention, it could then be discussed whether the mayor liked it or not.[39] Walker was thus reduced to a position of near impotence on the Chamber, as the puritan, 'oppositionist' elements seized control. On the very same day that this act was passed the Chamber set up a committee to co-ordinate 'the Parliament businesses'. The members of this body were directed to 'call every [one] of the commons to confer together about the . . . [Parliament], and to meet weekly every Tuesday'.[40] Greatly alarmed by the drift of events, the Chapter took further steps to safeguard their position. On 28 March they hired a full-time lawyer.[41] Six days later they ordered that £2 should be given to the mayor 'for the relief of the poor against this Easter'.[42] Once again, it seems, the cathedral clergymen were anticipating popular disturbances.

Their fears proved well-founded. It was lamented in the Chapter Act Book on 8 April that 'we find daily the church much abused and prophaned by the standing open of the doors all day'. Accordingly, the clergy agreed 'that the church... shall be kept shut and not opened but in the tyme of divine service'.[43] On 13 April, the very day that the Parliament opened in London, more trouble broke out in Exeter, when two men were reported for breaking the windows of St Sidwells church.[44] No more evidence about this incident survives but it is tempting to see it an act of deliberate iconoclasm. Quite possibly, those who broke down the decorated church windows hoped that such actions were about to be legitimized by the new Parliament. Indeed the destruction may well have been of a celebratory nature, designed to mark the opening of the assembly that was expected to cure the nation's various ills (of which excessive church decoration was perceived by zealous protestants to be one). If this was indeed the case the iconoclasts were to be disappointed. Charles I soon found that his newly-summoned Parliament was not prepared to grant him the money he needed to fight the Scots until many other grievances had been redressed. Within a few short weeks he decided to dismiss the Parliament and again try to go it alone.[45]

The next few months saw attempts to maintain the Personal Rule break down altogether, amidst humiliating failure for King Charles. During summer 1640 the King somehow managed to scrape together a second army, but the troops proved mutinous and unreliable, and in August the Scots took Newcastle.[46] Charles thus lost all hope of a quick victory; to eject the Scots from Newcastle would involve a major siege, with all the necessary expenses that that would entail. Without the help of Parliament, there was simply no way in which Charles could raise this sort of money. Accordingly, writs went out for the momentous assembly which would later become known as the Long Parliament.

In Exeter two important events had taken place between the dissolution of the Short Parliament and the summoning of its successor. The first was the death of Ignatius Jurdain, which occurred sometime between 2 June (when he attended his last council meeting) and 18 June (when he was buried in St Mary Arches Church).[47] Jurdain's death was a heavy blow to the godly party in Exeter, but it was not enough to shake their grip on power, a fact which was underlined by the election of Richard Crossing—a puritan—to take Jurdain's place on the city council.[48] The second important event was the election of John Penny as mayor in late September.[49] Unfortunately no hard evidence about Penny's politico-religious beliefs has survived. He died before the Civil War broke out, so there is no way of telling which side, if any, he would eventually have supported. It is possible that Penny was himself a puritan. Alternatively, he may have been a moderate whom the radical group found it easy to influence. What is certain is that the new mayor was by no means a committed supporter of the royal regime, as his predecessor Robert Walker had been.

For the first few weeks of Penny's mayoralty, there was little sign of any change in civic policy, but it was not long before national events again began to influence affairs at Exeter. Late in October writs were sent out for the new Parliament, and, once again, the freemen of Exeter returned two candidates with sharply divergent political views. On the one hand Robert Walker was re-elected, on the other, Simon Snowe, another member of the godly faction, was selected to replace James Tucker.[50] The new Parliament finally opened on 3 November 1640—and simultaneously affairs at Exeter entered a crucial new phase. Just as the opening of the Short Parliament had sparked off an act of celebratory recognition in the city, so did the opening of the Long Parliament. Yet on this occasion, the celebratory measure was taken by the city authorities, rather than by one or two isolated individuals as had been the case in April. On the very day that the Parliament began, Exeter's magistrates compiled an unprecedented list of seventy illegal ale sellers. All were severely cautioned and warned to cease their activities.[51] The compilation of this list marks a turning point in civic policy. Henceforth, tipplers, drunkards and unregulated ale-sellers were to be pursued by the city magistrates with renewed vigour and determination. Under Mayor Walker only eleven drink-related offences had been presented to the sessions court. Under his successor at least 105 such offences were reported.[52]

Nor was this aggressive campaign against drunkenness the only sign of a change in civic policy. Swearing was also increasingly clamped down on after 3 November. Under Mayor Walker only one Exonian had been fined for swearing, but under Penny twenty-five people were punished for this offence. Penny's mayoralty saw an upsurge in prosecutions for sabbath breaking too. On 11 November, just eight days after Parliament had opened, an Exeter man was fined for 'his acte of profanacion' in 'gathering of sand . . . on the Sabbath'.[53] Two days later the Chamber launched a new offensive against sexual immorality, noting that 'by the ancient custom of this city, whores and other such lewd people hath been used to be punished at the Cart's Tail up and down the streets for the more public show of the offenders'. During the 1630s this practice had ceased, but now, the dominant party on the Chamber agreed, 'it's much desired that the old custom be revived for such a common and notorious sin'. Accordingly the city treasurer was directed to provide a new cart.[54] The evidence from the city records makes it quite clear that a renewed campaign of moral reformation had been launched in Exeter—and that this campaign had been directly inspired by the summoning of the Long Parliament. We need not be surprised by this. Contemporaries believed that the new Parliament was about to undertake a thorough reformation in church and state.[55] In the light of these expectations, it is perfectly understandable that puritan groups across the country should have begun a similar, and simultaneous, reformation in their own localities once the national Parliament had actually begun to sit.

The puritans' expectations of the new Parliament were well-founded. At Westminster, the MPs not only refused Charles's pleas for money but quickly seized the political initiative. Rather than assisting the King against the Scots, they set to work to reform the state by dismantling the institutions on which the Personal Rule had been based. The King's chief ministers were arrested and the prerogative courts were voted down. Similar measures were taken to reform the English Church. Archbishop Laud was arrested and other allegedly Arminian clergymen dismissed, while orders went out that church decorations—stained glass, altar rails and painted frescos—should be removed. Needless to say Parliament's orders were obeyed with alacrity by Exeter's puritan city councillors. The Chapter party meanwhile, which had been able to rely on central government support against its local enemies during the Personal Rule, now found that the boot was firmly on the other foot. During 1641-42 the Chapter found itself coming under increasingly serious attack from Parliament, from the Exeter Chamber, and most frightening of all, from radical, anti-clerical, elements of the local populace.

These were heady days for the godly in Exeter, and from pulpits all over the city radical preachers like John Bond exulted in England's 'Deliverance' from the 'Babylonish captivity' of the Personal Rule.[56] Hundreds of ordinary Exonians clearly agreed with these sentiments, athough little evidence about their opinions has survived. Typical may well have been James White, a city merchant, who recorded in his private chronicle at this time that 'the Parliament affaires goe on prettie roundly and with good successe' (see document 1 (1640-1)). Yet not everyone felt the same way and a Parliamentary decree that a national fast should be kept on 8 December 1640 was received with contempt by a number of Exeter citizens. Several groups of men pointedly ignored Parliament's order and sat tippling in alehouses instead; for this they were later bound over by the JPs.[57] Significantly, the most prominent of these offenders, Hugh Hance, later went on to support the King during the Civil War—as did all four of the solid citizens who stood surety for the tipplers.[58] It is hard to avoid the conclusion that, even as early as this, a nascent anti-Parliamentarian party was beginning to form in Exeter.

This was certainly the impression of John Bond. In a sermon preached in 1641 he launched a bitter attack on those he termed 'a sort of Anti-Deliverancers amongst us' and told his auditors how to identify the enemies in their midst (see document 3). Bond's sermon provides a fascinating, and very unusual, picture of the proto-Royalist party in England in 1641: of those whose opposition to Parliament's proceedings would eventually lead them to come out in support of the King. Particularly important are the hints which Bond supplies about the political ancestry of the 'Anti-Deliverancers'. The faction included, he notes, 'all . . . [those] which in their sermons and discourses, by their pennes, purses or otherwise . . . [had] engaged themselves against the Scots'. Also represented were the 'Anti-Sabbatarians': those who had defended the traditional Sunday pastimes. Finally there were the conformist ministers and cathedral men: those who had 'vented the rising doctrine . . . [of] Arminianism' from their 'golden pulpits'.[59]

Bond's sermon shows that the proto-Royalist party in Exeter had deep roots, that the 'Anti-Deliverancers' of 1641 were directly descended from the pro-war party of 1638–40, and from the loose anti-puritan alliance which had opposed Jurdain's campaign for moral reformation throughout the early seventeenth century. Other sources make it clear that the links between the local anti-puritans and the Crown long predated 1638. As long ago as 1618, it had been hinted that Jurdain's enemies in Exeter looked to the King to support them against the godly, while similar comments had been made in 1622.[60] The fact that Robert Walker, leader of the proto-Royalist party in Exeter in 1641, was the son of Thomas Walker, Jurdain's most powerful local opponent during the 1620s, seems unlikely to be mere coincidence.[61]

If a proto-Royalist party had long existed in Exeter, its growth was undoubtedly encouraged during 1641 by the increasing prominence of religious radicals in the city. These extreme protestants sometimes went so far in their words and deeds that not even the moderate puritans on the Chamber were prepared openly to countenance them, while to religious traditionalists their activities were anathema. The resentment which such men could cause is clearly illustrated by an incident in March 1641 when John Vigures, a cordwainer, launched a passionate verbal assault upon the cathedral clergy. His outburst was heard by several scandalized onlookers and promptly reported to the justices. A day or two later Vigures was brought before the sessions court and accused of saying that part of the service used at the cathedral 'was popery', that 'the bowing at the name of Jesus was popery' and that most of the clergy 'were Arminians'.[62] The accusations seem unlikely to have been false; the cordwainer was convicted of iconoclasm in a subsequent incident and he clearly held radical religious beliefs. Vigures's words caused bitter controversy in Exeter. Not only were those whom he had abused deeply offended, but it was also suspected by some that the justices would allow him to get off lightly. On the day of Vigures's trial a yeoman named Robert Carter was bound over 'for questioning the ... Mayor and Justices of partialty, in saying that they will hear nothing against ... Vigures touching the foresaid premises'.[63] Carter's words confirm that, in some circles, Mayor Penny and the city JPs were perceived as being favourably inclined towards religious radicals.

In the event the magistrates did bind Vigures over, thus preserving at least a semblance of neutrality. Yet the incident had stirred up old suspicions and it was not long before fresh trouble broke out. A few weeks after Vigures's conviction a riot, which unfortunately remains very obscure, took place in the Cathedral Close 'on the Lord's Day'. During the course of this tumult one of the participants opined that 'Mr Mayor was a knave'.[64] Similar sentiments were expressed in April by John Sowden, of Broadclyst, who demonstrated his contempt for Penny's social origins by saying 'that Mr Mayor ... was but a hosier', adding that the mayor and the sheriff were 'loggerheads'.[65] Both comments are suggestive. Gibes about the allegedly humble origins of the Parliamentarians later went on to become a staple of Royalist propaganda, while the abusive term 'loggerhead' was applied to puritans on other occasions before the Civil War (perhaps with the meaning of 'one who spreads dissension'?) and may well have been a forerunner of the later soubriquet 'Roundhead'.[66] Sowden's comments thus tend to support the theory that Penny was puritanically inclined.

More trouble occurred in June when John Pince, fuller, was bound over 'for shouting at Mr Alderman Bennett and some of the constables of this city, and causing divers other boys to do the like in their going into the Bonhay ... [on] Sunday'.[67] This incident requires a little explanation. The Bonhay was an island in the River Exe, where the citizens of Exeter were accustomed to take their recreation. Brawling, drinking and fornication were common here, as were a wide variety of games: trap-ball, shuffle-board and nine holes.[68] Despite puritan disapproval, these games had continued to be enjoyed, albeit furtively, by many Exonians up until 1641. Now, with the new tide of moral reformation sweeping strongly through the city, strenuous efforts were made to halt the gaming. Adam Bennet, a leading puritan councillor, was at the forefront of this campaign and it seems probable that the incident referred to above occurred when Bennet—accompanied by the city officers—came to suppress gaming in the Bonhay and met with an angry response from the youths who were at play there. The episode provides further strong evidence of local opposition to the puritans' policies.

Bennett's efforts to secure a moral reformation in Exeter aroused more dissent a few weeks later, when Adrian Moore, a weaver, was reported to the magistrates 'for saying that no man hath done him more mischief than Mr Alderman Bennet and that he [Bennett] hath been the cause of two of his servants going away' (apparently because they had been forbidden from gaming on Sundays). When John Sprague, a puritan constable, reproved Moore 'for suffering his servants to play on Sunday last', the exasperated Moore replied 'that he knew no other day for them to play on but that'. For these unwise comments he was later bound over.[69] Further anti-puritan sentiment surfaced in August when a man was hauled before the sessions court for 'speaking of scandalous words of Mr Henry Paynter and his doctrine'.[70] Paynter was a well-known radical and this was not the first time that he had aroused the hostility of religious conservatives in Exeter.[71] However, he clearly had the support of the Chamber, which had appointed him to give the weekly sermon known as the 'Bodley Lecture' in St Lawrence parish.[72] Needless to say, the man who had spoken out against Paynter was bound over by the magistrates.[73]

The dominance of the godly party was confirmed in September 1641 when Penny was replaced as mayor by Richard Saunders (the man who had quelled the Broadgate riot four years before).[74] Saunders' election must have greatly cheered the Exeter puritans, for national events had now begun to take an alarming turn. Unhappiness at Parliament's activities—of the type which Bond had identified earlier that year—was growing across the whole kingdom, and during October several alleged 'plots' against the Parliament were exposed. Worse still, Ireland exploded into rebellion, as the catholic inhabitants of that country rose to free themselves from the English yoke. Many protestant settlers were massacred, and rumours of imminent invasion were soon flooding into western England, creating an atmosphere of terror and foreboding that was to endure for many months (see document 4).

It was in this climate of fear that serious disturbances began to occur at Exeter. On 29 October two London merchants were brought before the justices and accused of 'endeavouring to seduce divers of his Majesties subjects from their allegiance . . . and refusing to take the Oath of Supremacy'. These men were quite clearly religious radicals, and they frankly 'acknowledged that they had not been at any church this twelve months past, neither did they know any ground they should'.[75] The precise occasion of their arrest remains obscure but it was probably connected with a simultaneous outbreak of iconoclasm in Exeter. On the very same day that the merchants were arrested, John Vigures (the man who had earlier accused the cathedral clergy of Arminianism) was bound over in £60 for breaking the windows of St Mary Arches church, while Thomas Minshall, one of the Chapter, was reported for 'speaking against the House of Commons for the order that they had set forth for the taking downe of rails and images'.[76] According to the court's informants, Minshall had said that 'the images and rails in the churches cost blood in setting of them up, and he did think they would cost somewhat ado before they would be pulled down'. 'None but such fellowes as Paynter and Bond are would have the old order put down and put in new', added Minshall, reiterating that 'it would cost blood in taking of it down'.[77] Despite Minshall's efforts, the decorated glass in the cathedral was eventually destroyed, but his words show that some Exeter people were already coming to believe that England's religious divisions could only be resolved by bloodshed. Minshall's sinister forecast clearly rattled the justices, who bound him over in the very large sum of £150.[78]

Two weeks later further dispute broke out over religious issues, when Thomas Baker, parson of St Mary Major parish, complained to the judges about the behaviour of John Tucker, clerk, whom he had 'lately entertained . . . to be his curate there . . . but for some cause had dismissed'. According to Baker, the curate had refused to accept his dismissal. Instead he had carried on as before, giving notice to the parishioners that he would hold a communion service on Sunday 14 November. Learning of this, Baker sent a message to his erstwhile curate 'acquaint[ing] him that he [Baker] intended to officiate the place of the minister there at that time himself' and ordering Tucker 'not to meddle therewithall'.[79] Tucker received this message with a bad grace, 'us[ing] very reproachful terms and speeches'. Nevertheless Baker seems to have felt that the basic point of his message had been driven home for, following this exchange, he heard no more from his curate. Expecting no further trouble, Baker arrived at the church on Sunday as planned. He then took divine service according 'to those holy rites . . . which are appointed by the laws of this realm' and called his parishioners to draw near and receive the communion. Yet just as Baker was 'going towards the Communion Table to do his office' the irrepressible Tucker burst into the church and 'did rush into the pulpit to preach, to the disturbance of the people and hindrance of the administration of the Holy Sacrament'.[80]

This is the story as Baker tells it. It will be noted that he makes no mention of any doctrinal disputes. Yet other information given to the sessions court makes it quite clear that Tucker was a religious radical. In February 1641 the curate had referred to the prayer book as 'cold Common Prayer', to the outrage of many of the parishioners. In addition he had repeatedly refused to make the sign of the cross during the ceremony of baptism. An impressive number of Tucker's former parishioners lined up to testify against him, suggesting that his beliefs had aroused considerable opposition in the parish.[81] And once again, a clear link can be discerned between those who opposed puritan activists in 1641 and those who went on to support the King in 1642. Of the nine men who informed on Tucker, four were later prominent Royalists.[82] The JPs acted promptly on receiving this mass of information and Tucker was bound over in £60.[83] Once again the image of judicial impartiality had been preserved but it is hard not to suspect that some of the JPs felt a secret sympathy for Tucker.

Next month yet another religious controversy broke out in Exeter, when two young men barged into the cathedral during service time. Their entrance was loud and disorderly, and John Burnell, a worshipper who was standing in the choir stalls, asked them to be quiet, saying 'gentlemen, me thinks you might have a little manners'. This polite rebuke did not have its intended effect. The boldest of the intruders, an apprentice named John Crosse, retorted brusquely 'Manners? Wherefore?'. When Burnell replied that respect should be shown in the time of divine service, Crosse launched into an impassioned tirade, saying 'he lied' and 'it was no divine service and so it should be proved before the best in the land'. Crosse next went on to attack the music used in the cathedral service, saying that 'he would fetch three or four ragged tinckerly rogues that should make as good music as they [the cathedral clergy] did, with their horns and pipes'. Crosse then mockingly told another man that 'if the Dean would cause the choristers to play on', he (Crosse) 'would fetch some to dance'. When the man threatened to 'acquaint Mr Dean' with the matter, Crosse contemptuously replied 'let Mr Dean go shit'.[84]

These heated exchanges naturally attracted a good deal of attention, resulting in 'the congregating of many people together in the church to the great disturbance of that place', and it was not long before Henry Rowcliffe, the cathedral notary, felt bound to intervene. Rowcliffe later deposed that on the day of the disturbance he had seen 'divers people gathered together in the North Isle of the ... Church making great tumult and noise'. Accordingly, he had made his way to the centre of the throng 'and demanded what the cause of the said noise was and withall desired them to be quiet in the time of divine service'. Crosse immediately bawled out 'that he did not know whether it were divine service or no'. When Rowcliffe tartly enquired of the apprentice 'whether he did not hear the two chapters read and whether he did not think that to be part of divine service', Crosse replied darkly 'I think it be so, if it be not corrupted'. Further angry pleas for silence followed, and at length Crosse seems to have desisted. There matters rested until next day, when members of the Chapter came to the city court and made bitter representations against Crosse.[85]

The JPs took their complaints seriously and on 31 December Crosse was bound over in £120. This was a large sum; throughout the whole of 1641 only Minshall and some catholic recusants had been required to provide greater sureties by the Exeter bench.[86] The high level of bail set for Crosse probably reflects the fact that even moderate puritans regarded his conduct as beyond the pale. Yet the apprentice had his supporters, too, and it is interesting to note that the three men who stood surety for him all subsequently embraced the Parliamentary cause.[87] More intriguing still is the fact that John Crosse's master was none other than Nicholas Carwithen, grocer, one of the most radical of the city puritans, and a man who had himself been apprenticed to Ignatius

Jurdain's cousin.[88] Carwithen had been involved in several controversies before this time, and later went on to become one of Parliament's most fervent local supporters.

January 1642 found Exeter tense and divided. The fracas in the cathedral had amply demonstrated the animosity which was being generated in the city by disputes over religion. The national situation seemed ominous: on 4 January Charles I, accompanied by 400 soldiers, had made an abortive attempt to arrest John Pym and four other leading opponents in the House of Commons. This aggressive action sparked off hysterical scenes in the capital. Fearful of a military coup, vast crowds of Londoners protested on the city streets and, six days later, Charles I decided he had no choice but to abandon his capital. That night the King fled to Hampton Court, leaving London in the hands of his opponents. These momentous events had immediate repercussions in Exeter. On 11 January the Chamber ordered that the town walls should be inspected and the watch increased. Four days later 'five severall peticions' were presented to the Chamber:

> subscribed by manie of the . . . inhabitants of this cittie, expressing severall dangers apprehended by them to the decayes of their trades, occationed by the disturbances in London, & opposicions by Bishopps & Popish Lords in Parliament, with their desires that the same may be presented to his Majestie & the houses of Parliament.[89]

These petitions have not survived, but the précis given in the Chamber Act Book suggests that they were very similiar to the petitions which were sent to the Devon JPs by the inhabitants of Dartmouth, Plymouth, Totnes and Tavistock at around the same time.[90] The similarity in the wording of these petitions implies a degree of collusion, possibly even of pre-planning, on the part of their anonymous organizers. The fact that all the petitions specifically blamed the bishops for the trouble in London, moreover, suggests that the petitioners were not pushing a truly neutral line. Religious conservatives would have resented the tone of the documents, and this probably helps to explain why the five petitions presented to the Exeter Chamber initially aroused 'much debate'.[91] Even so, a majority of the councillors eventually agreed that the petitions should be adopted and 'fitted up . . . withall convenient speed'. On 17 January the final versions of the petitions were approved, and two members of the Chamber set off to deliver them to the King and the Parliament.[92]

As the dominant body on the Chamber cautiously began to manoeuvre Exeter into the Parliamentary camp, fears of imminent conflict grew. On 23 January George Macey, an Exeter grocer, was accused of spreading dangerous rumours. Passing through the mid-Devon village of Colebrooke he had allegedly told a local innkeeper that 'within fourteen days or thereabout it would be as bad and worse in England then ever they heard of Ireland'. Upset by these dark prognostications, the innkeeper replied that he hoped Macey was wrong. Yet Macey was undeterred and 'answered again he would warrant it'. When the man inquired further, asking Macey if 'he were doubtful of any troubles in the North ... the said Macey answered "it might be as well here as there" '. These ominous words evidently frightened the innkeeper. A few days later he reported Macey to the Exeter JPs and the grocer found himself being bound over in £150.[93] Was it just coincidence that Macey, like the radical apprentice John Crosse, was a resident of St. Mary Arches parish? Was it just coincidence that Macey's own apprentice—Otho Bastard—was the young man who had burst into the cathedral with Crosse in December 1641? And was it just coincidence that one of those who stood surety for Macey was Crosse's master, Nicholas Carwithen?[94] It seems at least possible that a hard-core group of radicals in Exeter were purposely spreading rumours of catholic plots and imminent bloodshed, in the hope of frightening the populace at large into adhering more firmly to Parliament's cause.

The city magistrates were not, as yet, prepared to sanction such extreme tactics, but as 1642 wore on their underlying sympathies became increasingly clear, and those Exonians who dared to voice their opposition to puritan/Parliamentarian policies were punished. When William Tayler barracked the mayor and justices as they were taking the Parliamentary-sponsored oath of Protestation (see document 2) and spoke 'uncivil words of Mr Henry Painter then present about the same service' he was promptly bound over.[95] A week later Robert Carter —perhaps the same man who had accused Mayor Penny of favouring the puritans in 1641—was punished for his 'seditious words', while, in March, Nicholas Jagoe was bound over for speaking 'dangerous words touching the Parliament'.[96] Jagoe's arraignment was quickly followed by that of Thomas Baker, the vicar of St Mary Major who had reported his radical curate to the court in 1641. Now it was Baker's turn to be reported—for preaching a 'scandalous sermon' at the March assizes. Baker's offence was obviously felt to be particularly heinous, for he was bound over in the unprecedented sum of £300.[97] Significantly, both the Devon gentlemen who stood surety for him later went on to become prominent Royalists.[98]

As anti-puritans continued to be punished in the sessions court, the pro-Parliamentarian group tightened its hold on the Chamber. On 15 February James Marshall—a resident of St Mary Arches and another of those who had stood surety for Macey in January—was elected to the council.[99] Marshall was soon to emerge as a leading Parliamentarian, and his election pushed the conservative party on the Chamber still further into the minority. More evidence of the puritan/Parliamentarian ascendancy appeared in April, when the Chamber agreed that a piece of plate worth £50 should be given to Nicholas Carwithen and others 'towards their severall charges in their late journye to London about the peticon to his Majestie & the Parliament'.[100] That the radical Carwithen should have been one of those entrusted with the delivery of these petitions suggests that majority opinion on the Chamber was now shifting still further to the political 'left'.

This impression is further reinforced by the fact that, during May and June, the city authorities failed to publish a series of proclamations which Charles I had issued from York in an attempt to explain his case.[101] The puritan/Parliamentarian faction was clearly growing bolder and it is perhaps significant that, on 23 June, the Chamber ordered that Henry Painter's Bodley lecture—hitherto held in St Lawrence parish—should be removed to St Mary Arches.[102] This parish was not only the spiritual centre of Exeter puritanism, it was also the home of the most important councillors. It does not seem too fanciful to suggest that, by establishing Painter's zealously puritan lecture here, in the heart of civic government, the dominant party on the Chamber was making a symbolic declaration of allegiance. Clear evidence that the city JPs were taking a more partisan stand emerged a week later, when a weaver named Lewis Stapledon was bound over by the court 'for speaking seditious words against Puritans and Roundheads'.[103] This is the first time that the hostile nickname 'Roundhead'—used to denote supporters of the Parliament—is recorded at Exeter, and that Stapledon should have been punished for using it is clear proof of where the JPs' sympathies lay.

Reports of the situation in Exeter had by now reached the King himself, and on 2 July Charles wrote a letter to the city councillors, taxing them with their failure to issue his proclamations, and reminding them, pointedly, of the many privileges which the Crown had bestowed upon the city.[104] Despite the King's implied threat, the dominant party on the Chamber remained unmoved. Instead they moved into a closer alliance with the Deputy Lieutenants of Devon, who were then preparing to secure the county militia forces for Parliament. By mid-July the Devon Deputy Lieutenants were active in Exeter, holding meetings at the New Inn and sending out commissions to Parliament's local supporters.[105] Further evidence of co-operation between the pro-Parliamentarians of Exeter and Devon appeared on 26 July, when the Chamber agreed:

> that 2 severall petitions shalbe foorthwith prepared, th'one for his Majestie, th'other for the Parliament, expressing the greate feares the petitioners have att present of the distraccions, & supplicating for a happie accomodacion.[106]

As had been the case in January, this petition from Exeter was obviously designed to appear in conjunction with other, very similar, petitions from Devon which were being drawn up at the same time. And although these petitions have sometimes been regarded as 'neutralist' documents they were, in fact, nothing of the sort. Instead, the Devon petitions, while deploring the prospect of war, showed clear 'support for Parliament and concern for the King's activities'.[107] It seems almost certain that the Exeter petition was written in the same vein.

On the same day that the decision to draw up this petition was made, the Chamber ordered that, '[as] the tymes growe more dangerous', the night watch should be strengthened.[108] This order reflected the fact that the pro-Parliamentarian faction was now facing the first real challenge to its authority since the year of Walker's mayoralty. The Earl of Bath had recently been sent into Devon by the King with orders to rally the local community to the royal cause, and had announced that—in order to convey his message to as wide an audience as possible—he would attend the summer assizes which were soon to be held in Exeter. This news must have delighted local conservatives, but alarmed their opponents. Speculation as to how the city's rulers would react was intense and in an assize sermon delivered on 7 August the puritan preacher Thomas Trescott beseeched the assembled councillors to keep their nerve. 'Oh let it never be said of you that the fire of zeal was quite put out by the death of one Holy Ignatius [Jurdain]', Trescott admonished them, going on to deliver a thinly-veiled plea that the councillors should stick together, eschew equivocation in public affairs and declare themselves openly for Parliament (see document 5). Such a strategy was easy to recommend, but much less easy to adopt, for—as Trescott himself acknowledged—the councillors were deeply divided. 'Do not enterfare and clash one with another', Trescott begged, for 'if we once fall a dashing, we shall all fal in pieces'. 'If magistrates be not well glued . . . together, their disagreement breeds nothing but mischiefe and confusion' he added, concluding, ominously, that 'if they doe not appeare together it presageth a storme'.[109]

With Trescott's words still ringing in their ears, and Bath expected to appear before the city gates at any moment, the pro-Parliamentary faction on the Chamber found themselves in a difficult position. They could hardly refuse the King's representative permission to enter the city without dropping their neutralist mask, yet if the Earl were admitted, he might try to impose firm royal authority upon Exeter. Eventually, on 9 August, the Chamber took two crucial decisions. First it was agreed that the city gunpowder magazine should not be handed over to 'any person or persons' (presumably a reference to Bath and his followers) without the Chamber's consent. Second, four councillors were sent out to meet the Earl on his way to the city. If they found that Bath came 'in an ordinarie way, unarmed' he was to be escorted into Exeter with all due respect. If, however, the Earl appeared 'in a warlick manner' with more than one hundred armed men, the councillors were to stall and send back word to the Chamber (see document 6 (9 August 1642)). In the event Bath's demeanour must have satisfied the Chamber's emissaries, for later that day he was admitted to the city.[110]

Bath's presence had a heartening effect on the King's supporters in Exeter and following his arrival tentative efforts were made to halt the city's slide into the Parliamentary camp. On 9 August one Simon Zeager was brought before the justices by a city loyalist and charged with speaking 'traiterous words of the King's Majestie . . . [namely] that the King . . . [encouraged] the Rebells in Ireland . . . and that the King mayntayne[d] Papists about him against the Protestants'.[111] Zeager was promptly committed to prison for this speech, his punishment showing that, for the moment at least, the city authorities dared not tolerate such open criticism of the King. Attempts to disseminate Royalist propaganda were also made in Exeter during this period, and on 12 August a musician was accused of having sung a 'scandalous songe . . . touching . . . the five members of the House of Commons' at the Bear Inn, to an appreciative crowd of gentlemen.[112] There was clearly a strong groundswell of support for the King in Exeter—yet in the end Bath failed to capitalize on this.

Once the assizes had actually begun, on 12 August, it rapidly became clear that 'the Devon Grand Jury . . . sided with Parliament against the King'.[113] Bath, realizing that he could not win over the county jurors, seems to have given up hope of securing Exeter too. Next day he rode out of the city, having achieved nothing, and most of the pro-Royalist county gentry probably went with him.[114] Bath's departure effectively handed Exeter over to the King's enemies. Hitherto, fears that royal control might somehow be re-imposed upon the city had ensured that open support for Parliament remained muted, but now the King's local representative had shown he was unable to control affairs. Indeed, his precipitate departure from the assizes seemed an admission of weakness. With the fear of immediate repercussions removed, the puritan faction on the Chamber could finally throw off what remained of its neutralist mask. Bath's departure marked the end of the period in which Exeter's allegiance could still be regarded as in any way undecided. Henceforth no more royal officers were to enter the city, no more individuals were to be punished by the city JPs for abusing the King, and no more measures were to be taken by the city authorities to protect the rites of the established church. Exeter was now effectively a city held for Parliament.

4

'Rebel City'
Exeter under Parliamentarian Control

The Chamber Divides

Following the Earl of Bath's departure the political splits which had long existed within the Exeter Chamber at last came out into the open. Its pro-Royalist members began to withdraw from council meetings. From 25 August until the period of Parliamentary dominance in Exeter came to an end, Robert Walker, the conservative ex-mayor, attended just two out of a total of thirty-five council meetings (see Table 2, p. 224). A similar pattern can be seen in the case of three other councillors—John Colleton, Nicholas Spicer and Hugh Crocker—who came to only five, eight and thirteen meetings respectively over the same period. Walker, Colleton, Spicer and Crocker all went on to become prominent supporters of the King and, intriguingly, it was these same four men who had been the least frequent attenders at Chamber meetings during the pre-war period (see Table 1, p. 223). It seems plausible to suggest that the Royalist group of 1642–46 was the direct descendant of a pre-war 'out-group', or minority faction, therefore, one which had been opposed to the puritan majority on the Chamber. The fact that Spicer had been castigated by the godly activist Nicholas Carwithen in 1632 as one who was 'neither good for church or commonwealth' tends to bear this theory out.[1]

If it was the future Royalists who had been the least regular attenders at pre-war meetings, then it was the godly and the future Parliamentarians who had been the most assiduous. Predictably enough, Ignatius Jurdain had topped the poll, attending no fewer than 97 per cent of all meetings held before his death. He was followed in regularity of attendance by James Gould, John Hakewill, Thomas Crossing, Richard Yeo, Richard Saunders, James White, Joseph Trobridge, John Acland, Walter White, Richard Crossing and Adam Bennet, all of whom attended over 75 per cent of pre-war Chamber meetings (see Table 1). Of these twelve individuals—presumably the most active and influential of the pre-war city councillors—two (Acland and Trobridge) died before mid-1643.[2] All the rest went on to support the Parliament however (although admittedly Thomas Crossing and Richard Yeo later turned their coats), and this in itself undoubtedly does much to explain why Exeter as a whole eventually went the same way.[3]

In London, effective Parliamentary control was only secured after many of the city's accustomed, conservative rulers had been displaced.[4] In Exeter no such drastic change in the civic hierarchy was necessary. Rather, the period 1641–42 saw an intensification of pre-existent trends, as the conservative councillors—already in the minority—were marginalized still further, while the members of the already dominant godly party began to play an ever more central role in civic government. This is well illustrated by the fact that almost all of those who had been the most frequent attenders at council meetings during the pre-war period, went on to attend even *more* frequently during the period of Parliamentary dominance (see Table 2, p. 224).

Tightening the Parliamentary Grip

The Parliamentary faction may have controlled the Chamber, but they could not yet feel confident of controlling Exeter as a whole, for many of the inhabitants—possibly even a majority—were opposed to them.[5] Faced with this widespread popular hostility, the Chamber Parliamentarians had to do all they could to neutralize alternative power-centres and, predictably enough, their first moves were made against the Cathedral Chapter. Devoid of military strength, the clergymen had no hope of resisting the Chamber's orders. On 13 August they were forced to agree that the city watchmen should in future be allowed to enter the Close while making their nightly rounds—a triumph which the godly town councillors must have savoured.[6] Having established its authority over this potential enclave of disaffection the Chamber next turned to deal with external threats, ordering that 'in these dangerous tymes' the city watchmen should be increased (see document 6 (25 August 1642)).

The porter of Westgate was also dismissed, to be replaced by someone whom the Chamber could trust.[7]

Towards the end of August a 'Committee for the Safetie of the Cittie' was elected by Mayor Saunders and 'some of the aldermen', presumably the Parliamentarian ones. This committee was a direct imitation of the similarly-named body which had been set up by Parliament's supporters in London eight months before.[8] Fifteen men were appointed to it, almost all of them being prominent Parliamentarians, and henceforth the committee was to oversee all preparations for Exeter's defence. In September its members proposed that 'some ingeneere or other person well experienced in marshall disciplyne should be procured to be here continuallie resident' (see document 6 (8 September 1642)) and this recommendation quickly resulted in the appointment of Captain Peter Bagster as Exeter's military engineer.[9] While the Committee looked to Exeter's physical defences, the Chamber redoubled its efforts to root out 'malignant' (i.e. Royalist) civic officials, ordering on 13 September that only 'honest persons' should be permitted to take the night watch (see document 6).

Meanwhile a major overhaul of Exeter's ancient defences had begun. The Chamber had been concerned about the state of the crumbling city walls for some time, and in September the members of the Committee for Safety were requested to view the wall along its entire circuit.[10] Repairs got under way almost at once and on 13 September it was ordered that 'the citties gunnes ... shall be foorthwith mounted' (see document 6). This process involved the cannon being dragged up onto the 'barbican' (the earth rampart which lay behind the city wall) and sited on specially constructed 'mounts', or batteries. The Chamber possessed only six pieces of artillery in September 1642.[11] More guns were swiftly procured, however, and within a month Exeter had '25 pieces of ordnance ready mounted'.[12]

Needless to say, these defensive preparations did not meet with the approval of local loyalists. On 20 September Robert Hore and Phillip Edwards, two of the city's new watchmen, deposed that, while 'comyng this evening towards the Guildhall ... to watch by command of the Maior' they had been 'misused and assaulted in their way by William Blight, gent, who gave them divers reproachful speeches touching their intended service, and stroke the said Edwards uppon the head with a staffe'. For this offence—and also for using 'unseemlie termes' of the mayor—Blight was thrown into a cell beneath the Guildhall. The prisoner remained defiant, however, declaring that 'he knewe there were two or three hundred upp at this present to take his parte'.[13]

As Blight obviously knew, Royalist activity was now becoming increasingly visible elsewhere and, as September passed into October, 'manie dangers' were said to be threatening Exeter. On 11 October the Chamber ordered that the main gates should be shut at 6 p.m. every night, while the aldermen of each ward were 'to take care that noe strangers be interteyned within their severall quarters' (see document 6). Meanwhile Parliament, almost certainly responding to a request from the city authorities, had ordered that Exeter's trained bands, or civic militia, should be got into a state of readiness (see document 7). These orders were swiftly obeyed and officers chosen for each of the four city companies. The appointees were all prominent Parliamentarians. Indeed, at least three of the four captains chosen were members of the Committee for Safety.[14] These appointments met with no overt resistance, but there were discontented mutterings, and one man asserted that he would rather be sent to South Gate prison than march into the field under 'the Coxcombe Evans' (a reference to Richard Evans, chosen Captain of the South Quarter).[15]

Parliament's order concerning the militia also authorised the Chamber to improve Exeter's fortifications, and this speeded up the work which had already begun. By mid-October defensive preparations were under way at the castle, and a week later the Chamber ordered that East Gate and South Gate should be repaired.[16] The complaints of the cathedral clergy (who owned much of the land in this area) were not permitted to delay the work, and Archdeacon Hall was brusquely commanded to remove an enclosure of his which was impeding access to the barbican. Special care was taken to block up the underground passages which brought water-pipes into Exeter beneath the city walls. The Chamber feared that an attacking force might make use of these 'vaults' to infiltrate the defences, and it was therefore ordered that both the cathedral and the city passages should be stopped up (see document 9 (25 October 1642)). Again, the members of the Chapter had no choice but to comply.[17]

The Admission of Roundhead Troops

The repeated violations of the Dean and Chapter's privileges, the constant hounding of Royalist sympathizers in the sessions court (see document 8) and the gradual appropriation of the most important civic offices by puritan/Parliamentarians all served to bring Exeter more firmly under the Chamber's control. The Roundhead faction was still not entirely secure, however. This was made clear towards the end of September when Walter White—the most strongly Parliamentarian of the two mayoral candidates whom the Chamber had put forward to the city electorate—was rejected by the freemen in favour of Christopher Clarke, whose position was more ambivalent.[18] The contest was clearly a turbulent one. A man was later bound over 'for disturbing of the election of a newe Maior', while scathing remarks were directed at White by local Royalists, one of whom declared 'that the said Mr White was *non compos mentis*'.[19] In the end Clarke proved willing to align himself with the Parliamentary cause, but the rejection of White had shown just how much opposition there was to the hardline Parliamentarians in Exeter. Accordingly they sought a further extension of their power.

On 21 October Parliament granted the city authorities full power to search the houses and secure the persons, arms and ammunition 'of all [such] inhabitants . . . as shall, by words or actions, declare themselves refractory to the ordinance[s] of the Parliament'. It was further ordered that, 'for the defence of the said city', the Parliamentarian deputy lieutenants of Devon should have 'power to . . . send in such . . . numbers of soldiers, out of the county of Devon unto . . . [Exeter] as they shall think fit, at the request of the Mayor'. Specific provision was also made for a troop of horse to be quartered at Exeter.[20] These orders opened the way for the Parliamentarian faction on the Chamber to subdue their opponents by force of arms—and the necessary arrangements were swiftly made.

On 2 November a troop of Roundhead cavalry from Somerset, under the command of Captain Alexander Pym, arrived before East Gate. Pym demanded that his men should be allowed to enter the city, and Mayor Clarke hurried to obey, ordering that the gate should be opened and the troopers let in.[21] At this crucial moment rioting broke out on the city streets, impressive testimony of the strength of Royalist feeling in Exeter. The trouble centred on East Gate, where the watchmen had ignored the commands of the mayor and were refusing to let Pym's troopers in. The most prominent protester was Jonathan Hawkyns, cutler, who was subsequently charged with 'opposing of Captayne Pym and his company from commyng into this cittie . . . to the great disturbance of the peace'.[22] When a group of pro-Parliamentary constables appeared on the scene,

Hawkyns, armed with a halberd, defied them. Eventually the constables managed to arrest Hawkyns, only to lose him again when he was rescued by some of the bystanders (including, significantly enough, Richard Comyns, the Cathedral porter, who had so often baited the godly town constables during the 1630s). Despite this setback the Parliamentary faction eventually managed to quell the disturbances. Pym's troopers were admitted and were soon helping to track down those who had opposed their entry. By the end of that day the recalcitrant watchmen had been thrown into gaol. A watch was set at Hawkyns' house, meanwhile, presumably to arrest him should he dare to reappear.[23]

It is instructive to compare this episode with the very similar affair which took place in Bristol just a month later, when a group of local men (unsuccessfully) tried to bar the city gates against a force of Roundhead troops whom the mayor and sheriff had ordered to be admitted.[24] Scholars might well be tempted to cite these incidents as evidence of the 'localist' mentality at work, as splendid examples of provincial 'neutrals' attempting to isolate their own communities from the spread of the war. Yet as soon as one scratches beneath the surface a very different picture emerges. In both cities, those who tried to shut the gates against the Parliamentarians emerge from other sources as committed Royalists. Their actions were prompted by partisan considerations, not neutralist ones, therefore, and—in Exeter at least—the fracas at the gates can in no way be seen as the response of a unified 'localist' community to the onset of war. Instead it was just the latest round in the long, grinding, battle between the city's puritan/Parliamentarian faction and their Royalist opponents—and another round which the Royalists had lost.

The First Siege

The troopers' arrival greatly strengthened the position of Exeter's pro-Parliamentarians, permitting the Chamber to adopt a more hardline stance. In the wake of Pym's admittance the house of William Glyde, a forthright Royalist, was searched, and his weapons confiscated.[25] It was also ordered that the fruit trees on the barbican—hitherto preserved in deference to their owners' feelings—should be chopped down, while the watchmen at the gates were given extra money for candles and firelight (see document 9 (3 November 1642)). Exeter's military preparedness was fast improving, and this was just as well for, although Devon was firmly held for Parliament, Cornwall had declared itself for the King. In November 1642 Sir Ralph Hopton raised a Royalist army here and led it over the border into Devon. It was widely expected that Hopton would move upon Exeter, and the Parliamentary authorities in the city began to send out warrants for men and supplies.[26]

According to a Roundhead news-pamphlet the anticipated attack came on 18 November when the Royalists arrived before the city, the Cornishmen 'flinging up their caps and giving many great shouts for joy'. Hopton summoned the city to surrender, the same source goes on, but the citizens refused to give in. Instead they launched a bloodthirsty attack on Hopton's men, killing 2,000 of them and putting the rest to flight.[27] These claims have been accepted by previous historians.[28] Yet the attack of 18–19 November never took place. An unpublished diary shows that on 18 November, the very day that the Cornishmen are alleged to have arrived before Exeter, they were actually marching into Tavistock, some forty miles to the west.[29] The pamphlet was a propaganda piece and the events it describes are completely fictitious. Far from advancing on Exeter, the Cornish army remained quartered around Plymouth for most of November 1642.

This delay gave the Parliamentary authorities in Exeter more time to crack down on internal dissent and, to this end, they sought a further extension of their powers. Early in November, the House of Lords received a petition:

> [from] the Mayor and . . . Captains of the city of Exon, shewing . . . the imminent danger the same is now in, by means of . . . an ill-affected and malignant party in . . . the said city, who, being men of great and wealthy estates, do not only refuse to contribute to the public work of fortifications . . . but neglect to perform the ordinary duty of watching.

Parliament responded to this by ordering the city authorities to make a general rate in Exeter, 'taxing and assessing every . . . inhabitant within the same' towards the city's defence. Anyone who refused to 'chearfully contribute' their share was to be proceeded against as a malignant.[30] The screw was tightening on the Exeter Royalists, but—even as Parliament issued its orders against them—Hopton's army had started to move eastwards, prompting an upsurge of hope among local loyalists and a flurry of defensive preparations by the city authorities. More guns and ammunition were bought on 29 November, while the newly-appointed military engineer was granted a gratuity of £10 'in regard of his extraordinarie paynes taken ... here of late'. On the same day the Chamber decided that a committee should be chosen to consider ways of raising money for 'the better defence of this cittie' (see document 9).

By early December the Cornish army was only thirty miles from Exeter and the city authorities had begun to prepare for the worst, erecting fortifications and calling in reinforcements from the surrounding countryside.[31] These precautions were well-advised, for Hopton—having learnt that 'the garrison of Exon was but weake for the guard of such a place'—had indeed decided upon an attack. Learning of this the Scottish Colonel William Ruthen (then commanding Parliament's forces in Plymouth) marched to the city's assistance. Avoiding Hopton's scouts, Ruthen arrived in Exeter shortly before Christmas 'with a good party of horse and muskettiers mounted'.[32] He was warmly greeted by the city authorities, who had been watching Hopton's movements with apprehension. A payment of £1 made by the city to 'Colonel Ruthen's trumpeter' at this time almost certainly represented a reward for announcing the reinforcements' arrival.[33]

Hopton's forces were snapping at Ruthen's heels and the Royalist advance guards soon arrived on the south-western outskirts of Exeter. By 26 December loyalist elements were controlling the village of Ide and Cornish troops occupied Alphington soon afterwards.[34] From here, the Royalist commanders sent in a message to Exeter, suggesting that they came as friends and should therefore be admitted. When this letter received but a 'slight answer' from the mayor, two Cornish regiments crossed the River Exe and seized Topsham, 'the sea-towne to Exeter'. The Roundheads were greatly alarmed by these developments. According to one source, the loss of Topsham 'bred so great a fear within [Exeter] that divers of the people got over the walls by night and so fled away'.[35] The Parliamentary commanders were made of sterner stuff, however, and on 28 December they launched a fierce attack upon Topsham. Shaken, the Cavaliers abandoned their position and fell back onto the west bank of the River Exe.[36]

By 30 December the main body of the Royalist army was concentrated at Alphington. From here Hopton sent another letter to the mayor, charging him to lay down his arms and admit the Royalist forces. Hopton promised all within the city full indemnity if they would return to their allegiance. Should the inhabitants continue to defy the King's authority, however, Hopton refused to answer for the consequences, 'you cannot but expect the bitter fruits of your own planting', he hinted darkly. The mayor remained unimpressed and returned a defiant answer (see document 11), so Hopton decided on another attempt to take the city by force. The Royalists had by now got possession of Cowley Hill, a mile or two to the north of the city, and it was probably from here that they launched 'a violent storm' on Cowley Bridge, a position held by Roundhead forces. Yet despite the ferocity of their attack the Royalists failed to take the bridge.[37]

Quite what happened next is unclear. A contemporary news-pamphlet —written by Abel Hyward, a Parliamentary officer—claims that, on the morning of 1 January, the Royalists launched another fierce attack. According to Hyward, the Royalists were on the brink of victory when Captain Pym sallied out with 800 men and attacked the Cornishmen in the rear, killing 1,000 of them and putting the rest to flight.[38] There are good reasons for doubting the accuracy of this account, however. For one thing the grandiose style of Hyward's letter is uncomfortably reminiscent of the pamphlet of November 1642, which has already been dismissed as spurious. Much more serious is the fact that none of the other surviving sources make any reference to an attack upon Exeter or a subsequent Royalist rout. Instead they all suggest that the Royalists had decided to retire without fighting because they realized that they had no hope of taking the city. Hopton himself claimed that he had retreated because of poor morale among his soldiers and a shortage of supplies.[39] A Royalist pamphlet blamed the decision to retire on the approach of the Earl of Stamford with a powerful Roundhead relief force. Most Parliamentary writers took a similar line, ascribing the retreat to the season of the year and 'the approach of the Earle'.[40] One or two pamphlets *did* claim that there had been some fighting as the Cornish withdrew.[41] But if the Royalists had really suffered a defeat of the magnitude which Hyward alleges, one can be sure that other Roundhead pamphleteers would have picked up on it. As they did not it seems fair to assume that the story was either false or greatly exaggerated.[42]

What is certain is that the Cornishmen abandoned their positions before Exeter on the morning of 1 January 1643, falling back along the snow-filled lanes towards Crediton. Hopton's soldiers were cast down by their failure to take Exeter, but their disappointment was as nothing compared with that of the Royalist sympathizers within the walls. Hopton's departure—together with the arrival of hundreds more Roundhead troops under Ruthen—had left them completely exposed to the mercy of their enemies.

Royalist Nemesis

Even before the dramatic events of Christmas 1642 there had been signs of an increasing willingness on the part of the city authorities to implement repressive measures against their internal opponents. In early December, four men—all described as 'ill-affected to the peace'—had been imprisoned by virtue of the Parliamentary ordinance of 26 November.[43] Far more worrying for the city loyalists was the drawing up of a special oath or 'covenant' a few days later. This document incorporated a solemn promise to uphold 'th[e] present happy Parliament . . . [and] to defend, preserve and protect this city . . . against . . . Sir Ralph Hopton and his adherents', and was clearly designed to flush out Royalist sympathizers (see document 10).

The covenant was just one more weapon in the armoury of Exeter's puritan/Parliamentarians, who were by now planning the final moves in their long campaign against the Dean and Chapter. Accounts had already been settled with the insolent cathedral porter, Richard Comyns—arrested for his part in the riot of 2 November—and soon it would be the turn of his clerical masters. On 12 December Parliament (again presumably acting at the request of its local adherents) authorized the mayor and deputy lieutenants to seize the cathedral bells and melt them down for ammunition. In addition they were to establish a magazine for provisions in 'such part of the cathedral church . . . as may best be spared'. As a crowning humiliation for the cathedral men, Parliament also ordered that:

> in these times of public danger . . . such part of the . . . service as is performed by singing-men, choristers and organs in the cathedral church [shall] be wholly forborn and omitted, and the same to be done in a reverend, humble and decent manner, without singing or using the organs.[44]

How the radical apprentice John Crosse must have exulted when these orders reached Exeter!

Just how long it took for Parliament's instructions to be put into effect is unknown, but the last entry made in the Chapter Act Book was dated

17 December 1642.⁴⁵ Three days later the name of Dr [William] Hutchinson, one of the cathedral Canons, appeared on a list of four men who had been 'assessed' (presumably as suspected Royalists) to contribute money to the Parliamentary cause, 'by order of Collonell Ruthin'.⁴⁶ No such assessments are known to have been made before this date, and the list is thus of considerable significance. It not only bear witness to a further turning of the screw upon the city Royalists, but it also shows that it was the arrival of Ruthen's forces which had permitted the puritan/Parliamentarians to take this decisive step. Intriguingly, no further assessments were made during the period of the siege itself, perhaps because the Parliamentarians were too busy, perhaps because they were unwilling to fleece their Royalist neighbours while the possibility remained that their positions might soon be reversed. Between 20 December and 1 January the authorities contented themselves with arresting just five men 'conceived to be persons ill affected to the peace'.⁴⁷ After Hopton's departure, however, the floodgates of repression opened wide.

Hitherto, there had been little that was genuinely 'revolutionary' about the outbreak of the Civil War in Exeter. The leaders of the puritan/ Parliamentarian faction—like their counterparts in London—had proceeded by relatively slow, measured stages, never permitting events to get out of the magistracy's control.⁴⁸ Yet in the immediate aftermath of Hopton's retreat, the pent-up frustration of the pro-Parliamentary soldiers and citizens combined with a surge of elation at the Royalist defeat to produce an explosion of violence. The week of 1–7 January 1643 saw the puritan/Parliamentarians enjoying a period of catharsis, almost one of carnival, in Exeter, as they paid off old scores and humiliated their enemies. Many of the godly town councillors clearly approved of, and took part in, these activities. Chamber moderates may well have been alarmed by the turn of events, however, while Royalist observers were quite simply horrified by what they described as 'the factious tumult of the city of Exeter'.⁴⁹

According to the author of the Royalist pamphlet *Mercurius Rusticus*, the city authorities quickly put Parliament's order of 12 December into effect. First, the cathedral was locked up and all services banned. Next, the Roundhead mob embarked on an iconoclastic rampage in the cathedral church: destroying the 'popish' decorations which had offended puritan sentiment for so long (see document 13). Finally, the Parliamentarians turned to the cathedral clergy. According to *Rusticus* they laid:

intolerable taxes on most of the members of the church, and whosoever refused to submit to these most unjust and illegal impositions, were threatened to have their houses plundered and their persons sent on shipboard [at Topsham], where they must expect usage as bad as . . . [in] the [Turkish] galleys.

Dr Burnell, 'a grave, learned man, and canon of the church, refusing to submit to their taxations, they gave command (though he were at that time sick and confined to his bed) to take him in the night and bring him away to prison'. Similarly:

> at twelve by the clock at night, they seized on Mr Hilliar [the man who had demonstrated such public enthusiasm for the Scots War in 1640] in his bed . . . [and] because he would not disburse such sums as they demanded, they carry him first to the prison, and thence to the ship. In the way to the prison they throw dirt in his face, and beat . . . [him] so cruelly that his roaring and outcries were heard and pitied by all his neighbours.

Finally:

> for the like refusal, they took Dr Hutchinson, another canon of the church, a man of weak, infirm body, and violently carried him towards the ship, there to imprison him. By the way, as they carried him along, he was . . . blasted and abused, and hooted at by the boys, and exposed to the affronts and revilings of the base, insolent multitude.[50]

Royalist news-pamphlets may be suspected of bias but *Rusticus*'s account is borne out by many other sources. Financial documents drawn up by the Parliamentarians themselves show that, on 4 January, forty-one Exeter residents—including Burnell and Hutchinson—were assessed to pay large sums of money towards the Roundhead cause.[51] An independent account has also survived of the treatment meted out to another of those whose names appear upon the list, Edward Gibbons. Writing in 1704, a relative recalled how Gibbons:

> aged about 88 yeares, was summoned before Mr Adam Bennet, Mr Richard Crossing, Mr Richard Saunders & others, Commissioners for the Parliament, and there ordered to pay them £50, which if he

refuse to pay he must forthwith be carried on shipboard & appeare in London at Goldsmyth's Hall'.

Gibbons refused to pay, so:

> next day they granted a warrant directed to . . . [three men] to seize all his goods, which they did, not leaving him a bed, nor so much as a dish or spoone, & turn'd him & his wife . . . [and] 3 Grand Children & 4 servants . . . to doore, & . . . seized all his estate.[52]

There is also the testimony of the Roundheads themselves, many of whom revelled in their enemies' misfortunes. A letter written from Exeter on 7 January reported that 'this weeke we had many great Delinquents apprehended . . . Doctor Hutchinson, Doctor Wilson, Canon Helliar . . . Isaac the Town Clerke . . . with many more; some whereof have againe ransomed themselves by £100, £200, £500 and . . . £800 fines to the Parliament'. 'The Cathedrall men look like ghosts, now their mouths are stopt that they can sing no longer', the writer crowed, adding that 'there was this week £400 found in that Church . . . and more they hope to find'.[53] This report was confirmed by another writer, who observed that:

> [because] the malignants in . . . Excester . . . would not contribute any moneys for the safety of the commonwealth, [they] were put into divers ships, and sent out to sea, which have made them to yield, and to submit themselves to a reasonable assessment.[54]

A New Governor

The orgy of anti-Royalist activity which had taken place in Exeter in the wake of Hopton's retreat calmed down somewhat following the arrival of the Earl of Stamford on 6 January.[55] Stamford—whom Parliament had appointed governor of the city and supreme commander in the South West—brought several regiments of Roundhead infantrymen with him, and his presence made the Parliamentary grip on the city still more secure. Soon after his arrival he was presented with a gift of £100 by the grateful Chamber.[56] But there was no room for complacency. Hopton's army had managed to make its way back to Cornwall intact, so the threat of further attacks remained strong, while the recent scare had exposed many weaknesses in Exeter's defensive preparations. During early 1643 determined efforts were made to remedy these defects. The organization of the trained bands had obviously proved unsatisfactory, so a sergeant major was appointed 'for the ordering of the militia within this cittie'.[57] It was clear, too, that more money was going to have to be spent on the fortifications. Alderman John Hakewill—a prominent upholder of the Parliamentary cause—wrote to the Speaker of the Commons on 14 January, pointing out that Exeter had already spent over £3,000 on its defences and that '[the] charges still continue'. He therefore requested that the large sums of money which pro-Parliamentary inhabitants of Exeter had pledged to contribute to Parliament's army earlier that year should be spent on the city defences instead.[58]

Hakewill's request was granted and, with substantial sums of money secured, the Chamber found itself able to undertake more ambitious defensive measures. On 23 January a detailed list of instructions was issued, ordering, *inter alia*, that Exeter's ancient defensive ditches should be deepened, various local strongpoints occupied and the city magazine re-supplied. Care was also taken to deal with Royalist sympathizers within the walls. 'Malignants' were to be disarmed, incorrigible troublemakers turned out, and Royalist prisoners—of whom there were now many in Exeter—restrained and prevented from having any communication with the townsfolk (see document 12). As these orders were put into effect during January and February 1643 Parliament's hold on Exeter became increasingly secure.

Backed up by the London 'Gray Coats' (as Stamford's foot soldiers were known), Exeter's puritan/Parliamentarians were now able to implement the thorough-going reformation of which they had dreamed for so long. The remaining anti-puritan members of the Chamber were driven away or frightened into silence, while conservative clergymen were identified through their refusal to take the covenant, and removed (see document 16). Following the imprisonment of the cathedral men and their local supporters Exeter's pulpits were—in the words of one scandalized Royalist—left 'open only to factious, schismatical preachers, whose doctrine was rebellion, and their exhortations treason'.[59] Established puritan preachers like Painter and Bond were joined by an influx of radicals from elsewhere—Thomas Trescott of Inwardleigh, for example, and George Hughes of Tavistock—and the city rang with the sermons of those whom one proud correspondent termed 'our godly ministers'.[60] Any further intervention from the Royalist field forces seemed most unlikely. Throughout this period a Roundhead army remained near Plymouth, holding the Cornishmen in check and preventing them from making any further incursions eastward.

This situation changed suddenly in March, when Royalist Cornwall and Parliamentarian Devon entered into negotiations for a local truce. Exeter was put into a difficult position as a result of these talks for, early on in the dialogue, it was agreed that the representatives of both sides should meet at Exeter's New Inn.[61] This decision was highly embarrassing to the city authorities; not only did it suggest that they supported the truce (which Parliament itself was strongly opposed to), but also the talks would provide an excuse for many Royalists to gather in Exeter. Stamford was in favour of the scheme, but the city authorities —spurred on by Henry Painter and the godly party—decided to appeal above his head to Parliament.[62] Mayor Clarke sent a letter to the House of Commons on 8 March, warning MPs that the meeting was scheduled to be held in six days' time, and next day Richard Saunders despatched a further alarming letter, in which he suggested that the Royalist delegates might incite 'the considerable number of malignant inhabitants' to rise up in arms and free the 'desperate . . . [Royalist] prisoners within . . . [Exeter], wherewith two prisons are full' . Once this had been effected, he hinted, it would be easy for the Royalists to seize control of the city. Saunders therefore asked the Commons to send 'such orders as they may think fit' to enable him to deal with the situation.[63]

Parliament reacted with swift and angry decision. Orders were at once sent to Exeter; under no circumstances whatsoever were any Cornish delegates to enter the city. At the same time two MPs were sent post-haste to Devon to ensure that Parliament's instructions were obeyed. These two weary emissaries arrived in Exeter on the evening of 13 March, just in time, for the first of the Cornish negotiators arrived next day.[64] Unaware of any change of plan, they knocked at the city gates, but the mayor, bolstered by the presence of the two MPs, refused to let them in. For nearly an hour the delegates waited outside, during which time they were roundly abused and harangued by a city clergyman, 'than whom', one of his victims later noted ruefully, 'I never saw man better like a furious mastiff'. Eventually the Cornishmen were told that no meeting was to be held in Exeter after all. Instead they were conducted to the West Indies Inn, in St Thomas, safely across the river. Here it was decided that the talks should be postponed and on the 17th the Cornish delegates returned to their own county. The peace negotiations had been wrecked, partly as a result of Parliament's orders, but chiefly because of the obduracy of Exeter's own puritan/Parliamentarian Party—including 'a company of zealous, holy, religious women' who had confounded contemporary stereotypes by circulating 'a petition *against* peace'.[65]

Throughout the rest of March–April 1643 the local truce remained in force, but everyone realized that a renewal of hostilities was now inevitable. Stamford—urged on by the godly—spent this time in strengthening his army and when the truce expired he launched a major expedition into the west, hoping that this time he would finally crush the Cornish. The Earl marched out of Exeter on 11 May. His men were well supplied (they carried over £70 worth of lead bullets, cast by an Exeter plumber) and a Parliamentary victory seemed assured.[66] Yet within less than a week, Stamford had been routed at Stratton, in Cornwall, and his army all but destroyed (see document 14).

Demoralized Roundhead troops were soon streaming back into Exeter, closely pursued by the victorious Cavaliers. It was clear that Exeter was about to face a real siege and the Parliamentarians launched themselves into a feverish round of activity. City gentlemen raised fresh companies of volunteers, while teams of labourers began to dig a deep trench—complete with earthen banks and outworks—around the entire southern and eastern side of the city, the area which was most vulnerable to attack.[67] The new trench was intended to act as the defenders' front line, as a forward position in advance of the already deepened city ditch, and its construction caused a great deal of destruction in the city suburbs. St Sidwell's parish was particularly badly affected and many buildings here were pulled down or burnt.[68]

As the victorious Royalists advanced ever closer, fear began to set in among the inhabitants. A letter written from Exeter on 27 May reported that 'we all stand upon our guard upon paine of death', and added, breathlessly, that 'now, at this instant, we have alarum given at Cowley bridge, where My Lord [Stamford]'s Graye Coates are at watch'.[69] The state of mind of the Parliamentary leaders is well illustrated by their reception of Dr William Coxe, one of the cathedral canons, who had been sent from the Royalist army with peace proposals. On his arrival Coxe was arrested, searched and—upon suspicion of having swallowed 'papers of intelligence'—forced to drink several purgatives. Half dead as a result of this treatment, he was then thrown into gaol (see document 15). Soon afterwards Parliamentary sources reported that Coxe had been hatching a plot, aimed at 'blowing up the Eastgate with [the] helpe of a vault under it, which was so ancient . . . that scarce any in the towne had knowledge of [it] or could remember [it]' (a reference to the underground passages).[70]

Loyalist writers crowed that their enemies were fleeing from Exeter like rats from a sinking ship.[71] Among those who left the city at this time were the troopers of the 'Devonshire Horse', Stamford's cavalry brigade, which had escaped the debacle at Stratton largely intact. Anticipating a siege, the Parliamentary leaders decided that the city was not well enough provisioned to feed this large body of horses and men, and it was agreed that the unit should leave Exeter while the roads leading east were still clear. Accordingly the troopers rode out of the city on 31 May, managing to elude Hopton's advance guards and escape.[72] They were only just in time. By the beginning of June, Hopton's advancing army had cut off Exeter's links with the outside world (see map 3, p. 79).

The Second Siege

Royalist units first occupied positions within a few miles of Exeter, then began to advance closer still. Soon the city was reported to be completely 'streightened, espetially to the east side thereof'.[73] Around 10 June the besiegers—who had been joined by substantial reinforcements under Sir John Berkeley—appeared on the outskirts of the city itself. The events which followed were recorded by one of Berkeley's officers; 'the first day wee came before [Exeter]', he observed, 'the enemy despising our small number sallied out, with a very considerable party, but was vigorously repulsed . . . and some of their out worcks, and the south subburbs possessed' (see document 20). The attackers held on to the positions which they had gained in this initial assault. By 14 June the Royalists claimed to have 'beaten the Enemy to the gates of Exeter' and three days later the King's forces were reported as being 'sate downe before the wals of the city'.[74]

Faced with this threat, the Parliamentarians did all they could to improve their defences. A great deal of work was carried out on the fortifications to the south of Exeter during the week of 10–17 June, while on the 18th the Chamber agreed that £2,000 should be borrowed to deal with the present 'extraordinary occasions'.[75] A major sally was also attempted; several hundred horsemen set out to drive the Royalists from their base at Topsham. The Roundheads were tricked and defeated, however, and many of their men captured.[76] As a result the defenders'

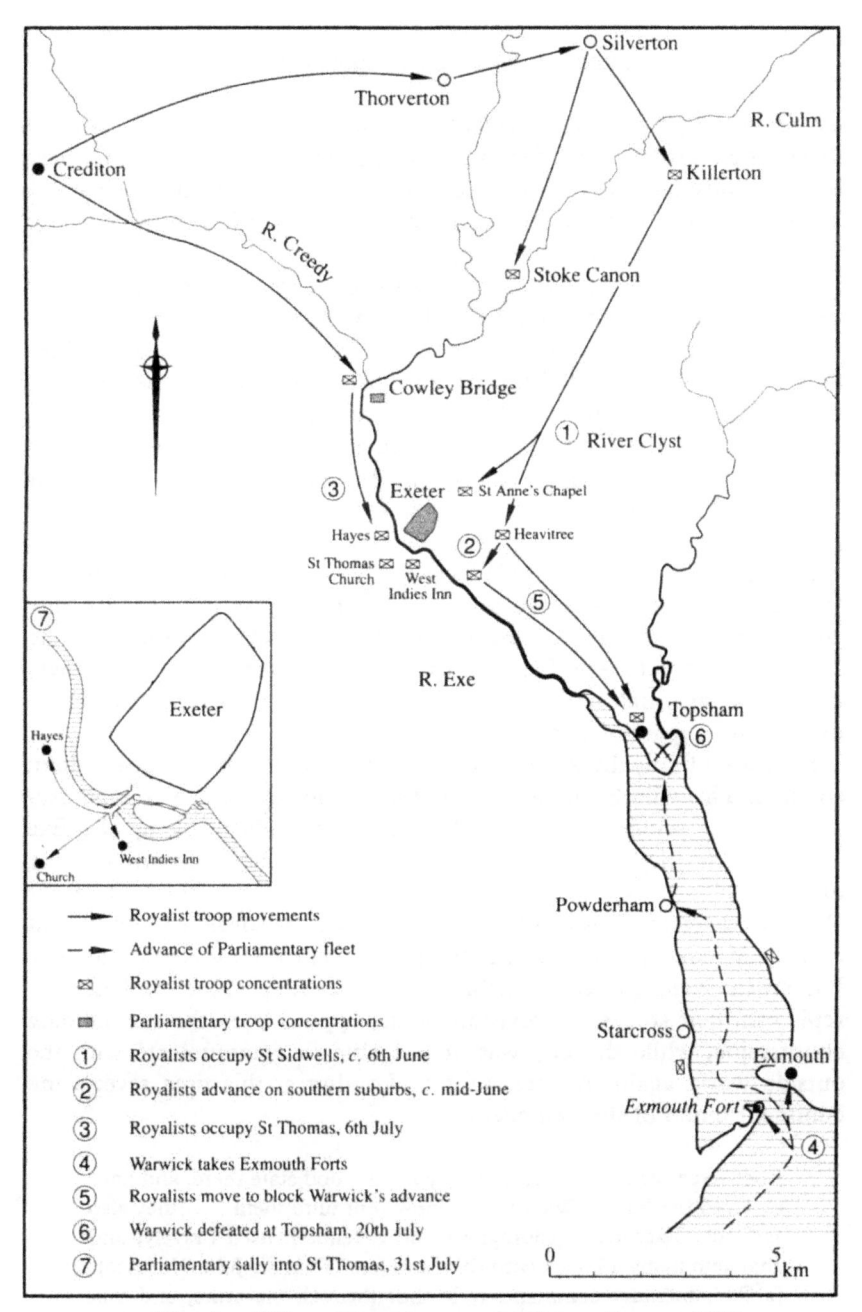

Map 3. Military Operations around Exeter, Summer 1643

cavalry strength (already inadequate following the departure of the Devonshire Horse) was depleted still further—and this was to have serious consequences. Two weeks later a Parliamentary news-book lamented that Exeter was in danger of being starved into surrender, 'for want of horse to open their passages'.[77]

Throughout the rest of June the besiegers kept up their pressure on the south side of the city, and the Parliamentarians threw all their energies into improving the fortifications there by digging trenches, demolishing houses and felling trees.[78] Unable to make any headway, the Royalists opened up a new front on 6 July, occupying the suburb of St Thomas, to the west of the river, in an engagement described by an onlooker as 'an exterordenary fight' (see document 17). The Royalists quickly occupied the church, the prison and the West Indies Inn. All these positions were within musket shot of the city, and it was soon being reported that the assailants were 'in a good way of getting . . . [Exe]bridge, being come close to it'.[79] Meanwhile Royalist pressure continued to be exerted on the south side of Exeter too, prompting the Parliamentarians to send fresh teams of labourers there and to pull down more buildings. Bales of wool were also placed against the city gates, to deaden the impact of Royalist cannon shot.[80]

Soon after 8 July the Royalists abandoned their position in the southern suburbs. This withdrawal was prompted by the news that Parliamentary naval forces, under the Earl of Warwick, were advancing up the Exe estuary to the city's relief (see map 3). The relieving force was a strong one—2,000 auxiliary soldiers were aboard Warwick's ships—and the Royalists diverted all available troops to oppose its advance.[81] As a result of these manoeuvres the immediate pressure on Exeter was reduced. The Parliamentarians gained something of a breathing space, and time to replenish their stocks of provisions with supplies from the surrounding countryside, while the city was at last able to communicate with the outside world again. A letter sent to London at this time reveals the confident mood of the defenders:

> from Excester they write, that they are in good state there, and have received the Earl of Warwick's supply sent unto them . . . [they also say] that Excester is couragious and defendeth itself bravely, and changeth many a knock with the Cavaliers. That Sir John Northcott [a Parliamentary commander] is shot through the arme, and that two captaines of the Gray Coates are slaine, and that the Cavaliers

have lost cart loads of their men, but in Exceter they have not lost above thirty in all.[82]

This estimate of Royalist losses may well be exaggerated but the figure given for Roundhead casualties seems perfectly credible. (Those of Exeter's parish registers which survive, over half the total, record the burial of only sixteen soldiers in the period preceding this date.[83])

Despite the defenders' optimism, Exeter remained in grave danger. Warwick had managed to send some supplies to the city, but he was still unable to break through in force—and Royalist troops were now massing at Topsham to resist the advance of his fleet. Warwick clearly hoped that Stamford would sally out of the city and combine with him in an attack upon the Royalists at Topsham, but Stamford—lacking an effective cavalry force—was unwilling to venture his foot soldiers so far from the protection of the city walls. In any case, Exeter was busy enough defending itself. Several Royalist units had remained in St Thomas, menacing Exeter's western defences, and measures had to be taken to deal with this threat. On 8 July work took place on the fortifications at Westgate and soon afterwards a battery was set up at Horsepool, nearby, to counter Royalist artillery on the opposite bank.[84] Shots continued to be exchanged across the River Exe throughout the next week, but, by now, all eyes must have been turning south to watch the slow progress of the Parliamentary relief force.

During the second week of July Warwick had gradually worked his way upstream, dislodging Royalist forces from their positions at Exmouth, Starcross and Powderham on the lower banks of the Exe. On the 18th he appeared before Topsham.[85] Even though there was no sign of the expected reinforcements from Exeter, Warwick determined to take the town by storm, and two days later he launched the crucial assault. Under cover of bombardment from the Parliamentary ships, Warwick tried to land a strong force of sailors on the strand nearby. But the Admiral's plan went badly wrong. The Royalists had sunk several small boats in the channel before Topsham, and this prevented Warwick's men from landing.[86] The Parliamentarians made several further attempts to disembark but their longboats were continually raked with musket fire, making a landing impossible (see document 20). Meanwhile the Parliamentary ships were being battered by Royalist cannon positioned in earthworks along the shore. Eventually Warwick was compelled to withdraw, leaving the Royalists in possession of Topsham. The relief force was shattered. Two of Warwick's ships had been sunk, a third had had to be set on fire lest it should fall into enemy hands and many of the sailors had been killed or wounded.[87] Warwick saw that he could no longer hope to batter his way through to Exeter and within hours the remnants of his relieving force had slipped out of the Exe estuary, leaving the beleaguered city to its fate.

With Warwick defeated, the King's forces were able to concentrate all their attention upon Exeter, and pressure on the city intensified markedly during late July. The Royalist positions in St Thomas now resumed their galling fire on Exeter with new vigour, prompting work on the fortifications at Stepcote Hill, 'Bidwells' Tower' (above Westgate) and many other places on the west side of the city.[88] Eventually this bombardment became too much to bear and on 31 July the Parliamentarians launched a major sally into St Thomas in which over 1,000 men took part (see map 3).[89] The aim of the operation was to destroy the Royalist strongholds in St Thomas and in this the Parliamentarians were clearly successful. One pamphleteer reported that the garrison had 'sallied out upon the enemy, made a great slaughter of them ... and burnt their workes and houses they had built for their shelter and defence' (a statement confirmed by recent archaeological excavation at Hayes Barton, St Thomas, which found the Tudor mansion house there to have been burnt down in the Civil War, following an attack from the direction of Exebridge).[90]

Conditions in Exeter at this time were well described in a letter written by a certain 'J.S.' to a friend in London. He noted that the Royalists had not yet re-occupied the positions which they had abandoned on Warwick's advance, and were largely confined to the west of the Exe. As a result the Parliamentarians were still able to bring in provisions from Tiverton and Cullompton 'but for how long this will continue', J.S. continued gloomily, 'God knowes'. The garrison feared that powerful Royalist forces would soon march into the west from Bristol, which had recently been captured by the King's forces (see document 18). Time was fast running out for the defenders of Exeter.

Royalist Triumph

By 27 August Prince Maurice (Prince Rupert's younger brother) had arrived at Heavitree with a powerful Royalist army.[91] Strengthened by these reinforcements, the besiegers increased the pressure. The city siege accounts record the Roundhead response to this new threat: between 26 and 30 August work was carried out on the fortifications at East Gate, at St Davids, at Southernhay and at Mount Radford (to the south of Exeter). Hedges were removed and new batteries built, while more work was carried out at the mills along the river.[92] It is clear that the Parliamentarians, uncertain of the direction from which the attack would come, were feverishly strengthening all sectors of the defences. One last message was also sent to Parliament at this time, setting out Exeter's desperate situation and pleading for help to be sent.[93] Meanwhile the Royalists were 'view[ing] all the . . . approches' in an attempt to discern where the defences were weakest. Prince Maurice was anxious to capture Exeter as quickly as possible, not only because he was 'desirous to make a short worke of the war in those parts', but also because the veteran troops who formed the core of his army were urgently needed elsewhere.[94]

On 3 September the Royalists at last moved into the attack. 'A very hot assault' was made upon the city, while a simultaneous artillery barrage 'did not onely shake the wals in severall places, but . . . fired a good part of the suburbs'. Demoralized by this bombardment, a Royalist source records, the garrison 'required a parley' (see document 21). It is tempting to suggest a degree of oversimplification here. That some sort of negotiations took place between the two sides is not in doubt, but the Roundhead call for talks may not have been prompted by fear alone. The defenders knew that Maurice had no time to conduct a long siege and may have hoped to entangle him in a time-wasting dialogue, one which would prevent him from accomplishing anything at Exeter until he was finally called away.

During the negotiations which followed Maurice offered the city honourable conditions of surrender, but the defenders refused to accept. Instead they offered an alternative, and rather remarkable, suggestion as to how the siege should be resolved. Their proposal was that Exeter should withdraw its allegiance from Parliament, but also refuse to admit the forces of the King; retaining its arms and defences, Exeter should 'stand newter' between the two sides.[95] The defenders hurried to point out that it was not 'want of courage, or sufficient meanes for our subsistence [which] hath drawne this from us, but an earnest desire to live & die in his Majesties favour'.[96] In fact it seems barely credible that the offer was made in a spirit of sincerity. Rather, this proposal to turn Exeter into a neutral zone was—like so many of the other apparently 'neutralist' initiatives of the Civil War—an attempt by one side to gain short-term advantage over the other. The defenders clearly hoped that Maurice's urgent need to rejoin the King would force him to accept such dubious terms. With the Prince's army gone, Exeter would soon be able to throw off its feigned neutrality and declare itself for Parliament once more. The Prince was not to be taken in. He refused to accept the proposal and by the end of the day his council of war had decided that an attempt must be made to take the city by storm. Colonels Bamfield and Chudleigh were chosen to lead the assault.

Bamfield himself has left a vivid account of the final Royalist attack (see document 20). 'Wee resolved', he records, 'with firelocks and pikemen ... to march silently an hower before break of day, to assault the [Parliamentarian] line ... by way of suprise'. The Royalists were completely successful, capturing the covered way which connected the defensive outworks to the south of Exeter with the city itself, so that 'all in the outworks were either killed, or taken'. 'Whereuppon', Bamfield goes on, 'wee lodged ourselves under the [city] wall ... soe neer ... that they durst not attempt to sally'. Meanwhile, other Royalist troops had turned the cannon in the captured outworks on their former owners (see document 21). Battered by their own guns and deprived of many of their best men, the Parliamentarians now felt their position to be hopeless. 'In this condition and consternation', Bamfield concludes, 'they beat a parley, desired a treaty, sent out hostages: Sir Richard Cave and I were employed to treat, and had the place rendered even on our owne tearmes'.

Terms of surrender were quickly agreed on (see document 22) and two days later Stamford and the Parliamentary troops marched out of the city. The Royalists were not over-scrupulous about observing the surrender terms. As the Roundheads marched 'from Westgate to Alfington, a long mile' the King's men stripped and plundered them, besides giving them 'many barres [i.e. blows] for resistance'.[97] Having dealt with Stamford's soldiers the Royalists next poured into the city, 'gathering together in the High Street and St Peter's Churchyard'. Here, a Parliamentary writer noted sourly, 'they wanted no tale-bearers to informe them which were for or against them during the siege'. The Royalist soldiers quickly acted upon this information and within minutes they 'began to break open Mr Prigg his house, a draper at Broadgate, whose house and shop of drapery was in lesse than halfe an houre rifled and spoiled, to the utter undoing of him, his wife and children, being valued neare upon £2,000'. (That Prigge had been a member of the Parliamentary Committee for Safety was presumably no coincidence.) Next 'they dispersed themselves and broke open other merchants houses, and tooke what they pleased, [and] ... many bloudy wounds [were] given to the citizens by the vulgar souldiers'.[98] Thus the King's troops took the revenge on those who had held Exeter against them for so long. The war in the west seemed over and the Royalists gloried in their triumph, calling all to witness that 'this proud city which had so long bid defiance to their ... soveraigne, was at last reduced into the power of his sacred Majestie'.[99]

5

'Reduced into the Power of His Sacred Majestie'
Royalist Exeter, 1643–45

> *Where is your God now, O yee hypocrites? Where is your holy cause, your cause and all your hopes?*

It was with these words ringing in their ears that the Parliamentary defenders of Exeter trudged out through the city gates on the day of the surrender and, to many, the jeers of Prince Maurice's soldiers must have sounded like an epitaph, not just for the Roundhead regime in Exeter but for over half a century of godly reformation in the city.[1] Alongside the dejected Roundhead soldiers stumbled Exeter's puritan ministers: John Bond, George Hughes (who had left his wife behind him, buried in a city churchyard) and Henry Painter, the latter in tears as he surveyed the wreckage of his hopes and dreams.[2] All the years of preaching, all the years of battling against 'profanity', all the years of ceaseless effort by Jurdain, his allies on the Chamber and so many other godly men and women, to turn Exeter into a beacon of light, a city upon a hill—all this seemed to have come to nothing, as the Royalist soldiers exulted in the departure of 'God's people' and the ungodly prepared to enter into their inheritance.[3] Even before Stamford's men had disappeared over the horizon, the Royalists began to pour in through the city gates.

The Establishment of Royalist Control

The first few days of the Royalist occupation were a confusing, chaotic time, about which little information has survived. There was clearly a certain amount of looting and disorder; the Chamber later rewarded Captain Bagster for 'securing' the civic regalia from unruly soldiers.[4] But the reports of indiscriminate pillage which appeared in the London press immediately after the surrender were almost certainly false, designed to frighten neutrals and 'malignants' in other towns held by Parliament rather than to give a true picture of the situation in Exeter (see document 23). The Roundhead news-book *Certain Informations* (published six weeks after the surrender) gave a very different account of events, not only conceding that Maurice's forces had 'forbor[n]e from plundering' after they had taken Exeter, but even going so far as to admit that 'those Cavaliers were famous at the first for their modesty and abstinence'.[5] There is no hard evidence to show that the Royalist soldiers plundered the citizens at random. Rather, their efforts seem to have been targeted against those, like Henry Prigge, whom the gleeful city loyalists identified as having been 'against them during the siege'.[6] The victims had become the persecutors and the persecutors the victims, as Exeter's politico-religious world was turned upside down.

What was the reaction of Exeter's civic rulers to this dramatic turn of events? Scholars working on other towns have found that, even when control of these communities shifted from King to Parliament or *vice versa*, the same local governors remained in power.[7] As a result, urban communities have tended to be portrayed as typically 'passive' during the Civil War, and town governors as 'time servers, ready to obey any government that safe-guarded local rights'.[8] In Exeter this was emphatically not the case. Instead, a dramatic power-shift took place thoughout the civic administration during late 1643, as Parliamentary sympathizers began to withdraw from public affairs and were replaced by supporters of the King.

The most obvious sign of this trend was the election of Hugh Crocker as Mayor. Crocker, a member of the pre-war 'outgroup', had remained in Exeter throughout 1642–43, but had kept a low profile, attending less than half of all Chamber meetings. Following the surrender he replaced the Parliamentarian Christopher Clerk as the most important of the civic officials. The first council meetings of Crocker's mayoralty, held in late September, saw the new mayor being joined by the other three members of the pre-war outgroup: John Colleton, Nicholas Spicer and Robert Walker. None of these men had attended a Chamber meeting for months and it is clear that they had been opposed to the Roundhead regime in

Exeter. Walker, indeed, had left the city altogether and joined the King's army.[9] Now that the puritan/Parliamentarians had been humbled, these men could take centre stage. Over the next two years Crocker, Colleton, Spicer and Walker were to emerge as the King's most important local supporters, playing a more central role in civic government than they had ever done before (see Tables 2–3, pp. 224–25).

As Crocker and his allies rose, so their rivals fell. During 1642–43 Exeter's civic government had been dominated by twelve men: Adam Bennet, Christopher Clerk, Phillip Crossing, Richard Crossing, Thomas Crossing, James Gould, John Hakewill, Richard Saunders, James Tucker, James White, Walter White and Richard Yeo. Each of these men had attended over three-quarters of the Chamber meetings held in Exeter during the period of Parliamentary control (see table 2). Had they been mere 'time-servers' they would surely have maintained this high attendance record after the city's surrender. Instead, eight of the group (Bennet, Clerk, Gould, Hakewill, Saunders, Walter White, Phillip Crossing and Richard Crossing), together with two more junior councillors (James Marshall and John Lovering), immediately began to withdraw from public affairs. Two more (James Tucker and James White) died in October. This left just two members of the former Parliamentarian in-group (Richard Yeo and Thomas Crossing) who were prepared to co-operate with the Royalist authorities.

Of the five remaining town councillors, two (Simon Snow and John Lynn) were in London—the first sitting as Exeter's Parliamentarian MP, the second having been sent up to prison as a Royalist. A third, John Martin, had left Exeter while it was under Roundhead control and only returned after the surrender; the Royalists could count on his support.[10] The positions of the last two men, John Cupper and Roger Mallack, were rather more ambivalent. Both had remained in Exeter during 1642–43, but had attended less than 70 per cent of all Chamber meetings, suggesting that they had hardly been committed supporters of the Parliamentary regime. Cupper's attendance record had been particularly low (see table 2), and the fact that he attended *every* Chamber meeting held after September 1643, and was also elected as a Royalist mayor in 1645, suggests that his sympathies had always been on the King's side. Mallack may have been a genuine neutral. He later deposed that 'there was imposed on me when the King's partie came into Exeter the some of £500 as an abbetor for the Parliament'.[11] This claim was made in an (unsuccessful) attempt to avoid being fined as a Royalist after the war, however, and other evidence suggests that Mallack played a key role in the administration of Royalist Exeter, attending 96 per cent of all Council meetings, and serving as a captain in the city's trained bands.[12]

Among the city councillors of Exeter, therefore, a partisan response to the war's events seems to have been far more typical than a passive one. Of the twenty-four individuals who sat on the Chamber in January 1642, eleven soon revealed themselves as committed Parliamentarians and six as committed Royalists, while three more died during the year. Only four men—Thomas Crossing, Richard Yeo, John Cupper and Roger Mallack—were prepared to serve under both regimes with anything like the same degree of enthusiasm, and of these four, only Crossing and Yeo were consistent in their attendance at meetings *throughout* the period 1642–44. Cupper and Mallack emerge rather as timorous Royalists than as genuine moderates (see tables 2–3). The middle ground at Exeter appears to have been surprisingly small.

The dismissal of long-established town councillors was rare before the Civil War, and in Exeter, as in many other places, there seems to have been considerable reluctance to take such a radical step during the early years of the conflict.[13] As a result, the official membership of the Chamber looked almost exactly the same in January 1644 as it had done a year before, with just three new councillors having been elected to replace those who had died. Beneath the surface, however, a quiet revolution had taken place. Half the surviving councillors had effectively withdrawn from Chamber business, leaving all the work to be done by the members of the rival, Royalist, faction. It was the same story in the sessions court. Although the official composition of the Exeter bench hardly changed between 1642 and 1646, the identity of those who carried out the work did. During 1642–43 Adam Bennet, Christopher Clerk, Thomas Crossing, John Hakewill, Richard Saunders and James Tucker had conducted the lion's share of judicial business. Between them, these six men appeared on the bench on 214 occasions during the period of Parliamentary dominance, while the other four magistrates (the Royalist aldermen Spicer, Lynn and Mallack and the Royalist Recorder, Peter Ball) appeared on just twenty-one. After September 1643 this position was reversed with Bennet, Clerk, Hakewill, Saunders and Tucker sitting on just seven occasions and Ball, Mallack, Spicer, Hugh Crocker and Robert Walker on 220.[14]

It was not just at the top of the civic hierarchy that the establishment of Royalist control brought about a change in personnel. Of the thirty-seven city constables in post in July 1643, no fewer than twenty-five had either resigned or been dismissed by mid-October.[15] Many of those who went are definitely known to have been Roundheads, while many of those who replaced them were Royalists, so it is hard to see this as anything other than a politically motivated purge.[16] Other civic officials appointed during the period of Parliamentary control were dismissed at the same time. On 2 October the Chamber ordered that Ralph Cooze, appointed keeper of the city prisons during July, should be removed and the old keeper reinstated.[17] The fact that Exeter's new governors felt it necessary to purge so many of the minor civic officials is telling, for it shows that principled political commitment was felt to be widespread in Exeter, even below the level of the Chamber élite.

It was not just a different set of councillors, judges, constables and gaolers who were swept into power on Prince Maurice's coat-tails. Also returning to Exeter amidst the Royalist baggage were many conformist clergymen, including Dr John Whynell—expelled from Exeter by Stamford in early 1643—and several members of the Dean and Chapter. (The first Chapter meeting for almost ten months was held in the Close on 9 September.[18]) It may not have seemed entirely coincidental to local puritans that the Royalist occupation also brought with it a virulent outbreak of disease, the worst to afflict the city since the great plague of 1625. The death rate in Exeter had been steadily rising throughout the last weeks of the siege; total monthly burials in the eleven city parishes for which registers survive climbed from thirty-one in June to forty-five in July and sixty in August. Yet it was only after the surrender that the epidemic reached its peak, burials rising to sixty-five in September and to a terrifying ninety-five in October.[19] The Chamber did its best to counter the disease, ordering that the streets should be swept and other measures taken to prevent 'the continuing and increasing of the contagious sicknes now raiging amongst us', but little could realistically be done except to wait for the infection to pass away.[20] The disease was almost certainly war-typhus (the infection which had swept away a fifth of Oxford's population earlier that year) and it continued to ravage Exeter throughout the rest of 1643.[21] The Royalist occupation could hardly have begun on a less auspicious note, and the appointment of a new military governor hinted at further hardships to come.

Royalist Demands

One of Prince Maurice's first moves upon entering the city had been to appoint Sir John Berkeley, an experienced soldier, as governor. Berkeley (who quickly established his headquarters at Bedford House, the imposing mansion of the Russell family, to the north of the cathedral) was to hold the post for the next two and a half years, and it was under his overall supervision that the Chamber and the Royalist military authorities had to work together to manage Exeter's affairs. The partnership was an an uneasy one at best. From the very beginning of the Royalist occupation the citizens' needs and aspirations were firmly subordinated to military necessity, and this was to become increasingly the case as the war dragged on.

Berkeley's most pressing concerns at the time of his appointment were financial ones. Maurice's troops were in desperate need of money and the citizens soon found themselves being forced to subsidize the Royalist war effort. On 21 September the Chamber agreed that £500 should be borrowed 'for a present to be bestowed on Prince Maurice . . . [and] the Governor'. This money was supposed to be reimbursed to the citizens 'out of the first loanes that shalbe brought in for his Majesties service', but—as an anonymous hand later recorded in the Chamber Act Book— 'this was never done'. Extraordinary payments aside, the people of Exeter were expected to raise money for the King on a more regular basis, and a few weeks after the donation of the 'present' to Prince Maurice the Chamber elected a special committee to consider 'the setling of the way for the raising of some considerable some of monie for his Majesties service'. The citizens were forced to pay up yet again next month, when Berkeley—who had by now assembled a large force of Royalist soldiers in the city—set off for the eastern front in Hampshire. On 4 November the Chamber agreed that £100 should be 'taken upp uppon the Citties securitie to be presented to Sir John Berkeley, the Governor . . . as a remembrance from this house, he being then to goe out of the Cittie'.[22]

Despite the departure of Berkeley's forces, many Royalist soldiers remained billeted in Exeter. These men would clearly have to be supported in some way and on 21 November two members of the Chamber were requested by their fellows to 'treate with the Commissioners for the Marshall affaires about the charge of such souldiers as either now live, or hereafter shalbe putt in garrison in this Cittie'. Soon afterwards it was decided that an extraordinary rate of £40 a week should be levied on the inhabitants in order to support the garrison. Six of the city councillors were requested to 'consider of the fittest way for raising thereof . . . And to prepare a rate in a proportionalle way for that purpose'.[23] This weekly rate was by no means the only financial burden which the Royalists imposed upon the people of Exeter. In September 1643 the Dean and Chapter found themselves faced with a request from the King for a 'gift' of £1000, while in March 1644 a commission was sent down to Berkley, Crocker and seven other local men, ordering them to persuade the citizens to contribute towards the loan of £100,000 which the Royalist Parliament at Oxford had recently agreed should be raised for the King's armies.[24] Crocker, at least, was quick to obey: five days after the commission was issued the Earl of Bath lent him £200 towards 'the 100 thousand pound ordered to be lent ye King'.[25]

As these demands for money poured in from all sides, the citizens strove to repair the damage which had been inflicted during the recent fighting. On 21 September the Chamber agreed that 'Exbridge shalbe foorthwith repaired in the defects thereof, especiallye in that parte which was of late pulled downe for the supposed safetye of this Cittie in the tyme of the late siege'. The waterpipes outside Eastgate, which had recently been 'broken upp and wasted by his Majesties forces lying thereabouts', were also ordered to be repaired. Finally three of the councillors were asked to 'take some care for the poore people in Mr Hurst's almeshowses' which had been pulled down 'during the tyme of the siege'.[26] A great deal of work was also carried out on the defences. During the period of Parliamentary control the city 'Receiver' (or treasurer) had laid out over £160 on Exeter's walls and gates. This was the highest sum to be spent by any receiver on the city defences since the mid-sixteenth century, but it paled into insignificance when compared with the amounts laid out by the Royalist authorities during 1643–44.[27]

Soon after capturing Exeter, the Royalists had drawn up a detailed list of the cannon which were mounted along the city walls (see document 24). The condition of the walls themselves was inspected at around the same time, and in January 1644 the Chamber issued a general directive ordering that 'the Citties walles that are nowe fallen downe or any other way defective . . . shalbe foorthwith builte upp againe and repaired'.[28] Over the next ten months £345 was spent on repairing the city walls in Southernhay. Total expenditure on the city defences during 1644 eventually came to £391, a quite unprecedented figure. A third of the city's annual revenue had been expended on the fortifications.[29] This massive outlay was made necessary by the continuing threat of a Roundhead attack on Exeter. Although the west country had been almost completely subdued by the Royalists during autumn 1643, strong Parliamentary armies still remained active on the region's eastern borders. This meant that the Exeter Royalists could not afford to neglect their defences. Nor could they allow 'ill-humours' to circulate within the city walls.

The Suppression of Internal Dissent

Despite the departure of Exeter's most committed Parliamentarians with Stamford, there were still many in the city who remained hostile to the new regime. These disaffected elements were potentially dangerous and the Royalists, like the Roundheads before them, did their best to flush such persons out through the administration of an oath. During early 1644 the Royalist-occupied counties of Devon and Cornwall—together with the separate county of Exeter—had entered into a formal alliance known as the Association, one of the articles of which stipulated that all adult males should be compelled to take an oath of allegiance to the Royalist cause (see document 26). This oath was generally known as the 'protestation' and copies of it were sent to clergymen throughout the two counties with orders to administer it to their congregations.[30]

The oath met with widespread resistance in Devon. There were protests in Dartmouth and Barnstaple and 'many' complained in Exeter, including Nicholas Kennycott, a weaver, who was bound over by the sessions court on 30 March 'for refusing to take the protestation'.[31] Most Exeter people took the oath, however, either because they wanted to or because they were too frightened not to. The exiled Exeter minister John Bond has left a vivid account of how the Oath of Association was enforced. 'The common practice of the enemy in those parts', he wrote:

> is thus: upon the Lord's Day, when there is a full congregation met together, then the civill and military magistrates and commanders doe . . . send their severe warrants and orders, requiring that first the church doores bee shut up, and strictly guarded by armed souldiers (onely the women and children are first let goe) then the cruell officers are sent in to the people with a new oath, which is exactly, in all points, contrary to our Covenant . . . which all those

poore soules have taken already in that place: And here the trembling, wretched creatures are put to this miserable dilemma, or choyce, either to take that perjurious oath, and so to sweare that they will fight against their religion, Parliament, lawes & liberties . . . or else to receive a brace of bullets from that . . . pistoll, which is there presented to their breasts.[32]

This account is obviously overdrawn (imprisonment, rather than death, was the usual punishment for recalcitrants) but Bond's words help to clear the many former Parliamentarians who took the oath from the charge of being turncoats. Bond observed that many were frightened into taking the oath against their wills, for 'such is the terrour of . . . imminent death . . . that divers godly persons, through infirmity, have tangled themselves verbally with that bloudy combination'. Many later repented their actions. Bond noted that 'after the taking thereof some . . . have been distracted with the terrours of their clamourous consciences', while others had 'locke[d] up themselves in darknesse'.[33] Here Bond touched on an aspect of the Civil War which has been little studied: the extent to which ordinary men and women were psychologically scarred by being forced to disavow their most deeply held beliefs. Bond was unusual among contemporaries in paying serious attention to the mental damage which was caused by the war. Many hospitals had been set up to provide for soldiers wounded in battle, he observed, 'but Alas, Alas! How many . . . hospitals . . . shall we need for [the] wounded consciences and maimed soules in the west?' According to Bond some west-countrymen so bitterly regretted their weakness in taking the oath that they eventually committed suicide.[34]

The Oath of Association was a relatively sophisticated means of identifying Parliamentary sympathizers, of course. Ordinary Royalist soldiers adopted a much more simplistic approach—forcing people to swear or blaspheme, in the knowledge that committed puritans would never agree to do so. 'There is one sure test or touchstone', Bond lamented, 'by which some . . . are wont to try a suspected Roundhead, "Sweare Dammee", say they, "and wee shall beleeve thee, that thou art a friend to the King" '.[35] Oaths aside, the Royalists also used the city sessions court to clamp down on Parliamentary sympathizers. In the immediate aftermath of the surrender, the Royalist faction on the Chamber had been too busy establishing their new regime to act against political disaffection in their capacity as magistrates. Between 9

September and 31 December 1643 only one person was brought before the sessions court for a politico-religious offence (Ursula Jefferies, who had declared that the Fast Day which the Royalists had ordered to be kept on Fridays was 'a Papiste faste').[36] During early 1644 the magistrates became much more vigilant. Maria Courtney, a spinster, was bound over on 11 January for predicting 'that the city would be besieged again etc', and a number of similar cases followed over the next three months (see document 25).[37] Needless to say, the activities of the pro-Royalist justices stirred up great resentment among the city's puritan/Parliamentarians, and Mrs Susanna Walplate—dragged before the sessions court for accusing a conformist minister of being a Jesuit—probably expressed the secret hopes of many when she told the Royalist aldermen Crocker, Walker and Mallack that 'it was theire tyme nowe, but it would be theirs againe shortlie'.[38]

Few Parliamentarian sympathizers in Exeter were as brave, or as foolhardy, as Mrs Walplate, and open defiance of the new regime was comparatively rare. Instead most city Parliamentarians contrived a superficial conformity by taking the Oath of Association, paying their contributions towards the Royalist war effort (albeit grudgingly), and generally keeping their heads down. Many of those who had particular reason to fear Royalist reprisals—notably the former members of the Committee for Safety—took advantage of article five of the surrender terms and requested 'particular pardons ... for all treasons and other offences' committed by them in Exeter during 1641–43 (see document 22). Royal pardons were accordingly granted in early 1644 to Henry Prigge and many others.[39] The fact that these men considered it worthwhile to procure pardons shows that they, like most of the pro-Parliamentarian members of the Chamber, still hoped to remain in the city. As time went by, however, more and more followed in the footsteps of those who had left with Stamford.

'About 500 exiles from Devon and Exon alone' were said to be in London by late 1644. John Bond spoke of them as an 'armie of Martyres', adding that 'they are such an armie and number ... of men, women and children, as I dare say cannot be parallel'd from any proportionable part of the land'. Many of these people had left 'in the beginning of the storm', Bond noted, but the flight of others had been hastened by the hostility of their local enemies.[40] Thomas Eles of Exeter, merchant—formerly 'attendant' to Captain Samuel Crocker's company of Roundhead volunteers—fled the city after being threatened with legal process by

Samuel Isaack, the Royalist town clerk, whom he had helped to carry to the prison ship at Topsham in January 1643.[41]

Royalist members of the Chamber were also active in driving out their pro-Parliamentary colleagues. Having been elected as Exeter's MPs in the Royalist Parliament of 1644, Robert Walker and Peter Ball lost little time in informing the King of 'the absence of some and the neglecte of others of the Common Counsell and officers of this Cittie in their severall places'. Accordingly, orders came down from Oxford that 'some speichle course' should be taken with such persons. This in turn led the Chamber to arrange an extraordinary meeting 'to . . . consider of the dismission of such members of this Societie as there shalbe reasonable cause to displace and then to make eleccon of others in their roomes'. The mayor was asked:

> to make knowne the same to Mr Bennett and Mr Gould, who by their letters have heretofore desired to leave their places, and to write to Mr Phillip Crossing and Mr Richard Crossing . . . requiring them to give their attendances att the said tyme, as they will answer their neglecte att their perills.[42]

If the Mayor's letters had any effect at all on Bennet and Richard Crossing it was simply to drive them still further into opposition. By July 1644 they, together with another member of the Chamber (John Lovering) and two former members of the Committee for Safety (Samuel Clerk and Richard Evans) had become members of what was effectively a government-in-exile: the Parliamentary Committee for Exeter, based in London.[43] The bitter antagonism which now existed between the rival factions on the Exeter Chamber could hardly have been made more clear.

The Campaign of 1644

As the splits between the Chamber men deepened, Exeter was again thrown into the national spotlight. During April 1644 Charles I's Queen, Henrietta Maria, had travelled into the South-West from Oxford. The Queen was expecting a baby, and she wished it to be born in the comparative tranquillity of Exeter, far away from the Parliamentary field armies. Her journey was accomplished in safety and on 1 May she finally arrived in the city, the bells of the cathedral pealing out in welcome.[44] The Queen received a warm welcome from both the city and cathedral authorities, the Chapter presenting her with £100 in gold and the Chamber, not to be outdone, agreeing 'that £200 shalbe presented to the Queene . . . as a testimonie of the respecte of this house unto her Majestie'.[45] The Queen remained in Exeter for the next two months, and on 16 June she gave birth to a daughter—later baptized Henrietta—at Bedford House. The birth of the princess was duly acclaimed by the citizens: the ringers of St Mary Steps parish received handsome payment from the churchwardens there for sounding the church bells 'at the delivery of our queens majestie'.[46]

The princess had come into an uncertain world. A Roundhead army under General Essex was now marching into the West, and Prince Maurice—who had been besieging the Parliamentary sea port of Lyme in Dorset—fell back before the enemy advance, retreating with his army towards Exeter. Meanwhile the Queen was becoming increasingly anxious, fearing that she might become trapped in the city. Once Essex's troops began to move into Devon, she decided that she must leave Exeter at once, even if it meant leaving her new-born baby behind her. On 30 June the Queen was carried out of the city in a horse-litter, escorted by a large force of cavalry under Prince Maurice. The rest of the Prince's army covered her retreat into Cornwall, and eventually took up quarters at Okehampton. Encouraged by these signs of weakness, Essex's forces advanced as far west as Tiverton.[47]

Essex remained at Tiverton for much of July 1644. A summons was sent in to the garrison of Exeter, but Berkeley refused to countenance any surrender. Morale in the city was high and the Royalists' spirits had been bolstered by news of a major victory which Prince Rupert was alleged to have won in the north of England. On 15 July a messenger arrived from Bridgwater, claiming that 'the fortunate Prince Rupert hath done wonders agaynst the Scotts . . . and . . . broken that terrible army'.[48] Berkeley at once ordered a day of thanksgiving to be held. Cannon were fired from the city walls, bonfires lighted on the tops of hills and the bells of the churches rung out in celebration.[49] The churchwardens of St Petrocks laid out 2s 'for ringing by order that came from Mr Maior for newes that came from the northeast', while the cathedral ringers were given no less than 13s 4d 'for ringing for Prince Roberts victory against the Scots'.[50] At Tiverton, Essex was greatly irritated by the Royalist celebrations. He knew very well that the fighting in the north had actually ended in defeat for Prince Rupert, at Marston Moor—but he was quite unable to persuade the Exeter Royalists of this.[51]

Soon after Berkeley's day of thanksgiving, Prince Maurice advanced from Okehampton to Crediton, having decided to march to Exeter 'and there encampe, under the shelter of the town, and River'. On the very same day that the Royalist army arrived at Crediton, however, Essex began to advance as well. Frightened that he would be cut off from Exeter, Maurice sent a force of 1,000 men under Colonel Bamfield to secure and fortify 'Exbridge' (probably Cowley Bridge, to the north of the city). Bamfield achieved his objective, and as a result Maurice was able to march into Exeter safely on 21 July. Foiled, the Parliamentary army moved further into the west.[52] By now, it was becoming increasingly apparent to the Exeter Royalists that events had taken a turn for the better. Not only had Maurice managed to reach the city in safety, but a second Royalist army under the King himself was now marching towards Exeter. Preparations accordingly began to be made to receive the Royal army. Large supplies of cash would, of course, be most welcome to the King and on 25 July the Chamber agreed that:

> whereas there is present and urgent occasions for the use of monies for the present affairs of this Cittie, And its conceived that the Citties plate wilbe hereafter of little use, it is therefore this day agreede and ordered that the Citties plate shalbe foorthwith sold and disposed of for the best profitt.

Next day the Chamber met again and decided that:

> whereas the Kings Majestie is this day to make his accesse to this Cittie, where for his manie gracious favours . . . he ought to be with all dutie & respecte attended on by the Cittizens. . . . It is further agreede and ordered that there shalbe £500 presented to his Majestie, And £100 more to the Prince his highness (who comes with hym) as a testimonie of the Citties service and joy of his Majesties presence here.[53]

Later that day Berkeley and other leading Royalists rode out of Exeter to welcome the King, eventually meeting him a mile or so to the east of the city. From here Charles rode on into Exeter, where he was received by 'the Mayor [Hugh Crocker, whom he promptly knighted], the aldermen and a very great confluence of people, with much joy and acclamation'.[54] Meanwhile, the bells of the city churches rang in celebration, for the third time in as many months.[55] Upon entering

Exeter, the King's first action was to ride to Bedford House to see his baby daughter. Next, he summoned a council of war, where it was decided that the King and Prince Maurice should pursue Essex into Cornwall, while Berkeley should remain behind in garrison at Exeter. Berkeley's main task would be to forward supplies to the King's army, and with this in mind, a magazine of provisions was ordered to be set up in Exeter.[56] Next day the King left the city for the west, heartened by a gift of £100 which had been presented to him by the Dean and Chapter.[57]

Things remained quiet in Exeter for the next few weeks. Berkeley had been left with few soldiers and could hardly have undertaken any major offensive action. Most of his energies went into supplying the Royal army with provisions. Meanwhile the citizens were helping to clothe the King's armies. On 30 July the Chamber agreed to purchase 3,000 pairs of shoes for the Royalist soldiers quartered in Bristol. This gift cost £200, bringing the total amount given to the King, his family and his soldiers by the citizens of Exeter since May 1644 to well over £1,000.[58] The city would soon have to brace itself for further Royal demands. On 1 September Essex's army surrendered to the King at Lostwithiel in Cornwall, and shortly afterwards the triumphant Royalist forces began to make their way back to the east. The city authorities were anxious to give the King due honour on his return and the mayor sent out two scouts 'to bring word which way his Majestie came into this Cittie'.[59] On 18 September the King finally rode back into Exeter. Rumours began to circulate that Exeter would now replace Oxford as the Royalist's winter headquarters. Charles was anxious to get back to the Midlands, however, and six days later he and his forces again marched out of Exeter.[60]

Changes in Civic Government

Before the King left the city he made Berkeley responsible for blockading the Parliamentary garrison at Lyme. Troops from Exeter were also ordered to assist in the Royalist siege of Taunton and in future Berkeley was to spend a great deal of his time directing operations against these two troublesome garrisons.[61] Day-to-day management of affairs in Exeter therefore devolved upon the new lieutenant governor, Colonel Philip Frowde, and upon Nicholas Spicer, who had replaced Hugh Crocker as mayor in September.[62] The choice of Spicer as mayor is only explicable in terms of his pro-Royalist credentials, for he had already served in this office once before and to be elected to a second term in the Exeter mayoralty was comparatively rare. The decision to recall Spicer, even though he was well over sixty at the time, hints at just how limited the range of candidates who were acceptable to the Royalists must have been. And this in turn helps to show that, although the accustomed civic government of Exeter did not collapse or fall into abeyance during the period of Royalist occupation (as it did in Newcastle and other places) it did become more narrow, more restricted and—ultimately—more inefficient.[63]

In Exeter, as in Bath, local government had continued very much as normal under the Parliamentarians, and it was only after the Royalists took over that really dramatic changes began to occur.[64] Before the Civil War Chamber meetings had been held, on average, three times a month, and this continued to be the case during the period of Roundhead control. After the Royalist takeover, however, the number fell to just two a month (see Table 3, p. 225)—and as the meetings became less frequent they also became less well attended. Before the war, Chamber meetings had been regularly attended by twenty or more councillors. Yet during the period of Roundhead control, average attendance fell to fifteen and under the Royalists it slumped still further, to just thirteen.[65] Had numbers fallen any lower, a quorum would not have been attained and—under the traditional rules of city government—business would not have been allowed to proceed. The fact that the Royalist Chamber met less frequently than the Roundhead one, therefore, probably reflects the fact that, after 1643, it became harder and harder to round up the minimum number of councillors who were needed to conduct Chamber business.

This in turn emphasizes the fact that the withdrawal of the pro-Parliamentarian members of the Chamber from public affairs had seriously weakened Exeter's civic government. The work-load of those councillors who remained active had been greatly increased by their colleagues' defection and although attempts were made to remedy this in late 1644—when four of the most prominent absentees were dismissed and replaced by pro-Royalists—further deaths and desertions meant that the Royalist Chamber was reduced by early 1645 to an effective strength of sixteen men.

A similar pattern emerges from the records of the city sessions courts. During the period of Parliamentary control this body had met on 104 separate occasions, but during the Royalist occupation—which lasted two and a half times as long—it met on just 127.[66] The reduced frequency of meetings partly reflected the fact that, owing to the pressures of war and the withdrawal of the pro-Parliamentarians, two or three aldermen now had to do all the work. Poor Nicholas Spicer, already serving as mayor and as a city militia captain, practically ran the sessions court by himself during much of 1645. Spicer eventually attended a staggering 60 per cent of all court sittings held between September 1643 and April 1646, while Hugh Crocker attended 47 per cent and Robert Walker 37 per cent.[67] Before the war anyone who had attended even 30 per cent of the meetings would have been regarded as unusually diligent.

The decline of the sessions court also owed much to the fact that many of its functions had been usurped by the Royalist Council of War, which sat under Sir John Berkeley's direction at Bedford House. The first reference to this body in the civic records appears in March 1644, when it was noted in the sessions book that William Coombe, fuller, had been bound over 'by order of the counsell of warre' for abusing the established church.[68] Next month Matthew Axe, a dyer, was 'committed by the counsell of warre for speaking of words' and in July, Elizabeth Robyns was likewise 'committed . . . by the counsell of warre' for 'speaking of mutinous and seditious words'.[69] Thereafter, the sessions court dealt with only isolated cases of disaffection; the military authorities had clearly taken over chief responsibility for dealing with such matters. The unease which was caused by the inexorable growth of military power in Exeter was voiced by the clerk of the sessions court in April 1645, when he observed that Anna Couch, widow, had been 'committed [to prison] by the Leiutenante Governor Froud, but for what, or by whose authoritie, *ignotum est*'.[70]

Dark Days

This comment is symbolic of a wider sense of disillusion which was now beginning to set in at Exeter, as the partisan passions of 1641–43 gradually ebbed away and even the King's most committed supporters grew to despair of a war which was becoming more bitter and destructive with each passing day. In Exeter, as in Oxford, it is notable that celebrations of Royalist military triumphs became much more rare as the war progressed.[71] During 1644 church bells had rung out in Exeter for Prince Rupert's victory at Newark, the King's victory at Cropredy Bridge, the alleged victory at Marston Moor and the King's triumph in

Cornwall.[72] In 1645 only one such victory peal was recorded: the ringing of the bells of St Mary Steps on 8 May, 'by command of Mr Maior'.[73] As these last words make clear, the bells were rung by official order, rather than as a result of spontaneous popular delight. And the fact that the victory which Mayor Spicer had ordered to be celebrated on this occasion—a successful Royalist assault on Taunton, later turned into a defeat when the attackers were beaten back—seems somehow appropriate.

The increasing war-weariness in Exeter was undoubtedly exacerbated by fiscal demands. As the Royalist garrison grew, so did the rate imposed on the citizens, and by early 1645 even the churchwardens of St Petrocks were paying 5s a month towards 'the Garisson rate'.[74] Payments seem to have been made at three-monthly intervals. In March 1645 two members of the Chamber were requested to 'auditt Robert Phippes his account for the East Quarter and South Quarter [of the city] touching the weeklie payments for the garrison for the three first monethes'. Other councillors were asked to audit the accounts for the north and west quarters.[75] The upkeep of the garrison and associated charges clearly weighed very heavily upon the citizens; Christopher Broadridge, a merchant, later recalled that 'rates, taxes, billeting [and] fortifications for 4 yeares and upward on both sides . . . cost me at least £300'.[76] The financial squeeze tightened still further in April 1645 when an official rate 'for fortification' began to be levied on the inhabitants.[77] At the same time pioneers (conscripted military labourers) were brought into the city from the surrounding countryside to work on the defences. One such group were digging trenches in Southernhay by the end of April, while two months later similar work was underway in the Bonhay.[78]

Work on the defences was hastened after news of Charles I's defeat at Naseby reached Exeter. The destruction of the King's main field army here left the Parliamentarians in full control of the Midlands. The west-country was now the only compact block of territory which the King still held outside Wales and the Marches, and Parliament therefore directed the New Model Army, under the command of Sir Thomas Fairfax, to advance into the region. Fairfax's first aim was to relieve Taunton. This aim was swiftly achieved and on 4 July the besiegers drew off from the town. Six days later the Royalist army which was supposed to shield Devon and Cornwall from attack was routed at the battle of Langport; the Royalist garrison of Bridgwater surrendered soon afterwards. No major obstacle now stood between the New Model Army and Exeter, and the inhabitants reportedly began to 'quake' in anticipation of an attack. Parliamentary writers reported that Exeter was 'very flat, by reason of our greate success before Bridgewater'.[79] Many of the inhabitants were said to be preparing to go abroad, while others had left already.

Fortunately for the Exeter Royalists, the New Model Army did not follow up its victories by immediately advancing westward but moved to besiege Bristol instead. Berkeley therefore gained valuable time in which to improve the defences. Throughout July and August provisions were brought into the garrison and stored at 'Exeter hospital' (probably St John's Hospital near East Gate).[80] Desperate efforts were made to secure gunpowder, both from within the city and from abroad, while work on the fortifications continued apace. A major survey was also carried out, to establish how many people were living in the city, and how well provided they were with food. The churchwardens of St Mary Steps laid out three shillings:

> for takeinge account of whatt peopell were in our parish, and whatt poore and what stranger, and what soldiers and what provizion every houskeeper hade, and what they could provide, by order from Sir John Barkley, and for takinge of the protestation.[81]

The 'protestation' referred to here was yet another oath, which the Royalists had administered to the citizens in the hope of winkling out disaffected persons (see document 28). Nor was this the only ruse which the King's local supporters employed to track down their enemies. Alan Penny—one of the new Chamber men who had been chosen to replace the Parliamentarian councillors dismissed in 1644—bribed a boy, one Robert Buncombe, to betray city Roundheads. According to Edward Laurence, one of Penny's victims, Buncombe:

> did cunningly come to this informant's house pretending hymselfe to be of the Parliament's partie, and to be much displeased with those persons and others that were then used in this Cittie, and expressing a great desire of goeing unto the towne of Plymouth [then under Roundhead control].

Convinced by the boy's story, Laurence duly procured him 'some notes or letters to some persons for his better passage and admittance into

Plymouth aforesaid'. Yet as soon as he had possession of these documents, the perfidious Buncombe took them to the Royalist authorities, 'which drewe . . . [Laurence] into great trouble and danger by fyne and ymprisonment'.[82] This episode not only provides a rare glimpse of Civil War espionage techniques at work, it also shows how ordinary Exeter people like Edward Laurence continued to act covertly for Parliament throughout the Royalist occupation.

Royalist Divisions

As the Royalist leaders strove to curb internal dissent, their problems were compounded by the erratic activities of George, Lord Goring, commander of the main Royalist field army in the west. Following the defeat at Langport, Goring's dissolute soldiers (most of whom were cavalrymen) had retreated into North Devon. Here the Royalist forces remained throughout the summer, looting, pillaging and indulging in 'unheard of rapine'. Towards the middle of August plans were made to bring these ill-disciplined troops into East Devon, in order to resist the anticipated Parliamentary advance. Goring therefore travelled to Exeter, where he made preparations for the reception of his men. At first Goring seems to have got on well with Berkeley. But once it became clear that Goring wished to billet his dissolute troopers within the city walls, the governor became alarmed. As early as 21 August Berkeley warned the Royalist high command that no more troops could be quartered at Exeter 'without the exhausting of the provisions of this garrison'.[83] Once Goring's troopers actually arrived near Exeter, moreover, they began to eat up the supplies which were intended for the city itself.

This situation was clearly intolerable and bitter complaints were made against Goring. The officers of the garrison sent an urgent appeal to the Prince of Wales (then nominal commander of the Royalist forces in the west) requesting him to intervene. Goring, too, asked the Prince to come up to Exeter, in order to co-ordinate plans for resisting the Parliamentarians. Accordingly the Prince and his entourage set out from Launceston, arriving in the city on the evening of 29 August. The Prince was evidently in desperate need of money; the Chamber agreed to present him with £100 'as a testimonie of the humble duties of this cittie to his Highnes'. To raise this sum, the hard-pressed citizens were forced to divert funds which had originally been set aside for charitable purposes, 'there being noo other meanes to raise the same but by orphanes monie'.[84] The arrival of the Prince had a temporarily beneficial effect on affairs at Exeter. A council of war was called, and plans were made to march to the relief of Bristol, while Goring's army was ordered to advance to the east of Exeter, thus reducing pressure on the countryside around the city itself. This period of purposeful activity came to an abrupt halt, however, when 'news came in of the fatal loss of Bristol'.[85] With the capture of this important Royalist stronghold, the ambitious plans of the Prince and his advisers collapsed. All thoughts of a march to the east now had to be abandoned, and the Prince hurriedly returned to Cornwall.

With the departure of Prince Charles, really serious disagreements began to break out in Exeter. Goring still wanted to quarter his men within the city, and from mid-September onwards it was regularly reported in the Roundhead press that he was trying to usurp Berkeley's position as governor. The thought of the debauched Lord Goring presiding over the city while his licentious troopers ran riot within clearly horrified the inhabitants and, encouraged by Berkeley, they stubbornly resisited Goring's plans. It was noted in London at this time that Goring had 'attempted to go into Exeter', but that the inhabitants had 'refused to admit him or any of his company'.[86] Goring apparently reacted to this by setting up a permanent blockade. A few days later it was reported that:

> the difference is grown to that height betwixt ... Barkly and [Goring] that unlesse he may have accesse to come and quarter in the city, (and if occasion be to be Governour of it) he refuseth to let any more provision to be brought into it, and hath made stop of the market people that were going thither.[87]

It is hard to be sure whether Goring had actually *ordered* his men to stop supplies from coming into the city, as the Parliamentarians claimed, or whether he was simply unable to prevent his ill-disciplined troops from taking what they pleased. Whatever the case, it is clear that the troopers' activities were having a damaging effect on local food stocks. Royalist sources later admitted that the Exeter garrison was forced to live off its own previously-accumulated supplies, while Goring's horse:

> possessed the other parts of the country to themselves, and would neither suffer provisions to be brought to the markets, for the replenishing their stores, nor any warrants to be executed for any

payments ... insomuch as ... there was not so much brought into the city in a fortnight as they spent in a day, which was only by reason of the disorder of our own horse.[88]

With Goring's dissolute forces at the city gates, bitter quarrels raging between the Royalist commanders, and the Parliamentary forces advancing closer every day, several Exonians decided that the time had now come to flee. 'Some of note' in Exeter, the Roundheads observed:

> suspecting the strength of that place, have already sent away their treasure, we heare of ten thousand pounds sent away at one time. Many of the merchants and inhabitants of quality in that city have stolen away, and provided for the security of their persons in France, in Flanders and in Holland.[89]

Independent evidence confirms this report. George Potter, an Exeter merchant, later recalled that he, 'observinge the approachinge and growinge troubles daylie more and more cominge on ... to that cittie' had taken ship for France in the autumn of 1645, not returning home until the war was over.[90]

Despite the claims of the pamphleteers, Goring himself does not seem to have been denied admittance to the city (although his troops most certainly were); by late September the troublesome Royalist general was comfortably ensconced in Exeter. From here he wrote to one of the Prince's counsellors, informing him that 'we are very busy providing for them [i.e. the Roundheads] ... and I am very confident that they shall neither hurt Exeter or us'.[91] Despite the easy tone of this communication, bitter conflicts continued to rage between the Royalist commanders. It was reported in London that 'Goring hath had many quarrelings with Berkley ... and sweares ... that he will be Governour of Exeter himselfe'.[92] The Royalist horse, meanwhile, continued to find the city gates barred against them. On 13 October it was reported that Berkeley 'will not permit Goring to come into Exeter, and saith he will turn his ordnance against him, if he offers to come into the city'.[93] Whether the dispute ever grew quite as serious as this is, perhaps, open to question. No doubt the pamphleteers exaggerated the Royalist divisions as much as they could. Nevertheless, it is clear that deep hostility existed between Berkeley and the citizens on the one hand, and Goring and his army on the other.

At this point Goring was distracted from his ambitions at Exeter by the advance of the Parliamentary forces. On 13 October the New Model Army occupied Axminster in East Devon. Afraid of being cut off, Goring resolved to break through their ranks and march to the King at Oxford. That day, he drew off his forces from before Exeter and marched as far as Honiton, hoping to slip through the Roundhead out-guards at night. It was a bold plan, but Goring had left it far too late and the Royalists were unable to break through. Although Goring managed to inflict a sharp defeat on the Parliamentary advance guard, the march to Oxford had to be abandoned.[94] Instead the Royalists fell back on Poltimore, a small village two miles to the east of Exeter. From here, Goring again began to exert pressure on Berkeley to let his horsemen enter the city, but once again he was refused.

In a letter sent to Berkeley at this time, Goring begged the officers of the garrison to lay aside past differences and 'joyne together in his Majestie's service'. He then informed the governor that 'for the safety of my men and this citie, I have desired most part of my infantry to come hither', adding, rather vaguely, that '[I] have given further orders to my officers of horse, according to . . . directions from the Prince'. Goring concluded his letter by describing the measures which he felt should be taken to prepare the city for a siege. Had they been adopted, these measures would have proved most unpleasant for Exeter's inhabitants, many of whom Goring suggested should be 'turned out of the citie' forthwith.[95] The events of the next few days are rather hard to piece together, but it is clear that Goring continued to make unacceptable demands of the garrison while Berkeley—supported by the citizens —continued to resist him. The struggle reached a climax on 18 October, when it was noted in the Chamber Act Book that:

> whereas Sir John Berkley . . . the present Governor of this cittie, hath in manie particulars expressed a greate care and respecte to the welfare of this cittie and cittizens, And is alwaies readie to performe the same, being att present of greate concernment, Mr Maior is desired to render hym hartie thancks, for those his favors, and to intreate of hym the continuance thereof.[96]

Two things are made clear by this: first, that the citizens regarded Berkeley as their protector and second that they felt themselves to be under particular threat at this time—presumably from Goring.

Exactly what happened next must remain a mystery, but it is clear that Berkeley eventually thwarted Goring's plans in some way, thereby winning the citizens' gratitude. Towards the end of that same day the Chamber agreed to give Berkeley the substantial sum of £100 'as a testimonie of the citties thanckfulness & respecte to him *for his respect . . . for . . . of souldiers*' (the last part of this entry has been heavily crossed out and obscured).[97] In the absence of any further information, it seems safest to assume that Berkeley's triumph had been to keep Goring's cavalrymen firmly outside the city walls. It is known for certain that, although Goring himself was eventually permitted to enter Exeter, accompanied by his relatively well-disciplined foot soldiers, the dreaded horsemen remained outside. Over 1,000 of them were later reported to be encamped 'on the west side of the city, close', presumably in St Thomas.[98] By keeping Goring's cavalry out, Berkeley had not only preserved the property and goods of the citizens, but had also safeguarded his own position as governor. For the moment, affairs at Exeter returned to an uneasy state of calm.

Meanwhile the Parliamentarians had taken advantage of the quarrel between Goring and Berkeley to advance still further westwards. On 20 October a brigade of Roundhead troops occupied the village of Stoke Canon, just four miles to the north-east of Exeter. Elements of this brigade next ascended Stoke Hill and set up outposts there, in order to 'hinder markets, and keep firing [i.e. fire wood] for Excester from comming to them from the east'.[99] Next day Fairfax himself went 'with a small party to Stoke, and so on towards Excester, till he came within less than a mile of the town, viewed that part of the city, and returned back that night'.[100] The Royalists were now becoming increasingly nervous and that same evening they burnt down hundreds of houses in the city suburbs, in preparation for a siege.[101] Goring, baulked in his attempts to become governor and 'perceiving that he was . . . like to be besieged', decided that it was pointless to remain in Exeter any longer.[102] On the night of 22 October he marched away towards Okehampton with the bulk of his cavalry, leaving his infantry behind under Berkeley's command.[103] The Exeter garrison was left to face the advancing Parliamentarian army alone.

6

'Close Begirt'
The Final Siege

Following Goring's departure the New Model Army attempted to march from Newton St Cyres to Alphington with the intention of blocking Exeter off from the west. Yet owing to the difficulty of the terrain and 'the extremity of wet and unseasonable weather which it pleased God to send' the Parliamentarians found themselves unable to reach their intended destination. Instead Fairfax was forced to retire to Crediton, where his army rested on 24 October 'horse and man being much wearied out with the extreme wet weather, and their carriages broken'.[1] Next day the army commanders decided to return to the eastern side of the River Exe and to settle their quarters around Topsham, a town which would serve as a useful base for operations against Exeter. Accordingly, on 26 October, the bulk of the New Model Army marched to Silverton. Next day the army arrived at Topsham (despite 'the great quantities of wet [having] made the wayes so foul') and that night the Parliamentary outguards lay well to the north of their headquarters, within two miles of Exeter.[2] Indeed an alarm was given to the Royalists in Mount Radford, on the very outskirts of the city defences (see Map 4, p. 110).[3]

These moves clearly rattled the garrison. Fearing an imminent attack from the direction of Topsham, Berkeley ordered the destruction of eighty houses in the southern suburbs of the city on 27 October. This action sparked off great indignation in the Parliamentary press. One pamphleteer commented that Berkeley 'makes fuell of the inhabitants houses, converting whole streets into ashes, to make the Town . . . the more tenable, turning out the people to the mercy of the besiegers'. With

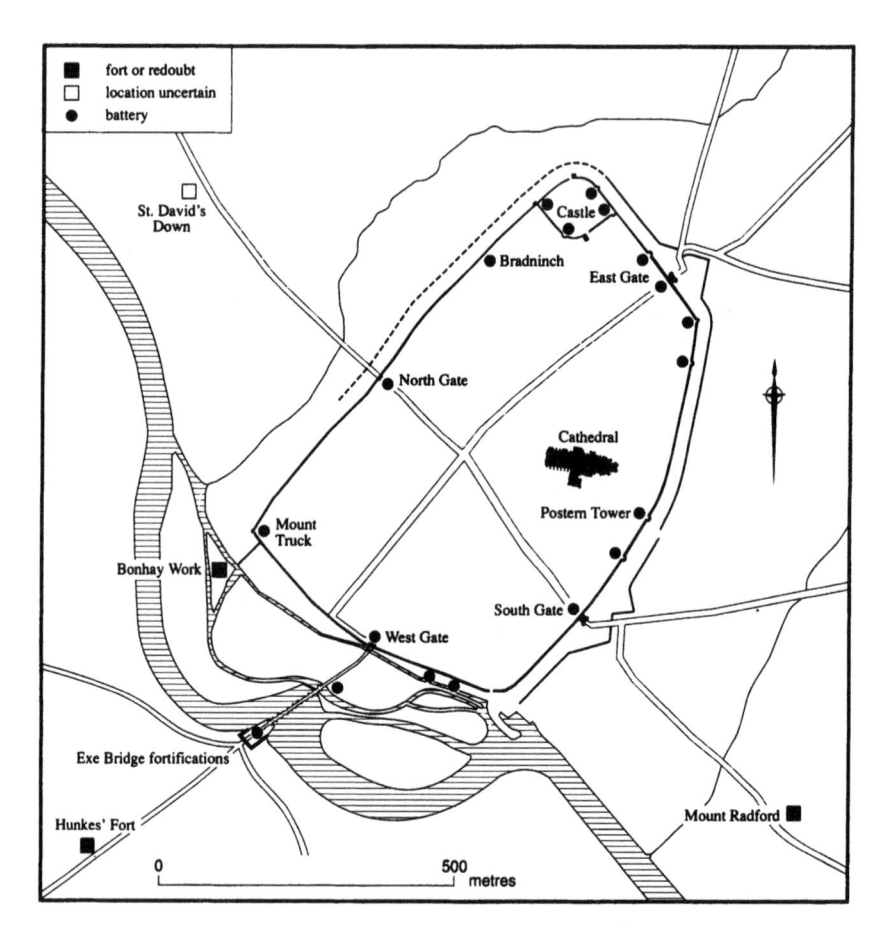

Map 4. Exeter's Royalist Fortifications

the city gates barred against them, the people whose homes had been destroyed were forced to travel to neighbouring towns for shelter. Many of them came in to the Parliamentary forces, complaining bitterly of 'the cruelty of the enemy'.[4]

On 28 October Fairfax held a council of war at Topsham. There was some dispute among the Parliamentary officers as to precisely what course they should now pursue. Some favoured the idea of establishing a permanent headquarters at Topsham. From here, they argued, a bridge could be built over the Exe towards Alphington, and this in turn would allow the siege of Exeter to be prosecuted on both sides of the river. Yet the majority were against this plan. They pointed out that the construction of such a bridge would be an immense task, while guarding it from attack would place heavy burdens upon the soldiers. It was also felt that, with winter coming on, offensive operations should be halted and a retreat into winter quarters made. Many of the common soldiers had already been 'killed by lying out' and to make matters worse a mysterious sickness had begun to spread through the Parliamentarian ranks. Fairfax therefore decided 'to refresh his [soldiers], who never stood in more need of it, by laying them in the best and most convenient quarters he could'.[5]

Fairfax felt that the Parliamentarians should 'secure all on the east of Ex, before such time as they possesed any quarters on the other side'. Several garrisons were therefore ordered to be set up on the eastern bank of the River Clyst, 'which being once finished, a few men might keep them and hinder provisions from going into the city'.[6] Once quartered in the villages which lay behind this defensive screen, the army could rest and recuperate in relative security. The first step towards implementing this plan was to determine precisely where the new garrisons should be located. Three sites were eventually chosen: the village of Stoke Canon (which lies beside an important bridge over the River Culm), the mansion house at Poltimore, and Bedford House, near Bishop's Clyst. All three sites stood near to main roads leading out from Exeter to the east.

Once these sites had been selected, a military engineer was sent out to fortify Bedford House. Colonel Hammond's regiment was given the task of fortifying Stoke Canon, while Poltimore House was occupied by a locally-raised regiment under the command of Colonel Ceely.[7] These frontline units were to be supported in depth by the other regiments of the New Model Army. On 29 October the army evacuated Topsham and marched to Broadclyst (a village within two miles of Poltimore).[8] Meanwhile Fairfax himself set off for Ottery St Mary, further to the east, which he had chosen to be his head quarters. The artillery train was ordered to billet itself here, and temporary fortifications were thrown up around the town.[9] Over the next few days Fairfax's men laboured to build their new fortifications along the line of the Clyst. A letter written from the Roundhead quarters on 8 November reported that 'we go on in our . . . fortifications neer Exeter, and shall settle our quarters so well . . . and so to receive or stop the Enemy, that he shall not be able to come this way, without great losse'.[10] Further defences were erected along the line of the River Exe, to prevent the Parliamentary positions from being outflanked.[11]

By 14 November the 'New Fortifications' were finished. A Parliamentary writer observed that 'the worke of these last eight daies hath been the compleating of our frontier garrisons of Stoake, Poultimore, and Bishops Cliffe, which . . . [now] are compleated'.[12] Behind this defensive screen the bulk of the New Model Army had spread itself out to quarter. Four infantry regiments were billeted at Bradninch, two more at Cullompton and another two at Ottery. Fairfax's own regiment was based at Honiton, while Major General Massey's forces had entrenched themselves at Tiverton. Four more infantry regiments manned the 'frontier garrisons': Colonel Hammond's regiment at Stoke, Colonel Rainsborough's at Rewe, Colonel Ceely's at Poltimore and 'the Taunton Regiment' at Bishop's Clyst.[13] The cavalry regiments were spread out across the countryside between Tiverton and Honiton (see map 5). Despite the great tract of land which the army was now occupying, provisions and lodging continued to be in short supply. 'Our quarters extend now some 24 or 25 myles in length, and yet are we streightned', one correspondent complained. The common soldiers were reportedly billeted 'ten and twenty in a single house'. Meanwhile the sickness in the Parliamentary ranks was continuing to gather pace, with dozens of soldiers succumbing every week to the mysterious illness termed the 'New Disease'.[14]

Lord Goring's Return

With the Parliamentarians clearly in no state to advance any further, the Royalists decided to reduce the strength of their garrison. Exeter was crammed with troops at this time: contemporaries estimated that there

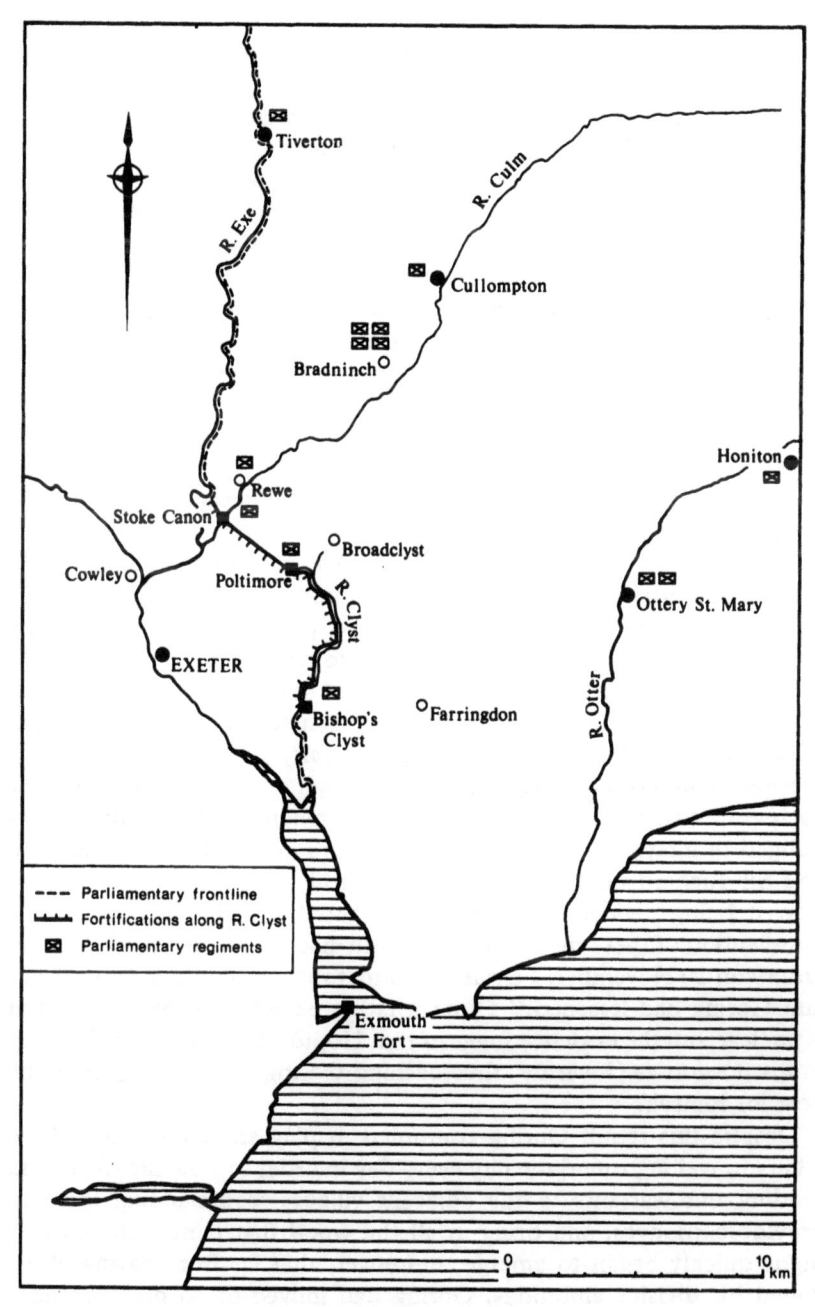

Map 5. Parliamentary Dispositions near Exeter, late 1645

were 1,500 regular infantrymen in the city, as well as 1,500 townsmen and six troops of horse.[15] Now that the Roundhead threat had receded, many of the regular soldiers were no longer needed and, in order to prevent the city from becoming overburdened, Berkeley resolved to send some of them away. On 6 November 600 veteran infantrymen were drawn out of Exeter and marched away to Crediton (probably by way of Cowley bridge, still in Royalist hands at this time).[16] Here they were met by a strong body of Goring's horse and escorted further west. The departure of these troops undoubtedly relieved the pressure on Exeter. Yet Berkeley's difficulties were by no means over. Not only could men be sent *out* of the city through Crediton, but, by using the same route, unwelcome guests could also come *in*.

This became apparent on 6 November, when Goring himself returned to Exeter.[17] Parliamentary writers ascribed his re-appearance to a continued desire to be made Governor. One pamphleteer reported that Goring had attempted to thrust Berkeley out of his position, and other writers confirmed this, asserting that 'now [Goring] is once in, he will never leave till Berkeley be out, meaning to take the Governourship . . . to himself'.[18] Two days later it was reported that 'there is like to be great difference betweene Gorings and Bartlets men, and the citizens that joyned with Bartlett'.[19] The townsfolk clearly remained as hostile to Goring's ambitions as ever. Indeed, the situation in Exeter soon became so highly charged that other Royalist commanders found themselves obliged to intervene. Parliamentary sources reported that Lord Hopton and Sir Richard Grenville 'are to go speedily [to Exeter] to settle that city, it being divided into the Gorian and Barcklian factions'.[20] The intervention of these mediators apparently had some effect; writing from Ottery on 10 November, Fairfax noted that the tension between Berkeley and Goring had lessened.[21] Quite what agreement had been arrived at is unclear, but the evidence suggests that Hopton had confirmed Berkeley in his postion as Governor, thus dashing Goring's hopes of gaining the post for himself.

Despite this rebuff Goring continued to play an active part in local affairs, travelling round the city every day in order to view the works and sending out warrants to the adjacent villages 'commanding them to provide carriadges, and bring in all the wood that is near the City'.[22] Signs quickly began to emerge, moreover, that far from having abandoned his divisive ambitions, Goring had moved on to much grander schemes. On 12 November he sent a letter to Fairfax, requesting a meeting between some of the senior officers of the two armies. The reasons for this meeting were left rather vague, but it was strongly rumoured that Goring hoped to arrange a separate peace between his forces and the New Model Army, and—with this achieved—'to have had both armies engage themselves to force both King and Parliament to conditions'.[23] Such a deal would have made Goring himself extremely powerful, of course. He and Fairfax would have become the arbiters of the entire realm.

Fairfax agreed to meet Goring's emissaries, but as soon as they arrived at Ottery he made it clear to them that he would not consider a separate peace 'whereupon . . . they returned back unto Excester, much unsatisfied'.[24] Goring's last throw had failed. He remained in Exeter for a few days longer, but with his schemes in ruins and his health apparently failing, he had little reason to stay. Soon afterwards Goring abandoned his command, riding to Dartmouth and from here taking ship to France. The citizens of Exeter cannot have been sorry to see him go.

Throughout the rest of November the troops of the New Model Army hardly stirred from their winter quarters. Fairfax himself stayed chiefly at Ottery, only 'riding out sometimes to see the finishing of the works at Broad Cliss and Poultimore, and disposing of the quarters for the foot'.[25] Meanwhile Berkeley continued to send troops out of Exeter in order to reduce the pressure on supplies. On 17 November one hundred soldiers marched out towards Crediton, and by the end of the month it was being reported that the Royalists 'have very much emptyed Excester, thereby to lengthen out provisions'. Those who came out of the city at this time told Fairfax that 'the inhabitants are the principall strength there'.[26] Further supplies were continually being procured, moreover. Hay was carried in daily, and correspondents asserted that the Royalists meant to 'fill the storehouses in the city full of provisions if possibly they can procure it'.[27]

Only fuel seems to have been really scarce in Exeter at this time. On 17 November the city was said to be 'in great want of fireing' and wood was the commodity which the Royalists were expected to run out of first.[28] By the end of the month the cost of firewood was growing higher, and prices continued to rise thereafter. Coal was also in great demand. It was reported that 'coals are very scarce with them in Exeter, they would give 10s a bushell for coals to be brought in for the publike service, if they could get them'.[29] Proof that the fuel shortage was beginning to bite comes from the city receiver's accounts; on 23 December the

Chamber paid 4s 6d for a horse-load of firewood, almost ten times the usual price.[30]

Optimistic Parliamentarian correspondents suggested that these shortages might soon bring the Royalists to their knees, but forecasts of an imminent surrender were misplaced. The Royalists knew that it was they, and not their weary opponents, who were in the strongest position. Hedgerows and country cottages contrasted most unfavourably with the snug billets available in Exeter, and the King's men boasted that 'we have our foot in the City and Towne who lie warm, and we shall spoile the Parliaments men, who have not so good quarter'.[31] The Royalists were further encouraged by the sickness which was raging through the Parliamentary ranks and, indeed they hoped that the New Disease would eventually 'consume th[at] army to nothing'. The Parliamentarians themselves admitted that their foot soldiers 'were sick in most places' during November: 'there dying of soldiers and inhabitants in the town of Autree [Ottery], seven, eight, and nine a day, for several weeks together, insomuch that it was not held safe for the headquarters to be continued there any longer'.[32]

Advance Across the Exe

Towards the end of November the Parliamentary headquarters were moved from Ottery to Tiverton. A few days later Fairfax—worried about the health of his men and anxious that the advance across the Exe should begin—ordered that several regiments should be sent to Crediton: 'a place that stood in good air, which likely would much conduce to the health of our souldiers, and lay conveniently for a strong quarter upon the west side of the river'.[33] Parliamentary dragoons occupied Crediton on 8 December and the next day they were joined by foot soldiers under Sir Hardress Waller making the town a permanent Parliamentarian base. Henceforth the Royalists were to find themselves under increasing pressure on the west side of Exeter, an area which had hitherto been shielded from Parliamentary attack.

On 14 December Roundhead forces launched an ambitious assault on Powderham Castle, an important Royalist garrison lying four miles to the south of Exeter. This position was vital to the Royalists because of its command of the River Exe. Although Parliamentary cannon mounted at Nutwell House, just across the river from Powderham, deterred Royalist shipping, they could not effectively cover the western side of the channel. As long as the Royalists held Powderham, therefore, small boats could continue to flit up and down the river, bringing in intelligence and supplies. Should the Roundheads capture the position, however, the river would effectively be blocked off and Exeter would become a wholly 'inland towne'.[34]

Fairfax decided that an attempt upon Powderham must be made. Troops were assembled and on the evening of 14 December Captain Deane led a force of 200 Parliamentary raiders across the river. The night was dark, snow was falling fast and the oars of the Roundhead boats were muffled. As a result Deane's men were able to land on the west bank without being challenged—only to find that 150 fresh Royalist soldiers had marched into Powderham just hours before. An attack on the castle itself now seemed out of the question, but the Parliamentarians were unwilling to return to Nutwell without having accomplished anything. Instead they decided to occupy Powderham Church, which stood on the river bank a mile upstream from the Royalist garrison and would serve as an excellent substitute for the castle itself. Urgent requests for assistance were sent back to Nutwell and, next morning, supplies and provisions were ferried across the river to the soldiers in the church.[35]

The Royalists were greatly alarmed by these developments, 'fearing the castle would be lost, as well as the river blocked up by the fortifying of this church'.[36] Berkeley immediately sent word to the Prince's army that reinforcements were needed, and within hours a crack brigade of Cornish infantrymen had set out for the city from Okehampton.[37] Meanwhile Berkeley organized a counter-attack. Around midday on 15 December, 500 Royalist soldiers set out from Exeter. These troops joined the castle garrison and at 7.00 p.m. that evening the combined Royalist force launched a determined assault on the Parliamentarians in the church, throwing in 'many hand grenadoes amongst them'. The Royalists 'continued storming till ten' but were eventually 'beaten off with much loss, leaving their dead on the place, and carrying with them many wounded, as appeared by the snow, that was much stained with their blood as they retreated'.[38]

Having beaten off this attack, Deane's men 'resolved to continue in their duty', notwithstanding 'the extremity of the cold, by reason of the great frost and snow'.[39] The Royalists were equally determined to recapture the church and their resolve was stiffened by the arrival of the reinforcements which had been called for: 600 veteran Cornishmen, under the command of Major General Wagstaffe. A second assault force was gathered together in Exeter and preparations for a new attack were made. But before the Royalists could sally out, Hardress Waller advanced from Crediton with three regiments of the New Model Army and occupied the village of Exminster, halfway between Exeter and Powderham. This move, the Parliamentarians claimed, 'took that effect as was desired; the enemy being so amazed, that they durst not march out . . . to attempt the church again, lest our men should get between them and home'.[40]

With the Royalists baulked, Fairfax decided to withdraw his men from their exposed position at Powderham. Next day more regiments were ordered to draw down from Crediton and distract the Royalists on the west side of Exeter. Elements of Hardress Waller's brigade fell upon the Royalist quarters in St Thomas that evening. 'Having slaine some, and wounded others', they captured 'the Maior of Excesters son, and five prisoners more'. Roundhead sources claimed that their men had advanced so close to Exe-bridge that they and the Royalist defenders had been able to exchange insults with each other.[41] Waller's men also took 'a convoy and 40 horse going to Exceter with wool', along with three packs of kersey cloth, which, the Roundheads crowed, 'should have been to cloath the enemy, but will now be of better use for our owne souldiers'.[42] The Royalists apparently put up little resistance. Parliamentary writers boasted that they 'made not one shot against our men' and that an entire Royalist cavalry troop had given itself up to Waller 'being weary of the service'.[43]

Once Waller received word that the troops at Powderham had completed their retreat, he abandoned his diversionary activities and withdrew to the north.[44] For a time it seemed that fresh assaults were about to be launched on Exeter, but the terrible weather conditions eventually forced Fairfax to abandon such plans. With snow lying thick upon the ground both Royalists and Parliamentarians remained chiefly in their own quarters for the next few weeks, contending with the elements rather than with each other.

The soldiers of both sides suffered greatly for want of winter clothing during this period. Parliamentary writers made frequent reference to the New Model Army's lack of coats and shoes and these vital accoutrements were scarce in Exeter too. On one occasion, Berkeley asked the city councillors to give him ten soldiers' coats which they had in their possession. The councillors demurred, pointing out that 'there are divers poore men of this cittie that do dutie and are unclothed and want those cloathes'. Nevertheless Berkeley's wishes clearly prevailed, for next day the coats were 'delivered to Lt. Coll. Piper by order of the Governor'.[45] This incident hints at the privation being endured in Exeter during the winter of 1645-46, a subject which was dwelt on at length by Roundhead correspondents. 'The town and souldiery is in great discontent for want of provisions', one such writer claimed in December, 'all, or the most part of their sheep being spent, [and] mutton at 8d per pound. [The common soldier] grudges at his 6d a day, victuals being dear, the Governour commands souldiers out to quarter, they refuse, we lie so to molest them, they say they will not be thus pent up . . . their horses begin to die apace, duty too hard, they run daily out of Excester, wants increase, wood scarce, no butter at all, nor oatmeal'.[46] This account of the garrison's sufferings is probably overdrawn, but the Royalists themselves admitted that 'Exiter is so close begirt, as very little or no provisions can passe into it, and it is not supplied for many moneths'.[47]

What supplies *were* brought into Exeter at this time came from the countryside to the south-west of the city which still remained relatively free of Parliamentarian troops. Messages from the Prince's army also came into Exeter from this direction; on 23 December the Chamber received a letter 'from Prince Charles['s] . . . Counsell . . . in Cornwall . . . touching the provision of shoes & stockings etc for his Majesties souldiers'.[48] Yet as time went by Exeter's communications with the Prince became increasingly tenuous. Several large houses to the south-west of the city were seized and fortified by Parliamentary dragoons during December and by the end of the month the journey from Exeter to South Devon had become distinctly hazardous.[49] On 3 January the Prince's steward was captured by Parliamentary troops near Chudleigh, while 'he was goeing from Cornwal to Exeter, to fetch the Prince his Buffe-coat and Arms'.[50]

Small-scale skirmishing took place daily around the city defences during this period, but the sheer strength of the Royalist works continued to deter the Parliamentarians from making any major assault.[51] Fairfax's men took some comfort from the damage which the winter frost was inflicting on the earthen banks which made up the Royalist line. It was reported in early 1646 that 'a great part of the works are fallen downe, that 20 men may enter abreast at one place, and the townesmen refuse to find tools to make them up'.[52] The besiegers hoped that the works would be damaged still further when the frost began to thaw, but before this could happen, matters were thrown into confusion by a major

Royalist advance. An attempt to relieve the city had been expected for some time and around Christmas 1645 it was reported that Royalist troops were massing at Tavistock. On 2 January news reached Fairfax that the Prince was at Dartmouth, and two days later it was confirmed that the Royalists were advancing in force.[53] For the moment, at least, attempts to take Exeter would have to be abandoned.

The Defeat of the Royalist Relief Force

On 6 January Fairfax and his officers held a council of war, at which it was decided to meet the relieving army head on, and to advance into South Devon 'where the greatest part of the enemy lay'.[54] Two days later the Parliamentary forces marched out of their winter quarters. By 9 January advance guards of the New Model Army had made contact with the Prince's cavalry in the Teign valley and for the next two weeks Fairfax remained tied up in operations around Bovey and Dartmouth. In consequence the Exeter garrison enjoyed something of a breathing space.

Although the Royalists were still hemmed in to the east of the city by the Parliamentarian troops manning the 'New Fortifications'—whom Fairfax had left behind when he marched away—in other directions they had more freedom of movement, and several scouting parties were sent out from the city towards the north-west at this time. On 10 January Berkeley sent out a party of horse towards Crediton to try to find out where Fairfax had gone. Berkeley was clearly worried by the Roundheads' sudden advance, and that night he wrote an anxious letter to the commanders of the relief force, asking for up-to-date information. 'I wish I could know what resolution is taken with you and what is expected from us', he wrote plaintively, adding that 'we shall put ourselves in the best readiness we can'.[55]

The garrison continued to make similar forays throughout the next week. On 15 January 'a partye of about 60 horse and 200 foot came from Exeter to Whitstone Church, drew up in St Thomas Parish, but returned back without doing any great harm', while next day three Royalist colonels were reported to be in Newton St Cyres.[56] Presumably, the Royalists were trying to gather intelligence. More particularly, they may have been hoping to pick up news of the relieving army's advance. If so they were to be disappointed. Fairfax had already put the Prince's army to flight and the scattered remains of the relief force were now spread out along the Cornish border, in a sad state of disarray. Meanwhile

THE FINAL SIEGE

Fairfax had moved against Dartmouth, the King's last stronghold in South Devon. On the night of 18-19 January the town was stormed and captured; over forty miles now separated the garrison of Exeter from the nearest friendly force.

The night after Dartmouth's fall a group of Royalist cavalrymen who had escaped from the town appeared before the gates of Exeter, clamouring to be let in.[57] This was probably the first intimation that the Exeter Royalists had had of just how disastrously their cause was faring elsewhere and Berkeley at once called an emergency council of war. At this meeting it was decided that all male inhabitants of Exeter between the ages of sixteen and sixty should be required to take up arms, that men, women and children should 'helpe repair the works in diverse places, where by reason of the frost they begin to fall down', and that troops should be sent out to gather intelligence.[58] The arming of the citizenry began at once. Parliamentary sources claimed that the Royalists had threatened to imprison those who refused to bear arms, and this may well have been true.[59] Certainly the Royalist recruitment effort quickly bore fruit, for the King's men were soon boasting that they had five new regiments in Exeter, each including five knights amongst its officers. With the garrison thus strengthened, the Royalists turned to the problem of supplies. Desperate attempts were made to gather up provisions from the surrounding countryside. The Royalists slaughtered 'lean oxen from the plow' for food, and also managed to squeeze some provisions out of the nearest villages.[60] Despite these temporary expedients, supplies were beginning to run short. Fuel was now selling at 6s 6d per horse load, and beef at 4d per pound, whilst there was a 'great want of salt'.[61]

As Berkeley battled with these problems of recruitment and supply, all eyes turned to South Devon. What would Fairfax do next? Would he build on his triumph at Dartmouth by marching to the west and engaging the Prince, or would he resume the interrupted siege of Exeter? The answer was not long in coming. Around 21 January Fairfax decided to return with all speed to Exeter and to engage 'in vigorous endeavours against that place'.[62] Exeter, not the dissolute and beaten forces of the Prince, was to be the next target of the New Model Army.

Preparations for a Storm

On 23 January Colonel Thomas Hammond marched out from Totnes with several Parliamentary regiments. His objective was to occupy the

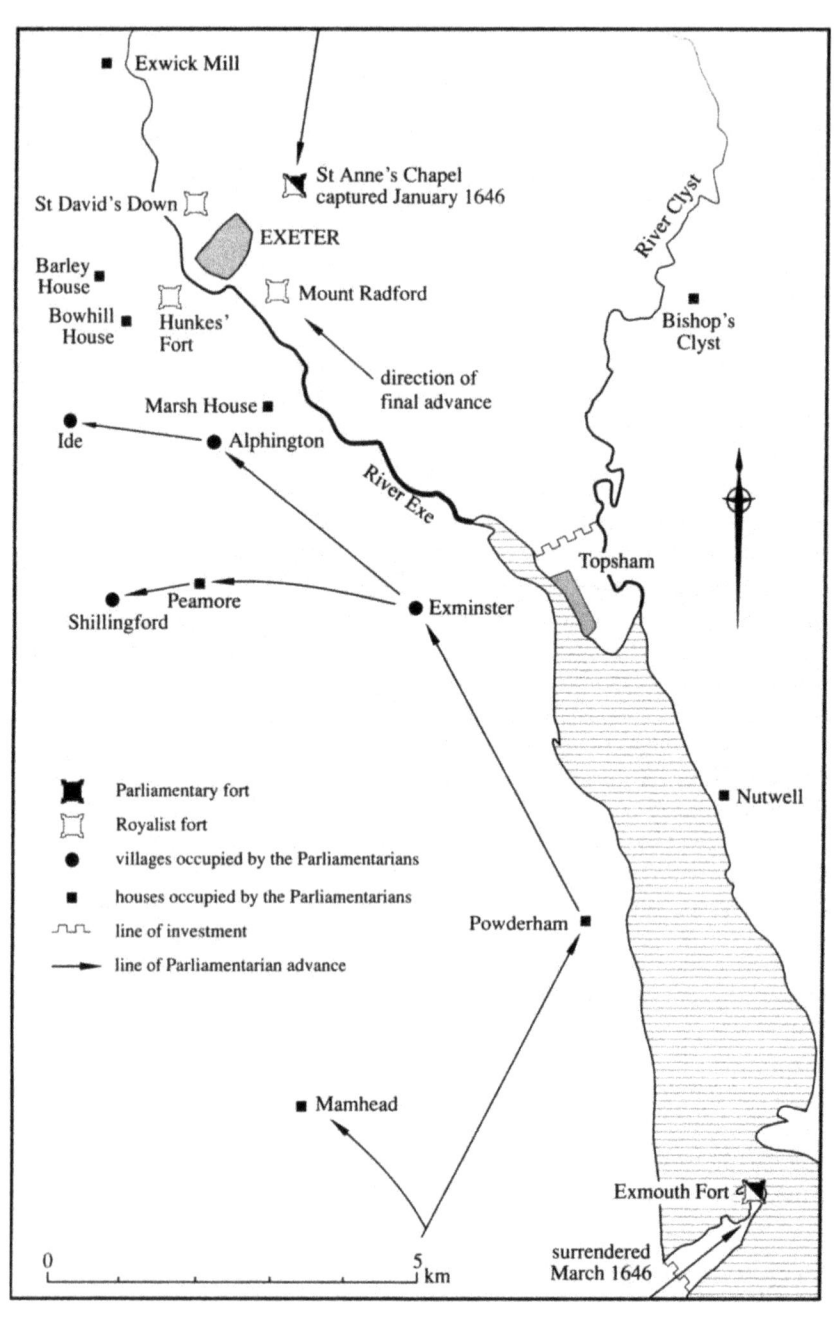

Map 6. *Military Operations around Exeter, early 1646*

countryside to the south-west of Exeter, hitherto used by Berkeley as a source of provisions. Advancing steadily northwards, Hammond's men quickly overran several small Royalist garrisons in this area (see map 6). Sir Peter Ball's house at Mamhead, near Dawlish, which the Royalists were beginning to fortify, was the first to be taken. Six Royalist troopers were captured here, whilst their companions fled 'into Exeter to tell tales'.[63] By the morning of 25 January Hammond's forces had arrived before Powderham Castle. Powderham's defences were designed to resist raids launched from the estuary, not a determined assault by an entire army, and the defenders quickly entered into negotiations. Within hours the castle was in Parliamentary hands.[64] Having dealt summarily with this obstacle, Hammond's men swept on towards Exeter early the next day, capturing further Royalist stragglers as they went. By 26 January New Model Army guards were stationed at Alphington, within sight of the city itself.[65]

Other elements of Hammond's force had taken up positions near Dawlish Warren and were threatening the Royalist fort on the sands there. The Roundheads probably expected another easy conquest, but this time they were to be disappointed. Exmouth Fort was a much stronger position than Powderham had been. Indeed one writer claimed that it was 'stronger than Oxford itself'.[66] Sixteen artillery pieces were mounted along its walls, and the garrison included a number of Cornish veterans. These men were not going to give up without a fight, and the initial Parliamentary summons met with a determined refusal. Somewhat taken aback, Hammond's men sent for reinforcements. These arrived the next day, when Fairfax himself came to view the situation on the Warren. A second summons was sent in soon afterwards but this had no more effect than its predecessor, the defenders returning 'a preemptory and stubborne' refusal.[67] Unwilling to waste any further time, Fairfax decided to leave the fort alone for the time being. Stopping only to ensure that the Royalist position was securely blocked up, he set off to join the main body of his army before Exeter.

Here, the Royalists were coming under increasing pressure. On learning of the victory at Dartmouth, the Roundhead troops in the 'New Fortifications' had advanced on the city and stormed the Royalist outwork at St Anne's Chapel. Many prisoners were taken in this assault, but far more important was the capture of the position itself. St Anne's Chapel lay at the far end of Sidwell Street, within a mile of the city gates, and as several observers pointed out, the keeping of a Parliamentary garrison here would 'much annoy the Enemy'.[68] Immediately after this setback to the east, moreover, the Exeter Royalists had to face the return of the New Model Army on the west. Peamore House, Barley House and Tothill House, all of which had been garrisoned by the Royalists, were swiftly abandoned in the face of Hammond's advance guards, on or around 26 January.[69] That night, Hammond's men took up quarters in Alphington and by the following morning large numbers of Parliamentary troops were massing on the western side of the city. An assault upon Exeter seemed imminent, but Fairfax—clearly hoping that his recent victories would induce the garrison to give up without a fight—decided to try negotiation first. On 27 January he sent in a summons to the Royalist governor (see document 29, Letter I).

According to the Royalist pamphlet *Mercurius Academicus*, Fairfax's summons was accompanied by a secret letter, promising Berkeley £40,000 if he agreed to give up Exeter to the Parliament. The governor was not to be tempted but, instead, called his officers together in the Guildhall, read the letter out to them and then 'desired their present resolutions'. At this, *Academicus* avers, 'every one of them, from the highest to the lowest, returned this answer with no little acclamation, [that] they would keep that city for his Majesty or loose their lives in the defence of it'.[70] Claims that Berkeley had been offered money to betray the city should probably be taken with a pinch of salt. Parliamentary sources make no reference to any attempts at bribery, simply recording that the Royalists sent a polite answer to the summons, in which they pointed out that 'in honour they could not surrender upon the terms offered, while they ... had such probable hopes of relief from the Prince'.[71] Fairfax apparently felt that there was some chance of persuading the defenders to change their minds, for on 29 January he sent in a second letter, restating his case (see document 29, Letter III). The Royalists were not to be persuaded, however. Negotiations continued, but there was little sign of the defenders' resolve weakening. Next day a Royalist drummer who had come out of Exeter under a flag of truce to confer with the Parliamentarians about exchange of prisoners irritated the besiegers by boasting 'very much of the strength of the city, that they are raising new regiments, and such like ridiculous stories'.[72] From this incident, and from the determined rejection of Fairfax's summons noted above, one gets the impression that Exeter's defenders remained relatively confident.

The garrison's spirits were undoubtedly buoyed up by the proximity of Prince Charles's army, still hovering on the Cornish border just fifty miles away. Berkeley expected relief from this quarter and his hopes seemed about to be fulfilled when Royalist cavalry units pushed forward to Barnstaple at the end of January. For a day or two it seemed that a relief attempt was imminent, but the threat quickly diminished when the Royalist cavalry failed to make any further offensive moves.[73]

Meanwhile preparations for storming Exeter went ahead. On 30 January Fairfax issued warrants to all the hundreds round about for ladders to scale the city walls, and these soon began to come in to the Parliamentary camp.[74] Work was also continuing at Topsham, where a temporary bridge was being built across the Exe. This structure was completed on 2 February, permitting the Roundheads to pass with ease from one side of the Exe to the other.[75] Fairfax's men were now 'very neer Excester; having intrenched themselves, and raised many strong forts within a mile ... [of the] City'.[76] At least four such forts were constructed—at Exwick Mills, Barley House, Bowhill House and Marsh House— and together they formed a formidable defensive screen, protecting the Parliamentary units camped at Alphington from any sudden Royalist attack (see map 6).[77] Meanwhile other units of the New Model Army—assisted by locally-raised auxiliaries—continued to man the 'New Fortifications' to the east. Fairfax's men moved closer to the city defences every day, Roundhead sources claiming that 'our souldiers are very cheerful, and desire nothing so much as to storm the city'.[78]

The Parliamentarians' forward position at this time was Barley House in St Thomas parish, a substantial mansion built in stone.[79] The house was initially occupied by Fairfax's troops in late January, when the barns, stables and outhouses were all burnt down in order to make the main building more easily defensible.[80] By 2 February there were four companies of foot soldiers stationed at Barley. These men were in an exposed position, for their new quarters were within musket shot of the Royalist works. A Parliamentary correspondent reported that the Royalists 'daily shoot into the house, and we against them; they can also talk one to another, they call our men Round-headed Rogues, our men return them answer'. On 3 February Fairfax himself visited this exposed position.[81]

The New Model Army had by now managed to occupy two more strongpoints in Saint Thomas: 'the hospital' (i.e. the Bridewell in Cowick Street), and the burnt-out shell of the parish church.[82] The church and the houses around it had been fired by the Royalists on 31 January in order to deprive their enemies of cover, yet these desperate measures proved unable to halt the Parliamentary advance.[83] Fairfax's men were soon digging themselves in around the ruins of the church and similar work took place at the hospital.[84] Both places were very close to the Royalist fortifications; the hospital, in particular, was said to be 'within half musket shot of the enemy workes'.[85] The main Royalist positions in St Thomas at this time were 'Hunkses Fort' in Cowick Street, and another 'worke' which guarded the west end of Exebridge. Musket fire raged back and forth between these positions and the strongpoints held by the Parliamentarians.

Fairfax's troops gradually moved closer to the Royalist defences. In one place, it was said, the besiegers had 'gotten within musket shot of the City workes' and, in another, they had 'possest [a] house under the very walls'.[86] Berkeley's men tried a sally in the hope of pushing the besiegers back, but were beaten in again with heavy losses.[87] Secure in their new positions, Fairfax's men now began to harass the Royalist outguards. Roundhead correspondents reported that 'our men perceiving the Enemy in their redoubts and sconces, do often fire at them and kill some of them in their owne workes, and make them so fearefull that they dare not let a light appeare in the night'.[88] This was not the only hardship which the Royalists had to endure. It was gleefully reported by the besiegers that 'provisions are so scarce [in Exeter] that mutton is sold at 10d the pound, butter at 12d, they have no cheese, [and] wood is at 7 or 8s a horse load'.[89] Many were unwilling to endure such privation and desertions began to occur. One Roundhead source reported that 'the enemy daily come out of the City to our army, 20 and 30 in a company', whilst another averred that 'those that escape out of Exeter and come to our quarters, assure us there's a great inclination in the city to capitulate'.[90]

Royalist morale may well have been falling, but letters sent from Berkeley to the King at this time displayed a firm resolve to 'hold it out to the utmost'. Berkeley assured the King that he had 2–3,000 men bearing arms in the city, 200 barrels of powder and 'good store of ordnance mounted'. In addition, he claimed, the disaffected elements amongst the populace had been cowed. Berkeley concluded his report by stressing that he 'feared not all the forces can come against him' as long as there remained some hope of relief.[91] As long as the Prince's army continued to menace Fairfax's western flank, in other words, Berkeley would refuse to give up hope. Nor did the Parliamentarians have everything their own way in the skirmishes around the city. During the first week of February Captain Wix, the Marshall General of Fairfax's army, was captured with ten others when he came too close to the city in a little boat upon the River Exe.[92]

Despite this minor setback the Parliamentary build-up continued and by 7 February a temporary bridge had been erected on the north side of the city as well.[93] The construction of this bridge allowed the besiegers to make a determined thrust into the northern suburbs of Exeter, an area which had hitherto remained relatively free from such incursions. Parliamentary troops on the west side of Exeter, meanwhile, were now within artillery range of the city itself.[94] Several observers felt that a full-scale attack was imminent, with only the terrible weather delaying the final push. 'Courage, ladders ... and all things [are] in readines for the storming of Exceter' wrote one reporter excitedly, adding that there '[is] nothing crossing the resolution of our soldiers but the wetnes of the season, in which the ladders cannot find fast footing, nor the climbing soldiers fast handing'.[95]

As this last comment suggests, the incessant rain was fast becoming a real problem for the besiegers. Not only was it dampening the Parliamentary soldiers' morale, it was also strengthening the city defences. Several correspondents observed that 'by meanes of the raine that fell, the ditches about the workes of Exeter are full of water, so that now the taking of it may be something more difficult'.[96] The works had been formidable enough already without this accretion of strength, and there are hints that the Parliamentary commanders were beginning to have second thoughts about the wisdom of attempting an assault. On 7 February Exeter's defences were described as being 'very strong and tenable ... the Enemy having made a deep ditch, and of some bredth, betwixt the out-works and the walls of the Citie, which walls being strong of themselves, are made more strong by art and armes'.[97] Fortunately for the Roundhead soldiers, events taking place elsewhere eventually saved them from having to assault these formidable defences.

On 8 February news reached Fairfax's camp that the Prince's army was marching into North Devon, under the command of Lord Hopton. The Royalists brought many provisions with them and openly boasted that these supplies were intended for Exeter. An attempt to relieve the city was clearly about to be made and faced with this challenge, the Parliamentary leaders decided that the attack on Exeter must be postponed yet again while the New Model Army moved to engage the Prince's forces.[98] Nevertheless, the blockade of Exeter was to be maintained. Strong guards were to be left at Alphington, Powderham, Barley and Peamore, while the 'New Fortifications' would continue to be manned. In this way, Exeter would remain completely blocked up on both sides, despite the absence of much of the Parliamentary army.[99]

Sir Hardress Waller's Blockade

Fairfax and his men set off for North Devon on 10 February, leaving the management of the blockade to Sir Hardress Waller. Waller's chief task was 'to straiten' the garrison of Exeter, to 'hinder them of provisions and keep . . . [them] from making incursions into the country'.[100] In addition he was to keep up the pressure on the fort at Exmouth. To accomplish these objectives, Waller had a cavalry regiment and three infantry regiments drawn from the ranks of the New Model Army. These units were assisted by 2,000 locally-raised auxiliaries, whose chief task was to garrison the 'New Fortifications'. The forces at Waller's disposal were surprisingly large. Following Fairfax's departure, it was estimated that the besiegers could muster some 5,000 men, while two further regiments were daily expected to arrive.[101] Waller probably possessed well over 6,000 troops by the end of February 1646, at least twice as many men as Berkeley could muster.

As well as these extensive human resources Waller possessed a good deal of firepower. Ten iron artillery pieces had been sent for from Lyme 'to beate downe the workes at Excester' and on 17 February these guns finally arrived in the besiegers' camp.[102] It seems probable that they were quickly put to use. No definite reference has yet been found to Waller's forces using cannon to batter the Exeter works, but it is known that some sections of the city wall were in ruins by the end of the war, quite possibly as a result of artillery fire.[103] Evidence that the citizens were worried about the effects of bombardment at this time appears in the civic accounts, which show that, towards the end of February, the receiver paid for the city's 'firecrooks' to be brought back to Exeter from St Thomas. These curious-sounding implements were metal hooks, mounted on long wooden poles, and were designed to pull the thatch off burning buildings. In March 1646 the Exeter firecrooks were repaired, probably because the citizens feared that enemy action might soon begin fires within the city.[104]

Following Fairfax's departure the garrison made several sallies. On

THE FINAL SIEGE

9 February a force of Royalists slipped out of the city but were driven back by Colonel Welden's regiment, while more of Berkeley's men sallied out near Exebridge two days later, killing one of Colonel Herbert's soldiers. Several Royalists were slain in this engagement and many were wounded on both sides.[105] The Parliamentarians remained very close to the Royalist outworks during Fairfax's absence. Pamphleteers reported that 'Exeter is close blockt up' at this time, adding that 'our men are in the subburbs on the east and north side, and have made fortifications to defend themselves and offend the enemy'.[106] Only to the south of the city did the Royalists have any room to manoeuvre.

Unfortunately, little more is known about the events of this period, either within or without the city walls. This is chiefly because the Parliamentarian pamphleteers (who represent our main source of information at this stage of the war) were far more interested in the exploits of Fairfax's army than in the slow progress of the siege at Exeter. Local sources are even less forthcoming. The Chamber Act Book records only one major decision between 10 February and 31 March: the creation of John Coventrie and Bullen Reymes as freemen of Exeter on 26 February 'in regard of their good respects they have shewed to this cittie'.[107] Both Reymes and Coventry were prominent Royalists, but what they had done to earn the Chamber's gratitude remains obscure.[108]

By mid-February Roundhead correspondents were reporting that 'the inhabitants of the city for the most part are weary of the warre and would fain hear of a composition'.[109] Discontent amongst the citizens was echoed by war-weariness amongst the military commanders, for in March it was reported that 'Sir Fulk Hunks and divers others in Exeter desire passes to go to France'.[110] Royalist morale must have plummeted still further with the surrender of the fort at Exmouth. This position had been under siege since 28 January and its supplies were running low. On 14 March the fort was summoned by the Parliamentarians and the governor agreed to surrender on terms. Next day the garrison marched out, leaving their guns and ammunition behind them.[111]

With Exmouth taken, Waller ordered his troops to advance against the southern defences of Exeter itself. Towards the end of March an officer in Colonel Ceely's regiment wrote to his commander informing him that 'we are now within musket shot of Mount Radford, and exchanging shot every minute, and God hath pleased to honour your [regiment] with the Frontier Quarters'.[112] Waller's advance was probably prompted by the news from Cornwall, where the New Model Army had finally drawn the net around Hopton's demoralized forces. The Prince had already fled abroad, and the Royalist soldiers were unwilling to go on fighting. On 15 March they laid down their arms. The last Royalist field force in the west-country was thus dispersed, leaving Exeter bereft of all hopes of relief. Word of the surrender quickly reached the Exeter garrison, and the Parliamentarians increased their pressure on the city, hoping to break the defenders' resolve. Yet Berkeley held grimly on. He would not surrender his position until overwhelming force had been brought to bear against him.

Fairfax's Return

After settling affairs in Cornwall the victorious New Model Army slowly made its way back across Devon. On 29 March Fairfax arrived at Crediton, while the vanguard of his army took up quarters at Newton St Cyres. That night orders were sent to Waller's men to occupy Heavitree, a village lying very close to Exeter, 'lest the enemy should sally out, and burn those villages upon the approach of the army'.[113] (Evidence that these orders were obeyed comes from the wardens' accounts of St Loyes Chapel, Heavitree, which record regular payments being made for firewood for the Parliamentary guards from 30 March onwards. These soldiers, apparently members of Colonel Shapcott's regiment, remained in Heavitree for another ten days.[114])

As Parliamentary soldiers advanced ever closer to Exeter, Fairfax remained at Crediton, drawing up a second summons. By the morning of 31 March this document was complete, and Fairfax resolved to accompany its delivery with a show of strength. Later that day the New Model Army was assembled at Newton St Cyres. From here the entire Parliamentary army marched on Exeter, with Fairfax himself at its head. The Royalists made one last show of defiance shortly before Fairfax's arrival, when Berkeley 'drew forth 500 Horse and Foote' from the city 'in a bravado [and] made a flourish'. As the besiegers began to draw towards them, however, the Royalists retreated. Soon afterwards the New Model Army drew itself up on a hill within sight of the city.[115] Meanwhile the Roundhead soldiers in the fortifications around Exeter were 'drawn forth in a compleat manner' within musket shot of the Royalist works. Fairfax then rode around the lines to inspect his men 'and as he passed by them, at every post, our men that lay there gave a volley of shot and a great shout'. Having demonstrated his overwhelming military superiority, Fairfax sent in a second summons. He then retired to Culm John, a mansion house to the north-east of the city, to await the Royalist response.[116]

This was not long in coming. Towards evening, Berkeley sent out a message promising that he would deliver a reply to the summons by 2.00 p.m. the next day.[117] Meanwhile he had arranged an emergency conference in Exeter, informing the city councillors that there would be an extraordinary meeting at Bedford House 'tomorrowe morning att eight of the clocke', in order to discuss 'a speciall occation of much concernement to this cittie'. Berkeley asked the councillors to appoint some of their number to attend the meeting, and the Chamber quickly obeyed, choosing Mayor Cupper, Robert Walker, Roger Mallack, and Hugh Crocker to act as their representatives.[118] It was not yet certain that the Royalists would accede to Fairfax's demands, for, as Berkeley told the councillors, the managing of the summons was to be left to the discretion of those who attended the council of war. The governor clearly felt that a decision to surrender was likely, however, for he advised the councillors 'that in case a treatie shalbe concluded uppon at the said meeting' they should name two persons to act on the city's behalf in any subsequent negotiations.[119]

To Parliament's supporters in Exeter, Berkeley's words betokened imminent liberation and they at once resumed an active role in local affairs, pressing for the right to select one of the two civic negotiators. It was later recalled that, of the two councillors whom the Chamber eventually chose to serve in this role—Robert Walker and Thomas Knott—Knott had been selected 'at the speciall instance of the Parliament's partie in this cittie'.[120] Walker, of course, was a hardline Royalist, while Knott was much more moderate, so it would seem that—in this moment of supreme crisis—the city authorities reverted to the pre-war tactic of choosing one official representative for *each* of the two main politico-religious groupings in Exeter.

With the New Model Army so close to Exeter the citizens must have been trembling in anticipation of a sudden surprise attack, followed by a savage sack of the city. The Chamber therefore took steps to ensure Exeter's safety while the negotiations were in progress by ordering that large sums of money should be spent on firewood and candles to provide light for the Main Guard.[121] With these precautions taken, the councillors could do little more but sit back and wait upon events. On 1 April the representatives of the garrison met at Bedford House to discuss the

Parliamentary summons. As Berkeley had expected, the majority decision was that negotiations should be entered into at once, and soon afterwards Berkeley's trumpeter rode out to Culm John with a letter for Fairfax. This expressed the garrison's desire to treat and was accompanied by a list of ten men whom Berkeley had selected to act as the city's commissioners, or negotiators. The list included Robert Walker, Thomas Knott and John Were (Exeter's counsellor at law).[122] That evening Fairfax returned Berkeley's trumpeter and sent out one of his own with an answer.[123] Fairfax expressed his pleasure at the Royalist decision, but suggested that the number of commissioners on both sides should be reduced from ten to six, 'that being as many as conveniently can be used in a business of this nature'.[124]

Berkeley now called another council of war, inviting representatives from all sections of the garrison to attend. The Parliamentarians reported that '[those] of quality on their part, and the clergy on theirs, made their addresses; and the like also did the inhabitants, [each] desiring to have their owne particular interests preserved in the treaty'. Eventually it was decided that the men who were to conduct the negotiations should be chosen 'part for the gentry . . . part for the souldiery, a third part for the clergy, and a fourth for the inhabitants of the city'.[125] Eight commissioners were then nominated, two for each of the different interest groups. Soon afterwards the Chamber agreed that 'the originall articles made uppon the late rendering of the Cittie to his Majestie shalbe delivered unto Mr Walker & Mr Knott to make use of them in the present treatie if occation require'.[126]

All seemed set for negotiations to begin, but on 2 April Berkeley held yet another council of war at which certain members of the garrison expressed themselves unwilling to treat.[127] For a moment it seemed that the Royalists might yet change their minds. Undoubtedly there was a small but determined group within the city who wished to see Exeter defended to the bitter end. The Roundheads termed these individuals 'the unwilling party' and their attitude was well summed up by one Mary Cholwill, who asserted 'that she had rather the Turks should come into the cittie then them, meaning the Parliaments Forces. And that rather then they should have the said cittie, the castle and cittie should be sett on Fyre'.[128] Such fanaticism was rare, however, and most of those at the meeting were utterly opposed to prolonging the struggle. They struck back with counter-arguments, pointing out that the defensive perimeter was large 'and that it would aske more men then was there to manage, besides the discouragement of being out of all hopes of reliefe, and beginning already to want victuals'. These arguments ultimately carried the day 'and accordingly all things were prepared in a readinesse that night, to treat the next morning'.[129]

Negotiations

On 3 April the city commissioners rode out to Poltimore House, a few miles north of Exeter. Here their opposite numbers joined them and the talks began. Little was accomplished on this first day, the Parliamentarians complaining that a small number of articles concerning the cathedral clergy had taken up a great deal of time and prevented any firm agreement from being reached. Perhaps as a result of these disagreements, the city commissioners went back to Exeter that night 'to have some amendments in their instructions'. They returned to Poltimore next day, however, and 'the treaty was hastened all that might be'.[130] The citizens were probably as anxious as anyone to see surrender terms agreed upon. Provisions were short in the city and considerable hardship was being endured. On 4 April the receiver paid Colonel John Buller £6 for a supply of bread, perhaps intended for the city poor.[131]

Several days passed and still the discussions continued, causing many on the Parliamentary side to grow impatient. 'I suppose you did think before this to have received news of the surrender of Exeter, considering the time since the treaty began', wrote one correspondent to a friend, yet, he continued, 'I cannot say two hours have been lost since the first entrance upon the same. The commissioners [have] sate two nights together ... in debating the businesse ... hoping to have compleated the Articles; but such were the Devices of ... the Enemies part, in ... putting many needless quaeres ... that it necessitated a consumption of time; and when any [points] were in a manner concluded, some further satisfaction was to be given, concerning some other point'.[132]

Despite the prevarication of the Royalists, progress was gradually being made and early on the morning of 9 April articles were finally agreed upon (see document 30). The city commissioners came out to Culm John to watch Fairfax sign the articles, while their opposite numbers went into Exeter to watch Berkeley do the same. Agreement seems to have been reached in an atmosphere of some cordiality, with Parliamentary writers reporting that there was 'very good correspondency' between the two sides and that the Royalists trusted very much in 'our faith in performing articles'.[133] As if to demonstrate a reciprocal sense of trust, Fairfax had no sooner received the Royalist agreement to surrender than he rode off to North Devon to see to the settling of affairs in those parts. The final surrender of the city was therefore overseen by his subordinates.

As soon as the articles had been signed, hostages were exchanged (Hugh Crocker being one of those who gave themselves up as guarantors for the Royalists' good behaviour).[134] Immediately afterwards the garrison began to surrender certain key positions. By the terms of the treaty the Royalists had agreed to hand over three of their outlying forts (Mount Radford, Hunks's Fort and the fort of St David's Down) before the city itself was given up. The transfer of these positions was carried out smoothly, and by the evening of 9 April the Roundheads were able to report that 'we are possesst of two works, and to enter a third'.[135] The third and last fort was handed over a little later that day. By nightfall all three positions were firmly in Parliamentarian hands.[136]

Surrender

Over the next three days the Royalist soldiers in Exeter packed up their baggage and made ready to depart. By the morning of 13 April all was in readiness. Berkeley mustered his men within the walls for the last time, and at midday the Royalist garrison marched out, drums beating, colours flying and lighted match in their hands. Princess Henrietta also left Exeter at this time. She was carried out in a litter, accompanied by Berkeley's wife and other high-born Royalist ladies. The Parliamentarian soldiers standing by adhered strictly to the terms of the articles, and no jeers or other injuries were offered to the departing garrison.[137]

Berkeley had permission to march to Oxford with his men, and the more optimistic Royalists undoubtedly hoped that the 2,000-strong garrison would form the nucleus of a new field army for the King. Such expectations were quickly to be disappointed. Among the departing Royalist troops were several regiments of Cornish infantrymen. These men had fought valiantly for the King hitherto, but now that his cause was so manifestly lost, they saw no point at all in marching to Oxford. The articles of surrender had expressly stated that all Cornish troops in Exeter should be allowed to return to Helston if they wished (see document 30), and as soon as the garrison had passed out of the city gates, the bolder spirits began to mutter that 'they had served long

THE FINAL SIEGE

enough, and now would go home'. These sentiments were echoed by their comrades and a cry of 'Every man to his owne home!' soon began to ring out along the Cornish ranks. As Berkeley and his officers looked helplessly on, the Cornishmen 'threw downe their Armes, and (in a great confusion) ran home'.[138] On this farcical note of confusion and disorder, the Royalist occupation of Exeter came to an end.

At 2.00 p.m. that afternoon the New Model Army finally took possession of the city which had defied it for so long, Oliver Cromwell riding in at the head of the Parliamentary troops.[139] The pamphleteers exulted in their army's triumph, boasting that Exeter's bloodless capture provided clear evidence of divine support for Parliament's cause (see document 31). 'And have we Excester!', they trumpeted, 'Excester, thou art this time as good as ten Excesters at another!'[140] Exeter's former reputation as a bastion of puritanism had clearly been forgotten by the Roundhead correspondents, and indeed two and a half years of Royalist occupation must have done much to alter the city. One writer noted disapprovingly that 'the citizens have learned like the Cavaliers, to sweare God damne them &c', adding that 'they want good ministers to teach them better'. Nevertheless, the Roundhead occupation passed off without incident. On 14 April the inhabitants 'opened their shops, and took money of [the] soldiers for divers things they wanted' and later that week, Fairfax and Cromwell were invited to supper by the Mayor, 'where', it was noted, 'they were entertained with great respect'.[141]

Fairfax, who had finally arrived in Exeter on the evening of 13 April, remained in the city for less than a week. During this time he took great pains to 'settle ... things in order to the safety of that place'.[142] Exeter was given a Parliamentary garrison and Colonel Thomas Hammond was appointed Governor. Fairfax also attempted to repair the damage which his army had inflicted upon the surrounding countryside, ordering that the Parliamentary siege works should be razed to the ground.[143] On 16 April the Roundhead soldiers began to leave the city, and two days later Fairfax, too, rode out.[144] For Exeter the Great Civil War was over and the city was left to lick its wounds, count its blessings, and accustom itself to Parliamentarian rule.

Conclusion

The city which Fairfax's troops left behind them in April 1646 was very different from the one which had declared itself for Parliament at the outset of the Civil War. In those heady days—days which by now must have seemed almost impossibly remote to the war-weary inhabitants —Exeter had presented a supremely pleasing prospect. The core of the ancient city had nestled snugly among its encircling suburbs, while they in turn had been lapped by the fields, woods and hedgerows of the surrounding countryside. Now this pleasant vista lay in ruins. The countryside had been laid waste, its hedges grubbed up, its orchards and coppices cut down, its very fields stripped of turf for use in the fortifications.[1] For miles about trenches and redoubts had been gouged, like livid wounds, into the rich, red Devon earth. Most shocking of all were the changes which had been wrought on the outskirts of the city itself. Exeter now stood in grim isolation from the landscape around it, set apart not only by the zig-zag scar of the former Royalist outworks (which ran right round the city walls) but also by the vast circle of ashes which marked the site of the former suburbs.

By the war's end the extra-mural areas of Exeter had been quite simply devastated. St Sidwells and St Davids had been flattened; there is no evidence that any houses close to the city in these two parishes survived. Every dwelling house in St Sidwells, from Eastgate to St Anne's Chapel (a distance of over a third of a mile) had been razed to the ground. In St Thomas, too, all the houses between Exebridge and the hospital had been 'utterly ruined by fire'. Trinity parish 'without the Southgate' was 'totally demolished by fyreing & pulling downe the howses'.[2] Things may have been a little better in St Edmunds and St Mary Steps, but even here a great deal of damage had occurred; George Leach, a brewer of

CONCLUSION

St Edmonds, later deposed that his brewhouse had been demolished, 'and my outhouses ... puld downe, and the trees of my orchard cut up, and all the walls and mounds pul'd downe, being worth at least £100'.[3] Gazing out from the city walls in April 1646, the inhabitants of Exeter would have seen a picture of utter devastation on every side. It was not just private houses which had suffered; churches, almshouses and inns had been demolished; the mills along the banks of the River Exe had been burnt to the ground, the city's complicated system of public water supply had been destroyed, the canal had been damaged and its barges sunk; roads had been churned up, bridges pulled down, gardens and orchards levelled.[4]

Turning away from this grim spectacle to survey the situation within the city walls, the inhabitants cannot have felt greatly comforted. Here too, many buildings had been damaged. Houses near Westgate still bore signs of the bombardment which they had endured in 1643, Watergate was 'fallen downe and so rotten and decayed that the wagons could not pass ... without great daunger', the roof of Southgate was 'gon in decaye through an extraordinary & unusuall waye' (perhaps as a result of Parliamentary bombardment?), while the inner drawbridge at Southgate was 'fallen downe and very dangerous for people and horses ... that passed under it'.[5] These major dilapidations aside, the city as a whole presented a sad, shabby appearance in April 1646. The destruction of the water-supply system had made it difficult to keep the streets clean. During the previous winter, moreover, Royalist soldiers—deprived of fuel by the Parliamentarian blockade—had carried away every piece of timber they could get their hands on to serve as firewood. Buildings all over Exeter now lay stripped of their furniture and fittings, and the Chamber had to lay out large sums of money during 1646–48 for the repair of the wooden crane at the quay, the doors of the water cisterns and the ceiling of the Guildhall: all 'broken upp and spoyled by ill-affected souldiers'.[6]

The general air of squalor was compounded by the fact that Exeter was now chronically overcrowded. Following the destruction of the suburbs, hundreds, possibly thousands, of homeless people had made their way into the city in search of temporary lodgings. Some had been fortunate enough to find refuge with relatives, or in the few surviving civic almshouses.[7] The rest had had to find shelter wherever they could: in the abandoned houses of the cathedral clergy, in the Bishop's Palace, in Bedford House, in the guardhouses which stood at the city gates or in any other unoccupied corner.[8] The displaced inhabitants of the suburbs were by no means the only new claimants on the city's limited housing stock; after four years of conflict Exeter was positively littered with the human detritus of war.

Up until 1642 the Chamber had been careful to prevent too many 'foreigners' from settling in Exeter, but with the outbreak of hostilities this system of regulation had inevitably broken down.[9] Thousands of soldiers from other parts of the country (not to mention their camp-followers and other assorted hangers-on) had passed through Exeter during 1642–46, and once the war was over it was found that many of these people had taken root. Some were too poor, too sick or too badly wounded to make the journey back to their former homes, while others were simply unwilling to exchange the billets which they had managed to secure in Exeter—however uncomfortable and uncertain these temporary quarters might have been—for the greater uncertainty of the outside world. The Chamber did its best to rid the city of such 'incomers', but the process took time. It could also be expensive; in July 1647 the Receiver paid a carpenter eight shillings 'for the makinge of a barrow for the carying away of a meamed souldier from the hospitall to bee convayed unto Cornwall to his home, from tithinge to tithinge, who hath layen longe at the citties charge, and cannot bee cured'.[10] The suffering which this poor man must have undergone as several dozen surly tithingmen took it in turns to push and manhandle his barrow along the notoriously bad roads from Exeter to Cornwall does not bear thinking about.

The Chamber could expel 'foreigners' from the city, but it could do little about the illegitimate children whom the soldiers had left behind them. Many Exeter women had formed romantic attachments with soldiers during the war. One such was Julian Trivett, whose father, John, served in a Royalist infantry company throughout the final siege. During that bitter winter, John Trivett struck up a friendship with one of his fellow soldiers, a certain William Chambers, and invited him to his house. Here Chambers met his host's daughter, to whom he took an instant liking. Matters developed from there and, as Julian herself later recalled, 'the said Chambers did . . . severall tymes . . . come to this deponent's fathers house & called her foorth to goe with hym on the Sabbath dayes in the afternoones'. These innocent-sounding excursions eventually resulted in Julian becoming pregnant, but she managed to conceal her condition until the siege was over—by which time, of course, Chambers had left the city and could no longer be found to answer for his misdeeds.[11] Some pregnancies resulted from altogether briefer liasons; Johan Dark, the servant of a city innkeeper, confessed to having been begotten with child 'by one Robert [blank], sometime a trooper, whose surname this deponent doth not nowe remember'.[12]

Refugees, ex-soldiers, and ex-soldiers' bastards: by April 1646 Exeter was positively awash with new faces. This was just as well, for over the last four years many hundreds of the city's pre-war inhabitants had disappeared. Some, driven out by the destruction of their houses, had begun new lives in the surrounding towns and villages.[13] Others had travelled still further afield in search of shelter, or had joined the Parliamentary armies, while a few die-hard Royalists had gone into exile.[14] But the vast majority of the missing were dead. The Civil War had taken a heavy toll on the local population; well over 1,200 people are known to have been buried in the city between 1642 and 1645 (compare this figure with 569 burials in 1630–33, 805 in 1634–47 and 786 in 1638–41).[15] The burial rates do not tell the full story, moreover, for the registers of several city parishes have been lost, while many Exeter men must have died while serving in the field, as soldiers. In April 1645 the Devon JPs were informed that 'Thomas Kelway, who dwelled without the Southgate in Exeter' had been 'slayne in his Majestie's service before Lyme', leaving a wife and three children.[16] Kelway's can hardly have been an exceptional case; post-war petitions survive from many Exonians who had been wounded while serving in the rival armies (see documents 32–34), and presumably these men were the lucky ones. Taking everything into account, it does not seem unreasonable to suggest that as many as 2,000 people—around a fifth of Exeter's pre-war population—may have either perished or left the city for good during the war years. Many hundreds more were temporarily displaced, and only gradually began to drift back to their former parishes during the 1640s and 1650s, as the suburbs were rebuilt.[17]

Four years of warfare had transformed Exeter in the physical sense and had brought financial ruin on many (see document 35). Yet how had it affected the politico-religious outlook of the inhabitants? Historians of the French Wars of Religion have observed that, although many cities witnessed frenzied outbreaks of inter-denominational violence at the beginning and end of each period of conflict, such episodes tended to diminish in their frequency and intensity as the fighting progressed.[18] The same general pattern is discernible in the English Civil War, and certainly the contrast between the manner in which Parliamentary sympathizers in Exeter greeted victory in January 1643 and in April 1646 is striking. The widespread popular disorders, the violent attacks on local Royalists which had marked the establishment of Roundhead control in 1643 were not repeated in 1646. Four years of war had, rather surprisingly, served to purge the city's body politic of some of its more violent humours. War-weariness, a desire to regain control of local affairs, and above all a sense that the battle lines, once so heroically simple, had now become strangely blurred (witness the Royalist Chamber's decision to support one of the King's commanders against another in 1645), all these things had contributed to a reduction in the political temperature at Exeter. The experience of war had been a deeply disillusioning one, and local people were now more cynical than they had once been, and more wary of expressing their opinions.

Partisan political commitment in Exeter was by no means dead, however. If the urge to hot-blooded, impetuous action had faded away, a cold, remorseless determination had replaced it—and nowhere was this more apparent than in the resolution with which the dismissed members of the Chamber sought revenge against their former colleagues. Two months after the surrender a Parliamentary ordinance was read out in the Chamber. This document noted that:

> whereas Richard Saunders, Adam Bennett, Walter White, James Gould, Richard Crossinge, John Loveringe, James Marshall and Phillip Crossinge ... were ... for their fidelitie to the Parliament ... displaced from beinge of the ... Chamber of [Exeter] ... the Lords and Commons assembled in Parliament, having received full and ample testimony of the integrity and abilitie of the said Richard Saunders and others, as likewise of their great sufferings for being faithfull in the Cause, doe [now] declare and ordeyne that such amoveinge and displacinge of them ... is voide, unjust and of none effect.[19]

As soon as this order had been read out, Saunders and his colleagues resumed their seats on the Chamber. They at once set about the congenial task of ejecting their enemies, and over the following months eight Royalist Chamber men — including Robert Walker, Hugh Crocker, Nicholas Spicer and John Colleton—were dismissed, together with a host of lesser officials.[20] The note in the Chamber Act Book recording Crocker's dismissal still rings with bitterness: 'Sir Hugh Crocker, for his

CONCLUSION

manifest opposicion to the Parliament and his crueltie to those that were well affected to their cause & procedinges is dismissed of this societie'.[21]

The Chamber reshuffle of June 1646 had more to do with local enmities than with an abstract desire for intervention on the part of the central government. In 1640–43 (and even, it might be argued in 1625–29) Exeter's godly town councillors had used the authority of Parliament to buttress and confirm their own local position. In 1646 they did exactly the same thing. These facts help to illustrate the central argument of this book: that the inhabitants of early Stuart Exeter were not mere witnesses to the political strife of the 1640s—uncomprehending victims of an imported conflict—but were rather committed players in a politico-religious game which possessed local, as well as national, dimensions. The removal of Robert Walker and his conservative allies from the Chamber in 1646 was the denouement of a long-running drama, one which had been dividing Exeter for almost half a century. And as the spiritual heirs of Ignatius Jurdain prepared themselves for a renewed moral crusade, it must have seemed to the Exeter puritans that the phoenix of deliverance had risen anew from the ashes of the city's destruction.

Notes

Introduction

1. R. Howell, *Newcastle upon Tyne and the Puritan Revolution: A Study of the Civil War in North England* (Oxford, 1967).
2. P. McGrath, 'Bristol and the Civil War' (Bristol Historical Association Pamphlet, 50, 1981), *passim*; and D. Scott, 'Politics and Government in York, 1640-62', in R.C. Richardson (ed.), *Town and Countryside in the English Revolution* (Manchester, 1992), pp. 46–68.
3. For a particularly influential statement of this point of view, see D. Hirst, *The Representatives of the People?: Voters and Voting in England under the Early Stuarts* (Cambridge, 1975), *passim*, especially pp. 54-59. The idea that political groupings in provincial towns post-dated, rather than pre-dated, the Civil War is still generally held, see J. Barry (ed.), *The Tudor and Stuart Town: A Reader in English Urban History* (1990), p. 28.
4. W.T. MacCaffrey, *Exeter 1540-1640: The Growth of an English County Town* (1958), pp. 1-2.
5. J.T. Evans, *Seventeenth-Century Norwich: Politics, Religion and Government, 1620-90* (Oxford, 1979), *passim*.
6. For a description of Norwich as 'the most "political" of the provincial centres', see R. Howell, 'Neutralism, Conservatism and Political Alignment in the English Revolution: The Case of the Towns', in J. Morrill (ed.), *Reactions to the English Civil War* (1982), p. 87.
7. See chapters 2–3 below; and D.H. Sacks, 'Bristol's Wars of Religion', in Richardson, *Town and Countryside*, pp. 100-29, especially pp. 102–04, and 108–11.
8. D. Underdown, *Somerset in the Civil War and Interregnum* (Newton Abbot, 1973), p. 117.
9. See D. Underdown, *Revel, Riot and Rebellion* (Oxford, 1985), *passim*.

10. See M. Stoyle, *Loyalty and Locality: Popular Allegiance in Devon during the English Civil War* (Exeter, 1994), ch. 5.
11. See D. Pennington, 'The War and the People', in Morrill, *Reactions*, pp. 115-35; S. Porter, *Destruction in the English Civil Wars* (Stroud, 1994); I. Roy, 'England Turned Germany? The Aftermath of the English Civil War in its European Context', *TRHS*, 5th Series, 28 (1978), pp. 127-44; I. Roy, 'The English Civil War and English Society', in B. Bond and I. Roy (eds), *War and Society* (1975), pp. 24-43; and I. Roy, 'The City of Oxford, 1640-60', in Richardson, *Town and Countryside*. Important recent additions to this burgeoning field are C. Carlton, *Going to the Wars: The Experience of the British Civil Wars* (1992); J. Morrill (ed.), *The Impact of the English Civil War* (1991); and P. Tennant, *Edgehill and Beyond: The People's War in the South Midlands* (Stroud, 1992).

1. 'The Centre, Heart and Head of the West': Exeter before the Civil War

1. J. Bond, *A Doore of Hope, also Holy and Loyal Activity: Two Treatises delivered in Severall Sermons in Excester* (1641), p. 49.
2. W.G. Hoskins (ed.), *Exeter in the Seventeenth Century: Tax and Rate Assessments, 1602-99*, DCRS, New Series, II (1957), p. ix.
3. See R. Pickard, *The Population and Epidemics of Exeter in pre-Census Times* (Exeter, 1947), p. 18; and W.B. Stephens, *Seventeenth Century Exeter: A Study of Economic and Commercial Development, 1625-88* (Exeter, 1958), p. 40.
4. DRO, Letter Book G, f.618; and DRO, Letter Book G, f.620.
5. For Hogenberg, see W. Ravenhill and M. Rowe, 'A Decorated Screen Map of Exeter', in T. Gray et al. (eds), *Tudor and Stuart Devon* (Exeter, 1992), p. 3. See also K.M. Constable, 'The Early Printed Plans of Exeter', *TDA*, 65 (1932), pp. 455-73.
6. For a detailed account of the city gates, see J.Z. Juddery et al., 'Exeter City Defences Project: Expenditure on the Walls and Gates, 1350-1700' (5 vols, Exeter Museum, 1989-90).
7. See M. Stoyle, 'Exeter's Medieval Aqueducts' (forthcoming, Exeter Museum, 1996).
8. See J. Brushfield, 'The Financial Diary of a Citizen of Exeter, 1631-43', *TDA*, 33 (1901), pp. 190-91.
9. S.R. Blaylock, 'Exeter Guildhall', *PDAS*, 48 (1990), pp. 123-78.
10. See Stoyle, 'Medieval Aqueducts'; and EQSOB 61, f.239.
11. F. Nicolls, *The Life and Death of Mr Ignatius Jurdain* (1654), p. 7; and S. Izacke, *Remarkable Antiquities of the City of Exeter* (1723), p. 167.
12. See, for example, DRO, Letter Book 60F, DD.391.42.

NOTES

13. ECAB, 8, f.85.
14. EQSOB 62, f.213.
15. See W.G. Hoskins, *Industry, Trade and People in Exeter, 1688-1800* (Manchester, 1935), pp. 111-22.
16. S. Lawrence, 'A Population Study of St Sidwells Parish, Exeter, during and after the English Civil War' (University of Exeter, certificate course dissertation, 1993—copy held in the Devon and Exeter Institution), p. 3.
17. Hoskins, *Industry, Trade and People*, p. 121.
18. Bod., J. Walker MSS, C.5, f.352.
19. Analysis based primarily on A.J. Howard (ed.), *Devon Protestation Returns* (privately printed, 1973), pp. 313-39.
20. See W.T. MacCaffrey, *Exeter, 1540-1640* (1978), pp. 1-53, especially pp. 28-32.
21. Ibid.
22. See M.E. Curtis, *Some Disputes between the City and Cathedral Authorities of Exeter* (History of Exeter Research Group, Monograph 5, 1932), *passim*, especially pp. 20, 23, 42, 46.
23. See Pickard, *Population and Epidemics*, pp.36-38, 44-45.
24. Brushfield, 'Financial Diary', p. 228.
25. See, for example, EQSOB 63, f.160.
26. See, for example, DRO, Petitions to the Chamber for Relief, File 4, No.1; and EQSR, 6 James I, roll 2, item 16.
27. See, for example, EQSOB 61, ff.162, 187, 356-58.
28. MacCaffrey, *Exeter*, p. 93.
29. Ibid., p. 92; see also EQSOB 61, f.10; and EQSOB 62, f.380r.
30. See EQSOB 62, ff.4r, 303, 319, 348, 356r; and EQSOB 63, f.27.
31. EQSOB 61, f.235.
32. EQSOB 62, f.316.
33. Ibid., f.360r.
34. EQSOB 61, ff.465-66.
35. *The Poems of Robert Herrick* (World's Classics edn., 1902), p. 37.
36. See EQSOB 61, ff.78, 119-21, 345; and EQSOB 62, f.53.
37. EQSOB 62, f.362r.
38. For a drunken fiddler being put in the stocks see EQSOB 62, f.385r.
39. See, for example, EQSOB 63, f.4.
40. For an outstanding introduction to this most controversial of subjects, see K. Fincham (ed.), *The Early Stuart Church, 1603-42* (1993), especially pp. 1-22.
41. See M. Stoyle, *Loyalty and Locality: Popular Allegiance in Devon during the English Civil War* (Exeter, 1993), pp. 186-88.
42. See ECAB 7, ff.208, f.271; and I. Gowers, 'Puritanism in the County of

Devon between 1570 and 1641' (University of Exeter, MA thesis, 1970), p. 151.
43. For Mico and Bartlet, see Gowers, 'Puritanism', p. 59 and Appendix H; for Manton, see WCSL, DCRS, C.A.T. Fursdon (ed.), 'Parish Register of St Mary Arches, 1538–1837', (unpaginated).

2. 'Zealous to Advance God's Glory': Ignatius Jurdain and the Puritan Dynamic

1. There are a number of short general accounts, see A. Brockett, *Nonconformity in Exeter, 1650–1875* (Manchester, 1962), pp. 1–4; W.C. Cotton and H. Woollcombe, *Gleanings from the Municipal and Cathedral Records of Exeter* (Exeter, 1877), pp. 76–78; I.W. Gowers, 'Puritanism in the County of Devon between 1570 and 1641' (University of Exeter, MA thesis, 1970), pp. 139–52, 265; W.T. MacCaffrey, *Exeter, 1540-1640* (1978), pp. 197–200, 274–75; and M. Stoyle, *Loyalty and Locality: Popular Allegiance in Devon during the English Civil War* (1993), pp. 186–88.
2. See F. Nicolls, *The Life and Death of Mr Ignatius Jurdain* (1654), p. 16.
3. F. Rose-Troup, 'An Exeter Worthy and his Biographer', *TDA*, 29 (1897), pp. 351–52.
4. Ibid., p. 352. In 1619 Jurdain was co-owner of a ship named 'The Virgin', see T. Gray (ed.), *Early Stuart Mariners and Shipping*, DCRS, New Series, 33 (1990), p. 47.
5. Nicolls, *Life*, p. 10.
6. G. Chapman, *The Siege of Lyme Regis* (Lyme Regis, 1982), p. 11.
7. Rose-Troup, 'Exeter Worthy', p. 371.
8. P. Collinson, *The Elizabethan Puritan Movement* (Oxford, 1990), p. 151.
9. Rose-Troup, 'Exeter Worthy', pp. 351–52.
10. Nicolls, *Life*, p. 3.
11. Ibid., pp. 5–6.
12. Ibid., introduction, pp. 4, 6, 14–17.
13. Rose-Troup, 'Exeter Worthy', p. 354.
14. Nicolls, *Life*, introduction, and p. 6.
15. For a wonderful evocation of this mentality, see D. Underdown, *Fire from Heaven* (1992), pp. 1–197.
16. W.J. Harte et al. (eds), *The Description of the Citie of Excester* (two vols, Exeter, 1919), II, p. 353.
17. Between June 1618 and June 1619, the examination of witnesses was undertaken by just two magistrates on average, see EQSOB 61 (1618–21), ff.1-220.
18. EQSOB 61, *passim*.
19. Nicolls, *Life*, pp. 12–13.

NOTES

20. EQSOB 61, f.11.
21. Ibid., f.25.
22. Ibid., ff.10, 19.
23. Between June 1618 and July 1620, for example, Jurdain sat on the bench on no fewer than eighty-three separate occasions, and was the third most regular attender of the ten city justices. See EQSOB, 61, ff.1–431.
24. EQSOB 61, f.405.
25. See EQSOB 61, ff. 141, 663; and EQSOB 62 (1621-30), f.74r.
26. EQSOB 61, f.174.
27. See R. Pickard, *Population and Epidemics of Exeter in pre-Census Times* (Exeter, 1947), pp. 36-38; P. Slack, *The Impact of Plague in Tudor and Stuart England* (Oxford, 1985), pp. 115–17; and D. Underdown et al. (eds), *William Whiteway of Dorchester, His Diary* (Dorset Record Society, 12, 1990), p. 76.
28. Underdown, *Whiteway*, p. 76; and Nicolls, *Life*, pp. 14–15.
29. Nicolls, *Life*, p. 15.
30. Ibid., introduction.
31. The parallels with Dorchester—where a catastrophic fire in 1613 provided the impetus for godly reformation—are striking, see Underdown, *Fire from Heaven*, passim, especially pp. 2-5, 90.
32. Nicolls, *Life*, p. 13.
33. Ibid., introduction. See also D. Hirst, *The Representative of the People?: Voters and Voting under the Early Stuarts* (Cambridge, 1975), pp. 204–05. Hirst claims that Jurdain was elected as a result of his behaviour during 'the plague year', 'rather than as a result of his puritanism', but both factors were surely important. Jurdain had already been elected as Exeter's MP once before (in 1621), so it is clear that—even under 'normal' circumstances—there was powerful support for him in the city. The freemens' acclamation of Jurdain as a man who was 'right for the Common-wealth', moreover, makes it tempting to suggest he was popularly regarded as a 'patriot'; i.e., as a committed protestant who would stand up for the rights of 'the country' against the incursions of a ideologically-suspect 'Court'. On the concept of 'the patriot', see R. Cust and A. Hughes (eds), *Conflict in Early Stuart England* (1989), passim, especially pp. 143–59.
34. J.J. Alexander, 'Exeter Members of Parliament, Part III', *TDA*, 61 (1929), pp. 202–03.
35. See W. Notestein et al. (eds), *Commons Debates, 1621*, (eight vols, Yale, 1935), III, pp. 105, 273, 430-32; and M. Jansson and W.B. Bidwell (eds), *Proceedings in Parliament, 1625* (1987), p. 362.
36. Nicolls, *Life*, p. 18.
37. For Jurdain's involvement with the adultery bill, see S. Clarke, *A Collection of the Lives of Ten Eminent Divines* (1662), p. 477; P. Collinson, 'A

Magazine of Religious Patterns: An Erasmian Topic Transposed in English Protestantism', *Studies in Church History*, 14 (1977), p. 239; R.C. Johnson et al. (eds), *Commons Debates 1628* (four vols, New Haven, 1977-78), II, pp. 323, 329; and III, pp. 22, 26, 30; and K.V. Thomas, 'The Puritans and Adultery: The Act of 1650 Reconsidered', in D. Pennington and K. Thomas (eds), *Puritans and Revolutionaries* (Oxford, 1978), pp. 257–82.
38. Nicolls, *Life*, passim; and Rose-Troup, 'Exeter Worthy', passim.
39. Rose-Troup, 'Exeter Worthy', p. 363; and Nicolls, *Life*, p. 2.
40. EQSOB 61, f.23.
41. Ibid., f.44.
42. Ibid., ff.331 and 369; EQSOB 62, f.142.
43. EQSOB 61, f.269.
44. Nicolls, *Life*, p. 1.
45. EQSOB 61, f.416-17.
46. Ibid., f.600.
47. Nicolls, *Life*, p.4; and EQSOB 63 (1630–42), f.151.
48. EQSOB 62, f.198.
49. EQSOB 61, ff.12-13, 29.
50. PRO, STAC 8, 161/10.
51. Councillors were sworn to secrecy about conversations which had taken place in the Chamber, see MacCaffrey, *Exeter*, p. 41.
52. PRO, STAC 8, 161/10; see also Nicolls, *Life*, p. 16.
53. EQSOB 61, f.13.
54. S.R. Gardiner (ed.), *The Constitutional Documents of the Puritan Revolution, 1625–60* (1971 edition), pp. 99-101.
55. EQSOB 62, f.74r.
56. *HMC, Exeter*, p. 131.
57. See T. Cogswell, *The Blessed Revolution: English Politics and the Coming of War, 1621–24* (Cambridge, 1989), pp. 6-53.
58. *CSPD*, 1625, p. 75.
59. P. Gregg, *King Charles I* (1981), p. 106.
60. EQSOB 62, f.253.
61. Ibid., ff.258–258r. Walter Yonge, a puritan Devon JP, noted darkly in his diary at this time that the prisoners had been delivered 'upon special command', see G. Roberts (ed.), *The Diary of Walter Yonge Esquire* (Camden Society, Old Series, 41, 1848), p. 83.
62. See M. Jansson and W.B. Bidwell (eds), *Proceedings in Parliament, 1625* (1987), pp. 375–76, 412.
63. DRO, Book 73/15, f.101.
64. *HMC*, 12th Report, *Cowper MSS*, volume I, p. 249.
65. Ibid.
66. See EQSOB 62, ff.284-84r, 293, 301r, 356r-58.

NOTES

67. *HMC, Exeter*, pp. 177–78.
68. Ibid.
69. EQSOB 62–63, *passim*.
70. Gardiner, *Constitutional Documents*, p. 103.
71. Nicolls, *Life*, introduction; and Underdown, *Whiteway*, p. 135.
72. Ibid.
73. Curtis, *Disputes between the City and Cathedral*, pp. 46–52. See also *HMC, Exeter*, pp. 115-33.
74. For Cotton, see I. Cassidy, 'The Episcopate of William Cotton Bishop of Exeter 1598–1621' (University of Oxford, D.Phil. thesis, 1963), *passim*. For Carey, see N. Tyacke, *Anti-Calvinists: The Rise of English Arminianism* (Oxford, 1987), p. 193.
75. Nicolls, *Life*, introduction.
76. See F. Rose-Troup, 'Biographical Notes on Doctor Matthew Sutcliffe, Dean of Exeter, 1588–1629, *TDA*, 23 (1891), *passim*, especially pp. 176–78, 183, 186–87, 191–92. Benedict Browning, whom Sutcliffe presented to a North Devon living in 1608, was a notorious radical, see Stoyle, *Loyalty and Locality*, p. 192.
77. See Rose-Troup, 'Biographical Notes', pp. 172, 189; and Rose-Troup, 'Exeter Worthy', p. 351.
78. *CSPD*, 1629–31, p. 5.
79. See Tyacke, *Anti-Calvinists*, p. 215.
80. There was a similar growth in tension in many cathedral towns during the 1630s, see A. Foster, 'Church Policies of the 1630s', in Cust and Hughes, *Conflict in Early Stuart England*, p. 208.
81. EQSOB 63, f.187r.
82. Ibid., f.193r.
83. ECAB, 8 (1634–47), f.83.
84. Ibid., ff.86, 88.
85. Ibid., f.121.
86. See Rose-Troup, 'Exeter Worthy', p. 371, and ECAB, 8, ff.85–86.

3. 'The Times Grow more Dangerous': The Descent into Civil War

1. J. Bond, *A Doore of Hope* (1641), B.14.
2. For events in Scotland during 1637–38, see K. Sharpe, *The Personal Rule of Charles I* (1992), pp. 769–91; and D. Stevenson, *The Scottish Revolution, 1637-44: The Triumph of the Covenanters* (Newton Abbot, 1973), pp. 58-87.
3. See Sharpe, *Personal Rule*, pp. 813–14; and, more generally, C. Hibberd, *Charles I and the Popish Plot* (Chapel Hill, 1983), *passim*.

4. M.C. Fissel, *The Bishops' Wars: Charles I's Campaigns against Scotland, 1638–40* (Cambridge, 1994), p. 112.
5. EQSOB 63 (1630-42), f.264.
6. Sharpe, *Personal Rule*, p. 795.
7. EQSOB 63, ff.266-67.
8. Ibid., f.269r.
9. Ibid.
10. Ibid., ff.269r-70.
11. Ibid., ff.271-71r.
12. See W.J. Harte *et al.* (eds), *The Description of the Citie of Excester* (two vols, Exeter, 1919), II, p. 797.
13. EQSOB 63, ff.270-70r, 271r.
14. Ibid., ff.271-71r.
15. Ibid., ff.270r, 271r.
16. Ibid., ff.266, 271r, 284.
17. PRO, SP 16/420/153, and APC, 2/50, ff.244, 294, 348. See also *HMC, Exeter*, p. 206.
18. *CSPD*, 1639, pp. 53, 160.
19. Bond, *A Doore of Hope*, B.13.
20. Ibid., B.13-14.
21. DCA, D&C 3557 (Chapter Act Book, 1635-43), f.142.
22. Ibid., f.143.
23. Sharpe, *Personal Rule*, p. 823.
24. ECAB, 8 (1634-47), f.180.
25. Ibid.
26. EQSOB 63, ff.294-94r, 298r, 300r.
27. ECAB, 8, f.180.
28. Ibid., ff.182-83.
29. Sharpe, *Personal Rule*, pp. 847, 851.
30. Ibid., p. 852.
31. DCA, D&C 3557, ff.170-71.
32. Ibid., f.175.
33. See *HMC, Exeter*, p. 80; *CSPD*, 1639, p. 85; and W.B. Stephens, *Seventeenth Century Exeter: A Study of Industrial and Commercial Development, 1625–88* (Exeter, 1958), p. 33.
34. DCA, D&C 3557, f.179.
35. Sharpe, *Personal Rule*, pp. 322-28.
36. The Chapter received a mandate 'for the appearing of the Deane ... in the Convocation' on 7 March, see DCA, D&C 3557, f.184.
37. J.J. Alexander, 'Exeter Members of Parliament, Part III', *TDA*, 61 (1929), p. 203.
38. For the freemen and their electoral rights, see M.M. Rowe and A.M.

NOTES

Jackson (eds), *Exeter Freemen, 1266-1967* (*DCRS*, Extra Series 1, 1973), pp. xiii-xxvi.
39. ECAB, 8, f.202.
40. Ibid., f.201.
41. D&C 3557, f.191.
42. Ibid., f.194.
43. Ibid., f.196.
44. EQSOB 63, f.315r.
45. Sharpe, *Personal Rule*, pp. 861-71.
46. For the military events of summer 1640, see Sharpe, *Personal Rule*, pp. 885-95; and Fissel, *Bishop's Wars*, pp. 39-61, 264-86.
47. ECAB, 8, ff.206, 208; and F. Rose-Troup, 'An Exeter Worthy and his Biographer', *TDA*, 29 (1897), p. 361.
48. ECAB, 8, f.216.
49. Penny was serving as mayor by 5 October 1640, see ECAB, 8, f.218.
50. Alexander, 'Exeter Members', p. 203.
51. EQSOB 63, f.337r.
52. Ibid., ff.298-374r.
53. Ibid., f.335.
54. ECAB, 8, f.223.
55. See A. Fletcher, *The Outbreak of the English Civil War* (1981), pp. 1-2.
56. Bond, *A Doore of Hope*, B.1-2.
57. EQSOB 63, ff.339r-40, 342r, 351.
58. Ibid., f.342r. The four sureties were Henry Dabynett, Robert Hawkyns, Anthony Salter and William Sampford. For their later Royalism, see M. Stoyle, 'Divisions within the Devonshire "County Community", 1600-46' (University of Oxford, D.Phil. thesis, 1992), Appendix IV.
59. Bond, *A Doore of Hope*, B.24, 29, 40.
60. See EQSOB 61 (1618-21), ff.13-14, and EQSOB 62 (1621-30), f.72r. The former source reveals that an Exeter man, accused of singing abusive songs about Jurdain in 1618, had not only boasted that the city councillor John Prouse was 'hys frend', but also that 'he had better frendes then he too ... the best in England save one ... and [that] God was the beste, and the Kinge was next'. Alarmed by the man's loquacity, Prouse 'strooke hym upon the head and sayd he hadd a muddy head to make such in songe'.
61. For Thomas Walker, see PRO, STAC 8/161/10. The parallels between the nature of pre-war opposition to 'the godly' in Exeter and in Dorchester are striking, see D. Underdown, *Fire from Heaven* (1992), *passim*, especially pp. 27-37, 149-66.
62. EQSOB 63, ff.351r-52.
63. Ibid., f.352.
64. Ibid., f.354.

65. Ibid., f.356.
66. See *CSPD*, 1639, p. 243 for a reference to the 'logger-headed ... puritanical crew of the Scotch Covenant'.
67. EQSOB 63, f.364.
68. See EQSOB 63, f.104r for a reference to men playing 'in the Bonehaye att Nyne Holes'.
69. EQSOB 63, f.368r.
70. Ibid., f.372r.
71. See *CSPD*, 1639, p. 69.
72. ECAB 8, f.275.
73. EQSOB 63, f.372r.
74. ECAB 8, f.243.
75. EQSOB 63, f.381.
76. Ibid., ff.380–380r.
77. Ibid., f.380.
78. Ibid.
79. Ibid., f.383.
80. Ibid.
81. EQSR, 1641/42, roll 1, items 7 and 8.
82. The four men who informed on Tucker and later became Royalists were Mark Browninge, William Dowriche, Thomas Newman and John Webbe. See ibid.; and Stoyle, 'Divisions', Appendix IV.
83. EQSOB 63, f.383.
84. Ibid., ff.385–386.
85. Ibid.
86. Ibid., ff.340r, 380r, 386.
87. The three men were John Elwill, Charles Hopping and Robert Sprague. For the wartime allegiance of Hopping and Sprague, see Stoyle, 'Divisions', Appendix V.
88. For Carwithen's apprenticeship to George Jourdain, see Rowe and Jackson, *Exeter Freemen*, p. 124.
89. ECAB 8, f.258.
90. See E.A. Andriette, *Devon and Exeter in the Civil War* (Newton Abbott, 1972), pp. 44–45.
91. ECAB 8, f.258.
92. Ibid., f.259. For the text of the petition which was sent to the Parliament see *LJ*, IV (1628–42), pp. 536–37.
93. EQSOB 63, f.391.
94. Ibid., ff.385–86, 391; A.J. Howard (ed.), *Devon Protestation Returns* (privately printed, 1973), p. 325; and Rowe and Jackson, *Exeter Freemen*, p. 135.
95. EQSOB 63, f.393.
96. Ibid., ff.393r, 397r.

97. Ibid., f.398r.
98. The two men were John Short of Ashwater and James Rodde of Stoke Canon. For their ultimate allegiance, see *CAM*, II, pp. 816, 1105.
99. ECAB 8, f.262.
100. Ibid., f.269.
101. See Fletcher, *Outbreak*, p. 324. Towards the end of June the mayor and sheriff of Exeter received official letters of thanks from Parliament for refusing to publish the King's proclamations, see *LJ*, V (1642-43), pp. 151-52; and *CJ*, II (1640-42), pp. 634-35.
102. ECAB 8, f.275.
103. EQSOB 64, f.1.
104. Fletcher, *Outbreak*, p. 324, citing BL, Harleian MS, 163, f.273r.
105. SRO, Wolesely MSS, 56/6, items 22, 23.
106. ECAB 8, f.275.
107. I.R. Palfrey, 'Devon and the Outbreak of the English Civil War', *Southern History*, 10 (1988), p. 33.
108. ECAB 8, f.275.
109. E.89 (4).
110. ECAB 8, f.276.
111. EQSOB 64, f.6.
112. Ibid., f.7.
113. Palfrey, 'Outbreak', p. 33.
114. See KAO, U269/A525/5.

4. 'Rebel City': Exeter under Parliamentarian Control

1. EQSOB, 63, (1630-42), f.63.
2. For the deaths of Acland and Trobridge, see ECAB, 8, ff.227, 298.
3. For Crossing and Yeo, see below, chapter 5.
4. See V. Pearl, *London and the Outbreak of the Puritan Revolution* (Oxford, 1961), pp. 132-34.
5. See M. Stoyle, *Loyalty and Locality: Popular Allegiance in Devon during the English Civil War* (Exeter, 1993), pp. 103-04.
6. DCA, D&C, 3557 (Chapter Act Book, 1635-43), ff.311-12.
7. ECAB, 8 (1634-47), f.278.
8. See Pearl, *London*, pp. 139-40.
9. For Bagster, see ECAB, 8, f.287.
10. ECAB, 8, ff.243, 281.
11. Ibid., f.281.
12. J. Vicars, *England's Parliamentary Chronicle* (1646), p. 172.
13. EQSOB, 64, f.11.

14. See ECAB, 8, f.279 and DRO, DD.391.34.
15. EQSOB, 64, f.18.
16. See EQSOB, 64, f.17; and ECAB, 8, f.285.
17. D&C, 3557, f.318.
18. See ECAB, 8, ff.283; EQSOB, 64, f.18; and Bod., J. Walker MSS, C.2, ff.252–252r.
19. EQSOB, 64, ff.12, 18.
20. *LJ*, 5 (1642-43), pp. 414, 427–28.
21. EQSOB, 64, f.18. Alexander Pym was the son of the Parliamentary leader, John Pym. I owe this point to David Underdown.
22. Ibid., f.25.
23. Ibid., ff.18, 21; and ERB, 1642–43, f.9.
24. See P. McGrath, *Bristol in the Civil War* (Bristol Historical Association Pamphlet, 1981), p. 15.
25. EQSOB, 64, f.18.
26. SRO, Wolesely MSS, 53/1/129 and 131.
27. E.128 (11).
28. See, for example, F.T.R. Edgar, *Sir Ralph Hopton: The King's Man in the West* (Oxford, 1968), pp.61–62; and E.A. Andriette, *Devon and Exeter in the Civil War* (Newton Abbot, 1971), pp. 74–75.
29. See BL, Additional MSS 35297 (John Syms's Day Book), f.19.
30. *LJ*, 5, pp. 461–62.
31. ECAB, 8, f.288; and SRO, Wolesely MSS, 53/1.
32. C.E.H. Chadwyck Healey (ed.), *Bellum Civile: Hopton's Narrative of his Campaign in the West*, Somerset Record Society, 18 (1902), pp. 26–27.
33. DRO, DD.391, f.35.
34. For Ide, see EQSOB, 64, f.28.
35. Bod., 4.M.68.art, *Mercurius Aulicus*, 1–7 January 1643.
36. Ibid.; Chadwyck Healey, *Bellum Civile*, pp. 26-27; and E.84 (8).
37. E.84 (4); and A. Fisher (ed.), 'The Apologie of Colonel John Weare', *DCNQ*, 4 (1907), p. 157.
38. E.84 (24).
39. Chadwyck Healey, *Bellum Civile*, p. 27.
40. Bod., 4.M.68.art, *Mercurius Aulicus*, 8–13 January 1643; E.84 (4), E.84 (29); E.84 (30), E.244 (42); E.244 (44); E.244 (45); and E.246 (6).
41. See E.244 (46); E.245 (7); and E.245 (11).
42. The final word on this subject belongs to Richard Izaacke, who lived in Exeter throughout this period and presumably knew what he was talking about. In his historical chronicle, compiled after the Civil War, he observes that the city was 'besieged . . . first by my Lord Hopton about Christmas [1642], who *having only viewed the same*, presently drew off his army and marched into Cornwall' (R. Izaacke, *Remarkable Antiquities of the City of*

Excester (1723), p. 157). This surely clinches the case against Hyward's version.
43. EQSOB, 64, ff.24–25.
44. *LJ*, 5, p. 487.
45. DCA, D&C, 3557, f.324.
46. PRO, SP.28, 153, f.18.
47. EQSOB, 64, ff.26–27.
48. For the situation in the capital, see Pearl, *London*, p. 279.
49. Bod., Wood Pamphlets, 376, *Sergeant Major James Chudleigh: His Declaration to his Countrymen* (1643).
50. E.122 (13).
51. PRO, SP.28, 153, f.18.
52. Bod., J. Walker MSS, C.2, f.308.
53. E.84 (36).
54. E.245 (11). See also *CSPD*, 1644, p. 448.
55. For the date of Stamford's arrival, see W.C. and C.E. Trevelyan (eds), *Trevelyan Papers: Volume III*, Camden Society, Old Series, 105 (1872), pp. 230–31.
56. ECAB, 8, f.289.
57. Ibid.
58. *HMC*, 13th Report, Volume I, *Welbeck MSS*, p. 89.
59. E.122 (13).
60. E.93 (7). For Trescott, see E.89 (4). For Hughes, see WCSL, DCRS, C. Fursdon and E. Searle (eds), 'Parish Register of St Olave, Exeter, 1601-1837: Volume II', (unpaginated), entry of 5 July 1643.
61. Andriette, *Devon in the Civil War*, p. 83.
62. CRO, Tremaine Papers, DDT, 1617A.
63. *HMC, Welbeck MSS*, pp. 101–102.
64. Ibid., pp. 102-103.
65. Ibid., pp. 103, 106; CRO, Tremaine Papers, DDT, 1617A; and E.94 (21). See also I.R. Palfrey, 'Devon and the Outbreak of the English Civil War', *Southern History*, 10 (1988), p. 40.
66. PRO, SP.28, 128, part 27 (entry of 13 May 1643).
67. See DRO, Miscellaneous Box 6, 'Accompt of Henry Gandy'; DRO, DD.391.12-20; and DD.391.39-40.
68. See M. Stoyle, 'Whole Streets Converted to Ashes: Property Destruction in Exeter during the English Civil War', *Southern History*, 16 (1994), p. 71.
69. E.104 (19).
70. E.104 (26).
71. BL, Burney, *Mercurius Aulicus*, 28 May to 4 June 1643.
72. DRO, 2065M, Add 8/F3/1.
73. BL, Burney, *Mercurius Aulicus*, 4–11 June 1643.

74. BL, Burney, *Mercurius Aulicus*, 11-18 June 1643.
75. DRO, DD.391, ff.40-40r; and ECAB, 8, f.294.
76. BL, Burney, *Mercurius Aulicus*, 18-25 June 1643 and DRO, Seymour MSS, 1392 L/42/12. See PRO, SP.28, 128, part 27, for payments made by the Parliamentarian county treasurer to the wives of soldiers killed and captured at Topsham.
77. Chadwyck Healey, *Bellum Civile*, pp. 50-51, note 1.
78. DRO, DD.391, ff.40-40r.
79. E.63 (2).
80. See DRO, DD.391, ff.40r-41; and W.B. Stephens, 'Roger Mallock, Merchant and Royalist', *TDA*, 92 (1960), pp. 289-90.
81. For the strength of Warwick's forces, see documents 16-17.
82. E.61 (16).
83. See WCSL, DCRS, Parish Registers of All Hallows Goldsmith Street, St Edmunds, Holy Trinity, St Kerrians, St Martins, St Mary Arches, St Mary Major, St Olave, St Pauls, St Petrocks, and St Sidwells; and W. Reynell and H. Tapley-Soper (eds), *Parish Registers of Exeter Cathedral* (Exeter, 1910).
84. DRO, DD.391, ff.41-41r.
85. E.62 (16) and E.62 (9).
86. R.W. Cotton, 'Naval Attack on Topsham', *DCNG*, 1 (1888), p. 154.
87. See document 17 and E.64 (11).
88. DRO, DD.391, f.42.
89. DRO, DD.391, f.22 and DD.391, f.42.
90. E.65 (9); and *Post Medieval Archaeology*, 26 (1992), pp. 115-16.
91. BL, Additional MSS, 18980, f.110.
92. DRO, DD.391, f.43.
93. E.67 (7).
94. E.67 (25); and E.67 (14).
95. E.67 (14).
96. E.67 (25). Parts of this communication are very reminiscent of a letter which Stamford had written to the King on 4 August, see Bod., Clarendon MSS, 22, 1720.
97. E.250 (13).
98. Ibid.
99. E.67 (25).

5. 'Reduced into the Power of his Sacred Majestie': Royalist Exeter, 1643-45

1. J. Bond, *Occasus Occidentalis, or Job in the West* (1645), p. 54.

NOTES

2. Ibid.; and C.A.T. Fursdon and E. Searle (eds), 'Parish Register of St Olaves, 1601–1837', II, (DCRS, 1937, WCSL, unpaginated).
3. Bond, *Occasus Occidentalis*, p. 10.
4. See ERB, 1642–43, f.9.
5. E.74 (6).
6. See above, chapter 4.
7. See R. Howell, 'Neutralism, Conservatism and Political Alignment in the English Revolution: The Case of the Towns', in J. Morrill (ed.), *Reactions to the English Civil War* (1982), pp. 84–85.
8. J.S. Morrill, *The Revolt of the Provinces: Conservatives and Radicals in the English Civil War* (1976), p. 39; see also Howell, 'Neutralism', p. 70.
9. *CJ*, III (1642–44), p. 85.
10. For Snow, see E.A. Andriette, *Devon and Exeter in the Civil War* (Newton Abbot, 1971), p. 185. For Lynn see E.244. (16) and *CSPD*, 1642/43, p. 490. For Martin, see tables 2–3.
11. PRO, SP.23, 183, f.488.
12. Ibid., f.492; and table 3.
13. See Howell, 'Neutralism', pp. 81–82; and J. Wroughton, *A Community at War* (Bath, 1992), pp. 174–76.
14. EQSOB, 64, ff.8r–71.
15. EQSR, 19 Charles I (1643/44), rolls 2–3.
16. Ibid. Puritan/Parliamentarian constables dismissed in October 1643 included Charles Hopping, Edward Snytall and Robert Sprague. Royalist replacements included Isaac Mawditt, John Pennington and Nicholas Robinson.
17. ECAB, 8, f.300.
18. See document 13; and DCA, D&C, 3557, f.324.
19. See WCSL, DCRS; transcripts of the parish registers of All Hallows Goldsmith Street, Holy Trinity, St Kerrians, St Martins, St Mary Arches, St Mary Major, St Olaves, St Pauls, St Peters, St Petrocks and St Sidwells.
20. ECAB, 8, f.302.
21. See R. Ransom-Pickard, *The Population and Epidemics of Exeter in Pre-Census Times* (Exeter, 1947), p. 44; P. Slack, *The Impact of Plague in Tudor and Stuart England* (Oxford, 1985), pp. 116–18; and I. Roy, 'The City of Oxford, 1640–60', in R.C. Richardson (ed.), *Town and Countryside in the English Revolution* (Manchester, 1992), p. 151.
22. ECAB, 8, f.307.
23. Ibid., ff.308–9.
24. DCA, D&C, 3557, f.329; *HMC*, Exeter, p. 13; and DRO, ECA, CIV.
25. KAO, Bourchier MSS, U269, A.518, 5.
26. ECAB, ff.299–301.
27. For patterns of expenditure on the city walls throughout the early modern

period, see J.Z. Juddery et al., *Exeter City Defences Project: Expenditure on the Walls and Gates, 1339–1700*, (five vols, Exeter, 1988–90), *passim*.
28. ECAB, 8, ff.305, 311.
29. See ERB, 1643-44, ff.4–12, 20. It is interesting to note that Bath, also under Royalist occupation at this time, spent an exactly similar proportion of its annual revenue on defensive work during 1643–44. See Wroughton, *Community at War*, p. 149.
30. See Andriette, *Devon in the Civil War*, p. 109; and, for the full articles of the Association, E.30 (1).
31. EQSOB, 64, f.53.
32. Bond, *Occasus Occidentalis*, p. 58.
33. Ibid., p. 59.
34. Ibid.
35. Ibid., p. 55.
36. EQSOB, 64, f.46.
37. Ibid., f.50.
38. Ibid., f.53.
39. W.H. Black (ed.), *Docquets of Letters Patent . . . of Charles I at Oxford, 1642–46* (1837), pp. 183-85.
40. Bond, *Occasus Occidentalis*, p. 37.
41. *CSPD*, 1644, p. 448.
42. W. Cotton and H. Woollcombe, *Gleanings from the Municipal and Cathedral Records of Exeter* (Exeter, 1877), p. 96.
43. E.54 (1).
44. DCA, D&C, 3780 (Receipts and Solutions, 1643–44, unpaginated).
45. Ibid., and ECAB, 8, f.157r. See also ERB, 1643/44, f.19.
46. DRO, DD.70973 (St Mary Steps Churchwardens' accounts, 1643/44).
47. Andriette, *Devon in the Civil War*, p. 113.
48. DRO, Seymour papers, 1392/L/1644/47.
49. E.3 (6).
50. DRO, St Petrocks Churchwardens' Accounts, 1643/44; and D&C, 3780.
51. *CSPD*, 1644, p. 350.
52. J. Bamfield, *Colonel Joseph Bamfield's Apologie* (The Hague, 1685).
53. ECAB, 8, ff.158-58r.
54. E. Walker, *Historical Discourses upon Several Occasions* (1705), p. 47; and C.E. Long (ed.), *Diary of the Marches of the Royal Army during the Great Civil War*, Camden Society, Old Series, 74 (1859), pp. 38–39.
55. DRO, DD.70973; and DCA, D&C, 3780.
56. Walker, *Historical Discourses*, pp. 47–48.
57. Long, *Diary*, p.39; and DCA, D&C, 3780.
58. ECAB, 8, f.159.
59. ERB, 1643/44, f.19.

NOTES

60. See Long, *Diary*, pp. 83–97; Walker, *Historical Discourses*, pp. 87–95; and E.10 (13).
61. See Walker, *Historical Discourses*, pp. 87, 95; *HMC, Hodgkin MSS*, pp. 101–02; and A.C. Miller, *Sir Richard Grenville of the Civil War* (1979), p. 108.
62. For Frowde, see T.E. Carte (ed.), *A Collection of Original Letters . . . Found among the Duke of Ormonde's Papers* (1739), p. 97.
63. For Newcastle, see Howell, 'Neutralism', p. 79.
64. Wroughton, *Community at War*, p. 148.
65. ECAB, 8, 1642–46, *passim*.
66. EQSOB, 64, ff.9–88.
67. Ibid., ff.44–88.
68. Ibid., f.53.
69. Ibid., ff.53r, 60.
70. Ibid., f.75.
71. Roy, 'City of Oxford', p. 154.
72. D&C, 3780; and DRO, DD.70973.
73. DRO, DD.70974.
74. DRO, St Petrock's Churchwardens' Accounts, 1644/45.
75. ECAB, 8, f.165.
76. PRO, SP.23, 184, f.813.
77. DRO, DD.70974.
78. DRO, 3004/A/PW 4/1; and ECAB, 8, f.166.
79. E.295 (6).
80. E.303 (26).
81. DRO, DD.70974.
82. EQSOB, 64, f.97.
83. Bod., Clarendon MSS, 26, f.93.
84. ECAB, 8, f.167r.
85. Hyde, *History*, p. 84.
86. E.302 (4).
87. E.302 (21).
88. Hyde, *History*, p. 83.
89. BL, Burney, *The Parliament's Post*, 30 September to 7 October 1645.
90. PRO, SP.23, 183, f.448.
91. Bod., Clarendon MSS, 25, f.202.
92. E.305 (16).
93. E.305 (10).
94. J. Sprigg, *Anglia Rediviva: England's Recovery*, (Oxford, 1854 edn), pp. 145–46.
95. E.306 (7).
96. ECAB, 8, f.169r.

97. Ibid.
98. BL, Burney, *The Moderate Intelligencer*, 23-30 October 1645.
99. E.307 (24).
100. Sprigg, *Anglia*, p. 158.
101. M. Stoyle, 'Whole Streets Converted to Ashes: Property Destruction in Exeter during the English Civil War', *Southern History*, 16 (1994), p. 75.
102. E.266 (12).
103. Sprigg, *Anglia*, p. 158.

6. 'Close Begirt': The Final Siege

1. J. Sprigg, *Anglia Rediviva: England's Recovery* (Oxford, 1854 edn), pp. 158–59.
2. Ibid., p. 161; and E.309 (2).
3. E.307 (27).
4. See M. Stoyle, 'Whole Streets Converted to Ashes: Property Destruction in Exeter during the English Civil War', *Southern History*, 16 (1994), pp. 67–84.
5. Sprigg, *Anglia*, pp. 161–63; and E.309 (2).
6. Sprigg, *Anglia*, p. 162.
7. Ibid., p. 163.
8. E.309 (2).
9. E.309 (11).
10. Ibid.
11. E.309 (15).
12. E.310 (7).
13. E.266 (21).
14. E.309 (25). See also R. Schofield, 'The Anatomy of an Epidemic: Colyton, November 1645 to November 1646', in P. Slack et al., *The Plague Reconsidered* (Local Population Studies Supplement, 1977), pp. 96–97.
15. E.308 (16).
16. E.209 (21).
17. Ibid.
18. E.309 (35).
19. E.266 (20).
20. E.309 (25).
21. E.266 (17).
22. E.266 (20).
23. Sprigg, *Anglia*, pp. 165–67.
24. Ibid.
25. Ibid., p. 167.
26. E.311 (21); and E.310 (16).

NOTES

27. E.310 (8).
28. Ibid.
29. E.266 (17).
30. ERB, 1645/46, f.2r.
31. E.311 (7).
32. Sprigg, *Anglia*, pp. 167–69.
33. Ibid., p. 170.
34. E.313 (21).
35. Sprigg, *Anglia*, pp. 171–72.
36. Ibid., p. 172.
37. BL, Burney, *The Moderate Intelligencer*, 25 December 1645 to 1 January 1646.
38. Sprigg, *Anglia*, p. 172.
39. Ibid.
40. Ibid.
41. E.313 (28); E.266 (34); E.313 (21).
42. E.266 (33).
43. E.313 (28).
44. Sprigg, *Anglia*, p. 173.
45. ECAB, 8, f.171.
46. E.315 (4).
47. Bod., Clarendon MSS, 26, f.96.
48. ECAB, 8, f.171r.
49. Sprigg, *Anglia*, pp. 173–75.
50. E.315 (15).
51. E.315 (14).
52. E.315 (4).
53. Sprigg, *Anglia*, p. 176.
54. Ibid.
55. Bod., Clarendon MSS, 26, f.193.
56. E.319 (8).
57. Ibid.
58. E.319 (21).
59. E.319 (8).
60. E.320 (7).
61. E.319 (8).
62. Sprigg, *Anglia*, p. 186.
63. E.320 (11).
64. Sprigg, *Anglia*, pp. 186–87.
65. E.320 (15).
66. E.506 (1).
67. E.320 (6).

68. E.319 (21).
69. E.319 (22).
70. Bod., Hope Adds. 1133, ff.135–36.
71. Sprigg, *Anglia*, pp. 188-89.
72. E.506 (4).
73. Sprigg, *Anglia*, p. 189.
74. Ibid.; and E.322 (3).
75. E.322 (3).
76. BL, Burney, *The Weekly Account*, 28 January to 4 February 1646.
77. E.322 (23); and E.322 (3).
78. E.322 (3).
79. Ibid.
80. PRO, SP.23.184, f.409.
81. E.322 (3).
82. BL, Burney, *Speciall and Remarkable Passages*, 6–13 February 1646; and Sprigg, *Anglia*, pp. 313–14.
83. WCSL, 'St Thomas Parish Church Wardens' Accounts'; and E.322 (8).
84. BL, Burney, *Speciall and Remarkable Passages*, 6–13 February 1646; and E.322 (8).
85. Sprigg, *Anglia*, pp. 313-14.
86. E.322 (15).
87. BL, Burney, *Speciall and Remarkable Passages*, 6–13 February 1646.
88. Ibid.
89. E.319 (16).
90. E.506 (8).
91. BL, Burney, *The Weekly Account*, 28 January to 4 February 1646.
92. E.322 (18); E.322 (35); and Bod., Hope Adds. 1133, f.114.
93. BL, Burney, *Speciall and Remarkable Passages*, 6-13 February 1646.
94. E.322 (8).
95. Bod., Hope Adds. 1133, f.2031.
96. E.322 (18).
97. E.322 (25).
98. Sprigg, *Anglia*, p. 191.
99. Ibid.; and E.323 (9).
100. Sprigg, *Anglia*, p. 251.
101. E.322 (29); and E.322 (30).
102. Ibid.
103. ERV, Box 2 (voucher of 13 January 1647).
104. ERB, 1645/46, f.2r.
105. E.322 (37); and E.323 (9).
106. E.322 (38).
107. ECAB, 8, f.173.

NOTES

108. For Reymes and Coventry, see H. Kaufman, *Conscientious Cavalier* (1962), pp. 156–57; and P.R. Newman, *Royalist Officers in England and Wales* (1981), p. 89.
109. E.322 (30).
110. E.327 (25).
111. J. Vicars, *The Burning Bush Not Consumed* (1646), p. 404.
112. Ibid.
113. Sprigg, *Anglia*, p. 240.
114. DRO, 3004/A/PW 4/1.
115. E.330 (20).
116. Sprigg, *Anglia*, p. 241.
117. Bod., Tanner MSS, 59, f.17.
118. ECAB, 8, f.175.
119. Ibid.
120. Ibid.; and PRO, SP.23, 183, f.871.
121. ECAB, 8, f.175.
122. Sprigg, *Anglia*, pp. 241–42.
123. Bod., Tanner MSS, 59, f.17.
124. Sprigg, *Anglia*, pp. 242–43.
125. WCSL, SB/EXE/1646/FAI.
126. ECAB, 8, f.175r.
127. WCSL, SB/EXE/1646/FAI.
128. EQSOB, 64, f.102.
129. WCSL, SB/EXE/1646/FAI.
130. Ibid.
131. ERB, 1645/46, f.1r.
132. WCSL, SDEV/1646/SEV.
133. Ibid.
134. E.506 (29); and E.506 (31).
135. WCSL, SB/EXE/1646/FAI.
136. Vicars, *Burning Bush*, p. 407.
137. E.322 (23); and Sprigg, *Anglia*, p. 251.
138. Vicars, *Burning Bush*, p. 412.
139. E.322 (23).
140. E.333 (15).
141. E.322 (23).
142. Sprigg, *Anglia*, p. 251.
143. E.322 (23).
144. Sprigg, *Anglia*, p. 252.

Conclusion

1. See M. Stoyle, 'Whole Streets Converted to Ashes: Property Destruction in Exeter during the English Civil War', *Southern History*, 16 (1994), pp. 71, 73, 74-75.
2. Ibid., pp. 75-76.
3. Ibid., p.76.
4. Ibid., *passim*; ERV, Box 2; ECAB, 8, ff.361 ff; M. Stoyle, 'Exeter's Medieval Aqueducts' (forthcoming, Exeter Museum, 1996); and W.B. Stephens, *Seventeenth Century Exeter: A Study of Industrial and Commercial Development, 1625-88* (Exeter, 1958), pp. 63-64.
5. ECAB, 8, f.165; ECAB, 9, f.28; and ERV, Box 2 (vouchers dated 18 January and 14 February 1647).
6. ECAB, 8, f.344; and ERV, Box 2, (vouchers dated 8 August 1646, 30 March 1647 and 4 April 1647).
7. See S. Lawrence, 'A Population Study of St Sidwell's Parish, Exeter, during and after the Civil War' (University of Exeter, certificate course dissertation, 1993—copy held in the Devon and Exeter Institution), p. 9; and Stoyle, 'Whole Streets Converted to Ashes', p. 77.
8. Stoyle, 'Whole Streets Converted to Ashes', p. 78.
9. See DRO, ECA, Book 102, *passim*.
10. ERV, Box 2 (voucher dated 9 July 1647).
11. EQSOB, 64, entry of 6 November 1646.
12. Ibid., f.47.
13. Stoyle, 'Whole Streets Converted to Ashes', pp. 78-79; and Lawrence, 'St Sidwells', p. 9.
14. One prominent Royalist exile was John Colleton, who by June 1646 was reported to have 'absented himself out of the kingdom', see ECAB, 8, f.353.
15. Statement based on analysis of the burial registers of All-Hallows Goldsmith Street, St Kerrians, Holy Trinity, St Martins, St Mary Arches, St Mary Major, St Olaves, St Pauls, St Peters, St Petrocks and St Sidwells (transcripts housed in WCSL).
16. QSOB 1/8, (1640-51), entry for Pasch 1645.
17. See Stoyle, 'Whole Streets Converted to Ashes', pp. 78-80; and Lawrence, 'St Sidwells', pp. 11-14.
18. M. Greengrass, *France in the Age of Henry IV* (1995), p. 6.
19. ECAB, 8, f.352; see also W. Cotton and H. Woollcombe, *Gleanings from the Municipal and Cathedral Records of Exeter* (Exeter, 1877), p. 116.
20. ECAB, 8, ff.353, 359, 361, 366, 387.
21. Ibid., f.361.

Documents

Document 1: *Extracts from the chronicle of James White, 1640–41*

These extracts from the private 'chronicle' of James White, an Exeter merchant, reveal just how well informed about national events some of the city's inhabitants were. White belonged to a rich puritan family and was a member of the Chamber; he later became a Roundhead captain. His chronicle demonstrates clear support for the proceedings of the newly-summoned 'Long Parliament' (see chapter 3, p. 49).

1639–40, Mayoralty of Robert Walker
'The sectaries of Anabaptistes and Seperatistes rise, and severely punnisht in the High Commission Court.

The First Parliament began and was within a while dissolved. Heerein the Bishopp of Excester [i.e. Joseph Hall] was called to a Barr in the Lords howse, for speakinge in the behalfe of the Bishopps.

The Kings Majesty made an expedition towards Scotland.

An Army was leavyed, and went to Barwick.'

1640–41, Mayoralty of John Penny
'The First Parliament beinge dissolved in August the second began in November 1640. One Mr Lenthall a lawyer, was chosen speaker, for the Howse of Commons. The Seaventeenth of November was solempnized a Fast, for the good successe and prosperous proceedinge of the Parliament.

The Parliament affaires goe on ['prettie roundly and' crossed out] with good successe.

The Earle of Strafford and the Archbishop of Canterbury were both impeached of high treason, in the Moneth of December, and they were likewise commyted to the Tower.

Commissioners came from Scotland, to signify the condition and case of busines there.

The Londoners resorted in a tumult, to the Parliament to desire justice on delinquents.

The Lord Keeper and the Kinges Secretary fledd the Kingdome.

The Howse of Commons did publish theire Articles, whereby the Earle of Strafford, and the Archbishopp were severallie impeached.

The cause of Episcopacy & Litturgie were greatly disputed, and discussed by the pen. The defendant was thought to bee the Bishopp of Exon, the opponents named themselves by the name Smectimnuans, the whole dispute was printed.'

1641–42, Mayoralty of Richard Saunders

'The Howse of Commons made an order for the better observeing the Lords Day.

In May came forth the Parliamentes Protestation, required to bee taken by all persons, throughout the kingdome, against Poperie and Innovations [see document 2].

A daungerous plott was discovered of bringeinge about the Army in the North, and to sett it against the Parliament, and to sieze on the Tower of London. By Godes mercy prevented and discovered.

The Earle of Strafford, the Lord Deputie of Ireland, was condemned and beheaded on Tower Hill in Julye.

The Archbishopp of Canterbury was degraded of all his dignity and orders.

The Parliament published an order, for remooveinge all manner of scandalous picktures, Images of the Trinity, and crucifixes, likewise,

DOCUMENTS

remooving the Communion Table and takeinge awaye the Rayles about it.'

Source: DRO, Book 73/15 (James White's Chronicle)

Document 2: The Parliament's Protestation

The 'protestation' (or oath) which appears in the following extract from the parish register of St Mary Arches, Exeter, was originally drawn up by the King's opponents in the House of Commons during May 1641. Although at first sight it seems a very moderate document, committed to upholding the powers of both King and Parliament, the protestation actually undermined the King's position, for it was accompanied by an 'explanation' stating that the rites and ceremonies of the established church—so dear to Charles I's heart and so disliked by zealous protestants—should not necessarily be regarded as part of the 'true reformed protestant religion' which the oath swore to defend. Towards the end of May a drive began to have the protestation taken across the kingdom as a whole, and predictably enough it was the godly who were the quickest to subscribe. The fact that the parishioners of St Mary Arches not only took the oath as early as August 1641, but also honoured the document by transcribing it into their parish register provides clear evidence of their commitment to the puritan/Parliamentarian cause. In January 1642 Parliament ordered the protestation to be taken by all adult males. Most Exeter men complied, but there was some resistance and a number of individuals —including many of the cathedral clergy—refused. The protestation was the first formal test of allegiance to be imposed on the people of Exeter, and its influence can be traced in a number of the documents reproduced below (see especially document 9 and document 11 (letter 2))

'Upon the 22d daye of August Anno 1641 being the Lords Daye, in the Parish Church of St Mary Arches in Exon, this Protestation was performed solemnlie according to the order of the Honourable house of Commons in Parlament, by all the Parishioners whose names are subscribed.

I, A.B., doe in the presence of Almighty God promise vowe and protest to maintaine & defend, as farre as lawfully I may, with my life, power & estate, the true Reformed Protestant Religion expressed in the Doctrine of the church of England, against all Popery and Popish Innovations within this Realme contrary to the same Doctrine & according to the duty of my Allegiance, his Majesties Royall Person, Honour and Estate; As also the Power & Priviledges of Parliament, the lawfull Rights & Liberties of the Subject, & every person that maketh this Protestation, in whatsoever he shall doe in the lawfull pursuance of the same. And to my power, and as farr as lawfully I may, will oppose & by all good waies & meanes indeavour to bring to condigne punishment all such as shall either by Force, Practice, Councells, Plots, Conspiracies, or otherwise doe anything to the contrary of any thing in this present Protestation contained.

And further that I shall in all just & Honourable waies indeavour to preserve the Union & Peace betweene the three Kingdomes of England, Scotland & Ireland: And neither for hope, feare nor other respect, shall relinquish this Promise, Vowe & Protestation.'

The names of 115 male inhabitants of St Mary Arches parish follow.

Annexed 'Explanation' of the religious clause of the oath, as issued by the House of Commons on 12 May 1641
'Whereas some doubts have been raised by severall persons ... concerning the meaning of these words contained in the Protestation lately made by the Members of this House (viz) "The true reformed Protestant Religion expressed in the Doctrine of the Church of England against all Popery & popish Innovations within this Realme, contrary to the same Doctrine"; This House doth declare, That by those wordes was & is meant onely the publick Doctrine professed in the said Church, so farr as it is opposite to Popery & popish Innovations; And that ye said words are not to be extended to the maintaining of any forme of Worship, Discipline or Government, nor of any Rites or Ceremonies of the said Church of England'.

Source: WCSL, C.A.T. Fursdon, (ed.), 'Parish Register of St Mary Arches, Exeter, 1538–1837', (DCRS, 1926)

Document 3: Extracts from a sermon by John Bond, 1641

John Bond, less than thirty years old when he gave the sermon from which these extracts are taken, was the most fiery preacher in Exeter on the eve of the Civil War. Born at Crewkerne in Somerset, he had only arrived in the city towards the end of the 1630s, when he took up the post of lecturer of St

DOCUMENTS

Sidwells. Bond was loathed by city Royalists (see chapter 3, p. 53) and the passages reproduced below make it easy to see why. Part of a sermon delivered some time during the summer of 1641, Bond's words are remarkable, not only for their frank admission that an anti-Parliamentarian party already existed in Exeter, but also for the fervour with which he urged his audience to winkle such 'delinquents' out (see chapter 3, pp. 50). Bond began by praising the newly-summoned Parliament and all its works, exulting in England's 'deliverance' from the 'Babylonish Captivity' of the Personal Rule. But, he warned his auditors, Exeter was not yet out of danger, for the 'honest, godly' citizens had traitors in their midst:

'[There are] a sort of Anti-deliverancers amongst us, men that care not to heare talke of any such great deliverance that hath bin wrought for us, but are up with their "What?, How? and Wherein?". Tell them . . . that the Lord hath done great things for us, and they are angry presently and part companyes. Tell them of a captivity of Zion that is turned, and they laugh as much at the turning as at the Zion. But are ye aware of their reason? I conceive it to be this: the men are delinquents, perhaps in person or else in party, and therefore should they acknowledge a Deliverance, next it will be enquired from what, and whom are we delivered. And the answer to this question might start new *queres* (i.e. questions) which may reflect upon themselves, their friends or faction. I therefore commend the pollicy of the men, though . . . [not] their piety . . . they doe trample unparalel'd Nationall Mercies under foot, and so are unworthy to breath in these blessed times which we see . . .

Who are they which doe now suffer, but Delinquents and Delinquencies? . . . And yet we have men, who either expresly or about the bush, dare tell the people of a kind of persecution, afflictions, hard times now, and I know not what . . . Deliverance is publicly proclaimed . . . yet . . . durst [they] still to bite the lip, to shake the head, or to grumble secretly at such proceedings? Brethren (I speak to all true Protestants and cordiall subjects) I charge you . . . that ye observe, marke out and pursue (lawfully) to the uttermost all such murmurers and repiners at the present blessings of Deliverance and Reformation . . .

In a word, do but marke (my Brethren) what persons (lay or clergy) are most dull and backward to the means and pieces of this Reformation; as first, to dayes of publike humiliation injoyned, next to the late Vow and Protestation (see document 2), and finally to this last duty of publike joy and thankesgiving; but on the contrary, are very quick, free and forward to promote or favour Arminian, Antisabbatarian, licentious papers, pamphlets or practises; mark these, and then ye have found them (ten to one) which I call Anti-Deliverancers, Anti-Reformists.'

Source: J. Bond, *A Doore of Hope: Also Holy and Loyal Activity, Two Treatises Delivered in Severall Sermons in Excester*, (1641)

Document 4: Extracts from the chronicle of James White, 1641-42

These extracts show how White perceived the gradual slide into Civil War. Unfortunately the entries come to an abrupt halt in autumn 1642, presumably because White—who had recently been appointed to the Parliamentary Committee for Safety (see document 6, pp. 174)—was now too busy with public affairs to keep his private chronicle up to date.

1641

'In October this yeare the rebelion in Irelande brake forth on the First November, the Lord Keeper made the whole relation of it in the House of Commons.

The Parliament made an order for the setlinge of the militia of the Kingdome, and chose Deputy Leiftennants for the severall shires of England and Wales.'

1641/42, Mayoralty of Christopher Clarke

'The Seaventh of February the Bishopps were voted out of the House of Lords, and not to sitt in Parliament any more, or to exercise any temporall Jurisdiction.

Petitions are framed and presented from severall Counties to the Parliament, expressing thankes for their great care and paynes.

A combination was reported to bee betweene them of Lancashire and the Rebells in Ireland to strike and joyne with them when they should come over and lande in those parts, but this was discovered by one of the plotters.

The King in his iourney to Yorke.

Forces preparing in Denmark and Fraunce against England. Report was of 30,000 well armed to goe into the province of Munster. They have taken Wexford.

The diurnalls of the passages in Parliament were prohibited, because soe much falsehood was printed in them.

The King came to Hull about the ende of Aprill, and Sir John Hotham, intrusted to keepe that place by the Parliament, shutt him out.

The ende of this moneth was great newes from Ireland, Five hundred of the Lord Musgroves men slayne. Many prisoners and bootie alsoe taken . . . My lord of Baramore hath slaine of men, woemen and children twoe hundred and eighty.

In Maye divers Lords left the Parliament, and went to the King att Yorke.

In June the Commission of Array was first sett on foote and first executed in Leicestershire by one Mr Henrie Hastings. The Parliament voted against this Commission of Array in Twoe votes that it was illegal.

The Parliament ordered 10,000 men, to bee raysed in and about London, to be disposed of by them.

The Parliament in July appoynted A Lord Generall over their Forces, the Earle of Essex, and signifyed theire cheerefull resolution, to live and dy with him.

Sentence was given in Parliament against Nyne Lords, that repayred to Yorke, where the King made preparations of warr against the Parliament.

An order came forth for volunteers.

About this tyme were great stirrs in Somersetshire, by pressing on the Commission of Array, the power of the Country was risen to suppresse them to the number of two thowsand.

The furtherers of the Commission of Array in Somersetshire were sent to the Parliament.'

Source: DRO, Book 73/15 (James White's Chronicle)

Document 5: Extract from an assize sermon, 1642

The sermon from which these extracts are taken was preached at Exeter Cathedral on 7 August 1642, before an audience including the assembled city councillors (see chapter 3, pp. 59–60). Its author, Thomas Trescott, was a committed puritan, and his aim appears to have been to persuade the members of the Chamber to declare themselves unequivocally for Parliament. The reverence with which Trescott invoked the name of Ignatius Jurdain is significant; even two years after his death, the 'Arch Puritan' clearly continued to exert a powerful influence on affairs at Exeter.

'As for you, the worthy senators of this honourable city, keep up the credit of your owne motto, *Fideles in Aeturnum* [i.e. 'Ever Faithful'], to bee faithfull in the discharge of that trust which God and the King have imposed in you, in a due execution of those that doe evill, and for the prayse of them that doe well. Oh let it never bee sayd of you, that the fire of zeale was cleane put out in the death of one holy Ignatius, you know my meaning ... [marginal comment: 'Mr Ign. Jurdain, a late worthy Alderman of that City, you are men, you are christians, you are magistrates, then quit yourselves like men, like christians, like magistrates.

Two things I may recommend unto you. First, do not enterfare and clash one with another in the execution of Justice. The States of the United Provinces (upon some difference between them and us) gave for their Impresse two pitchers, floating upon the water, with this word, *sic collidimur, frangimur*, if we once fall a dashing, we shall all fal in pieces. If magistrates be not well glued and sodered together, their disagreement breeds nothing but mischiefe and confusion, like Castor and Pollux, if they doe not appear together it presageth a storme.

Secondly, doe not strain courtesie in matters of publique concernment, whose tongue shall moove first, whose hand must subscribe first, and others like pieces of ill-placed good manners ... often times you will conclude tis fit this should be done, fit this order made, and that order confirmed and the like, yet none will move their hand to the worke, though everyone move his tongue: Just like the rats in the fable, they all agreed twas fit the cat should have a bell about her neck (that they might have warning of their enemies comming) but the demurre was, who should put it on, and none would doe that.

Doe not chalke up more sinnes over and above your owne score by a bashful connivance, or a sinfull silence: let the world see and know that your sword is steele to the back, able to cutt the strongest barres of iron in sunder. That Magistrate which shall bee carefull to execute Gods

DOCUMENTS

Lawes ... shall have no need to run to Paris or the Hague for refuge, he carries a sanctuary in his own bosome ... *Up then and be doing and the Lord be with you.*'

Source: E.89 (4)

Document 6: Extracts from the Chamber Act Book, August-October 1642

These extracts reveal the steps which the Chamber took to protect the city during summer and early autumn 1642 (see chapter 4, pp. 63–65). The measures included resupplying the civic magazine, appointing a Committee for Safety, and hiring a military engineer. Note the order of 13 September that only 'honest persons' should be permitted to serve as replacements on the night watch, and that a list of such persons should be compiled. The order hints at a view that it was already possible to divide the inhabitants into 'honest', Parliamentarian sheep and 'dishonest', Royalist goats—a view which later directives would make explicit.

9 August 1642

'This day it is agreede that the maggazyne of powder &c nowe in the Common Treasurie in this cittie which was provided att the common charge of the cittizens, shall not be delivered unto any person or persons without the consent of this house.

This day Mr James Tucker & Mr John Hakewill, Aldermen, Mr James Gould & Mr John Colleton are desired to meete the right honourable the Earle of Bath who is this day expected to this cittie, And to deliver this message hereunder written according to the direccions hereunder written &c.

If the Committee ... doe fynde that the Earle of Bathe doe come in an ordinarie way unarmed that then they or one of them or some messenger from them under their hands hasten their retorne to give notice thereof to the Captayne attending the gate where he is to come in att, that he may be received with all due respecte. But if they fynde he comes in a warlick manner with more then one hundred of armed men, that they then informe his Lordship of this order & desire hym, that if he intends to enter into the cittie in that manner that he will first before his entrie give them leave to informe Mr Maior & his bretheren thereof, And they

173

will foorthwith retorne his Lordship their resolucions. And the Committee to have a coppie of this order under the townclark's hand.'

16 August 1642
Whereas some propositions have byn made this day to this house by divers cittizens of good qualitie touching the dangers of the present tyme & for the better preservacon of the peace hereafter. This day Mr John Lynne, Mr Sheriff, Mr James Gould, Mr Richard Crossing, Mr Richard Yeo & Mr John Colleton, the Chamberlaine & Towneclark or any fower or more of them shall seriouslie consider of the said proposicons. And to reporte to this house what they conceive fitting to be done in the same with all convenient speede.'

25 August 1642
'[Ordered] . . . that there shall be 32 persons charged to warde everie day & 32 persons to watch everie night. And householders enjoyned to performe these services in these dangerous tymes & none to be excused therein but for just cause.

Alsoe it is agreede that a charge shall be drawne upp in writing to be delivered to the constables in everie quarter for their better direccions to the persons everie day that are to warde. And the warde to be continued from sixe in the morning untill the watch come att night.'

30 August 1642
'Whereas on Saterday last there was an elecion made by Mr Maior & some of the Aldermen of this cittie of 15 committees persons of this Chamber & others viz: Mr Hakewill, Mr James Tucker, Alderman, Mr James Gould, Mr James White, Mr Richard Crossing, Mr John Cooze, Mr John Lovering, Mr Richard Evans, Mr Thomas Ford junior, Mr William Holmes, Mr Henry Prigg, Mr Samuell Crocker, Mr John Butler, Mr Thomas Pitt & Mr John Gill, or any 8 or more of them, who were desired to consider of some fitting course to be foorthwith taken for some provision of corne [i.e. corned gunpowder] & other ammunicion for the better supplie & preservacion of this cittie & the inhabitants thereof, and from tyme to tyme to make reporte to this house of their doings therein, this day the said elleccion is approoved of & confirmed.'

DOCUMENTS

8 September 1642
'Alsoe it is agreede that 500 pounds waight of match shall be provided & bought for the common store of this cittie, such powder being nowe offered to be solde by Mr Vaughan the muster master.

Alsoe that such elmes & ashes shall be taken downe, in fitting places, as be needfull for the making of wheeles & carryiages latelie provided for the defence of this cittie.

Alsoe materialls to be taken out of Duryard Wood of the toppes of the trees for the making of gabyons & such things for the carrying of earth & mounting of the said ordnance.

Alsoe whereas it hath byn propounded by the committee for the safetie of the cittie that some ingeneere or other person well experienced in marshall disciplyne should be procured to be here continuallie resident for the better defence of this cittie & to be assisting & attendant on the captaynes here in these tymes of combustion, It is agreed that if such a person may be procured from London or any other place that shall be approoved of by this house for that service, that this house shall be ingaged to pay unto him £30 yerely towards his pencion & expences.'

13 September 1642
'Alsoe whereas complaynt hath byn made of divers disorders in the night watches in respecte that divers disorderlie persons are allowed of as spells to supplie those places, This day it is ordered that there shall be some convenient number of honest persons selected out in everie quarter within this cittie who shall be onlie allowed of to serve in those places in such persons' roomes as are to be excused of their owne personall service.

Alsoe it is this day agreede that the citties walles against Northinghay shall be repaired foorthwith.

Alsoe it is this daye agreede that the citties gunnes, vizt; three ordnances & three stock fowlers shall be foorthwith mounted att the charg of the cittie. And alsoe that a barrell of the common store of the powder to be used for the triall of those & other gunnes latelie brought and bestowed uppon this cittie for the defence of the same.

Alsoe it is desired that the before named committee for the safetye of this cittie in these tymes of publick danger doe viewe the walles about this cittie howe the same may be made passable &c.'

22 September 1642
'Whereas the porters of the severall gates of this cittie have byn of late inforced to spend much candlelight, and the like course is like to be continued, it is this day agreede that there shalbe five shillings a peece allotted & paid unto everie of them towards their extraordinarie expence.'

11 October 1642
'For the preventing of the manie dangers threatned to this cittie, it is agreede & ordered that the . . . gates of this cittie shall be shutt everie night from hencefoorth att sixe of the clock, & the wicketts of the said gates att eight of the clock, & none to be permitted to goe in or out after those howers, And that notice hereof be publicklie given to the inhabitants & all others that they may order their buisinesses accordingly.

Alsoe that all inhabitants be againe publicklie warned to watch & warde in person as their turnes doe come & as they shall be required to performe that service, & none to be excused, but such as are to be exempte by lawe.

Alsoe the Aldermen of the severall wards or quarters of this cittie are desired to take care that noe strangers be interteyned within their severall quarters, but such as be well knowne &c, and to cause search to be made everie night to that purpose in all innes &c.'

Source: DRO, ECAB, 8 (1634–47), ff.276–84

Document 7: Parliament intervenes in affairs at Exeter

By virtue of this order, dated 12 October 1642, Parliament authorized its local supporters to step up their defensive preparations. The document is typical of a number of similar orders which were issued by both Houses of Parliament during late 1642, all of them designed to strengthen the power of the pro-Parliamentary faction in Exeter (see chapter 4, pp. 65–66, 68, 71)

'It is this day ORDERED, by the Lords and Commons in Parliament, That the Mayor, Aldermen, and Common Council of the city of Exeter, within the county of Devon, for the time being, shall have power to assemble together, muster, train, and command, all the Trained Bands, and other persons able to bear arms, in that city, and county of the same; and, by the advice of the Mayor, Aldermen, and Common Council of the said city, to nominate and appoint such persons as are fit, to be Captains, and other officers, to conduct, lead, and command the said Trained Bands; and that the said Mayor and Aldermen, with the consent of the Common Council, do cause the said city, and castle of Exeter adjoining to the city ... to be fortified, and their ordnance there to be mounted, and the said city and castle put into a posture of defence; and to raise strong watches, by armed men, to set by day and night, in such places as are necessary and fitting; and that they do not permit any soldiers to come into the said city or castle, without authority of Parliament; and that the said Mayor, Aldermen, Common Council, and Justices of Peace of that city ... do apprehend, and commit to safe custody, as well all such persons as, being Commissioners of Array, do put in execution the same Commission, or that do promote or endeavour to put the same Commission in execution; as also all such persons as do lend money, plate, or arms, to His Majesty, for the maintaining of a wicked and unnatural War against His Majesty's good subjects, and that do disturb the peace of the Kingdom.'

Source: LJ, 5, p. 398.

Document 8: Information given to the City Sessions Court, 1642

These depositions were made against two Exeter men who had been unwise enough to voice their Royalist sympathies. Francis Gyles's reference to 'booke[s] or paper[s]' (extract I) reveals just how angered some local people were by the propagandist material which was now spewing forth from the London presses—and just how much such material had started to affect political opinion in the city. Also significant is the boast of Richard Rosser (extract II) that he would go to the Cavaliers 'at Lanceston'. Rosser's words make it clear that, by October 1642, Exeter's beleaguered Royalists were already looking to Cornwall for assistance.

Extract I—9 October

'Thomas Hill of Bishopps Nympton in the Countie of Devon husbandman informeth that yesterday being the viiith of this instant October he was att the Beare [Inn] in this Cittie, where he hearde Francys Giles of this Cittie gent to saye (speaking to other persons then and there alsoe present with hym) that it was exprest or sett foorth in some printed booke or paper that King Charles had poisoned his Father . . . and said Be not these roages that sett foorth such things, and is it not pittye that such roagues should be suffered.

Abell Hooper of this Cittie weaver informeth that he met casuallie with the said Thomas Hill this present day being Sunday. And goeinge in the streete with the said Hill, the said Hill tolde this informant that the said Giles had spoken against the Parliament, and had saide that the Parliament as he did think had declared or sett foorth that King Charles had poysoned his Father'

Extract II—19 October
'Richard Rosser of this Cittie Yoman being charged yesterday before Mr Alderman Bennett by one Mr Willes of Salt Ashe for speaking divers seditious words yesterday last to the said Mr Willes att the house of Richard Kellye of this Cittie Innkeeper, videlicit, that he would goe this day to Lanceston to the Cavalliers there, And that he knewe three severall places in this Cittie where they might enter. And being thereupon examined wither he spoke those words or noe denyeth that he said he would goe to Lanceston, but sayth that he being att the house of the said Kellye and in company of the said Willes, and speaking of the fortificacons that were making att the Castle and of those att Lanceston, confesseth he said that he thought they [i.e. the Cavaliers] might more easilie enter the Cittie att the Eastgate, Westgate or Norgate of the said Cittie then att the Castle, And that in the speaking therof he meant noe hurte to the Cittie, But in regard that those words are conceived of such ill consequence as may occation too much freedome in others to further the surprisal of this place, he is ordered to be committed to his Majesties prison.'

Source: DRO, EQSOB 64 (1642–60), ff.15–17

Document 9: Extracts from the Chamber Act Book, October-December 1642

These extracts reveal some of the steps which the Chamber took to improve the city defences during the last three months of 1642. The order of 25 October concerning the destruction of Archdeacon Hall's enclosure is particularly worthy

DOCUMENTS

of note. As the Parliamentary grip on Exeter tightened, the Chamber began to adopt an extremely high-handed attitude towards the ancient rights and privileges of the Dean and Chapter (see chapter 4, pp. 65, 71)

18 October 1642
'It is agreede that the charge of the chaynes for the severall gates of this cittie shall be paid for by Mr Receiver.'

25 October 1642
'[City officials ordered] . . . to view the vauts about the Eastgate & the defects about the walles betweene Eastgate & Southgate, and to reporte to the house . . . And it is ordered that the said dampes shall be foorthwith stopped upp by Mr Receiver . . . And that some buttresses be made there for the said walles in places needfull.

It is ordered that notice shall be given to Mr George Hall Archdeacon of Cornwall of an inclosure heretofore made neare the house belonging to his Archdeaconrie, being an auncient and common way to the citties walles neare adioyning thereunto, and to desire hym that the same may be laid open againe, which if he shall refuse or neglecte to doe, it is thought fitt & ordered that the same shall be taken downe.'

3 November 1642
'Uppon reporte of the Committee of the last meeting about the orchards & gardens adioyning to the citties walles betweene Eastgate & Southgate, it is agreede & ordered that all the owners of the said gardens shall foorthwith be warned to take downe all such trees within any of the said gardens that stand within 16 foote of the said walles which if they doe not performe within some convenient tyme, in these tymes of soe great danger, otherwise they will be cutt downe.

Whereas for the fortefying of some places about the cittie some stakes are wanting, it is agreede that 34 stakes shall be spared out of the common store for that purpose & delivered unto the persons intrusted therin by the Deputie Lieutenants of this cittie.

It is agreede that Mr Receiver shall pay unto the troopers that watchte Jonathan Hawkins house the last night by order of the Deputie Lieutenants the some of 20s.

It is agreede that there shalbe 2s 6d allowed unto the captayne of the

179

night watch everie night towards the charg of candlelight & fire &c, over & above the 12d a weeke to the porters of the gates formerlie appointed.'

29 November 1642
'It is agreede that there shalbe £10 bestowed on Peter Baxster the ingineere latelie interteyned by this cittie in that place, in regard of his extra- ordinarie paynes taken in those services here of late.

To Mr Baxster for his quarterlidg—£7 10s
& the payment above for a gratuitie—£17 10s
for charge of the chaynes of the gates &c—£60
for mounting of the greate gunnes—£30
for match latelie bought for the common store—£8
for other extraordinarie charges present—£10

Whereas it is desired by divers of the commons that a Committee should be chosen of this house & of the cittizens, for to consider of some fitting course for the raising of monie for the poore, & the better defence of this cittie, this house have elected of their owne societie these persons;

Mr Adam Bennett
Mr James Tucker
Mr Walter White   who are desired to joyne with 10 of the
Mr James Gould   commons to be likewise elected by them
Mr John Cupper   for the purposes before mencioned.'

13 December 1642
'This day it is agreede that the keyes of the powder houses att the Guildhall shall be & remayne in the custodie of Mr Maior.'

20 December 1642
'[Ordered] that Mr Receiver shall make a barracado or some other engiyne in the key lane for the stoppage of the passage of horses that way &c.'

Source: ECAB, 8, ff.284–88

Document 10: *The Exeter Covenant*

This oath was drawn up by the Parliamentary authorities in Exeter as Sir Ralph Hopton's Cornish army advanced on the city in December 1642 (see

DOCUMENTS

chapter 4, pp. 67–69, 71). Initially taken by the mayor, deputy lieutenants and Chamber men alone, it was later proffered to the rest of the city's inhabitants as well (see document 16). The wording of the document helps to illustrate the motivation of the city Roundheads and their deep-rooted fear of 'Popery and Tyranny'.

'The Covenant entered into by the Mayor of Exceter, Deputy Lieutenants . . . and Common Councell of the Cittie.

In regard of the extraordinary danger the city and county of Exceter now stands in, by reason of the near approach of the enemy whom we understand to be on his march hitherward, and may within a few daies be before our gates, we the Mayor, Deputy Lieutenants and Common Counsell of the said City and County, Do solemnly promise and vow according to our late general protestation [see document 2], to defend his Majesties honour and person, the priviledges of Parliament, the Laws of the land, the liberty and propriety of the subject, all which are declared by the Lords and Commons in Parliament assembled to be actually invaded by Sir Ralph Hopton, Sir John Barkly, Sir William Ashburnham, their accomplices and adherents, who have gathered together great forces for the accomplishment of their wicked designes, to the ruine of this present happy Parliament, and in it to lay the Foundation of Tyranny and Popery.

We therefore do firmly and constantly resolve by the blessing and assistance of Almighty God, as we shall one day answer the contrary before him at his Great Tribunall to discharge our duties and consciences in the exact performance of the said Vow and Protestation by our unwearied labours and indeavours, though with the expence of our Lives and Estates, to defend, preserve and protect this City and County, against the said Sir Ralph Hopton and his adherents in this their Rebellious Insurrection: And we do further promise, vow and protest, according to the true intent and meaning hereof, without any equivocation or mentall reservation, never to desert this Cause, but mutually to joyn with and support each other in the maintenance of it, in testimony whereof we have subscribed this Protestation.'

Source: E.130 (20)

Document 11: *Summons and response, 1642*

These documents trace the course of the correspondence between the commanders of the Royalist army and the city authorities in December 1642 (see chapter 4, pp. 69–70). Like the Exeter Covenant (see document 10), the Mayor's answer does much to illuminate the considerations which had prompted the city Parliamentarians to take up arms in the first place.

Letter I

'The true copie of
A LETTER
sent from
Sir RALPH HOPTON, Colonel ASHBURNHAM
and Sir JOHN BERKLEY
To Mr: Christopher Clarke, Maior of the city
of EXCESTER
. . . .
With the answer which the Maior returned . . .

Mr Maior,
Neither your slight answer to our last letter, nor your no answer to our former, (in which wee sent you a copie of our Commission), nor your neglect of the knowne lawes, in leavying armes without his Majestie's leave, nor your imploying those armes to the destruction of His Majestie's good subjects, and such as proceed by His lawfull Commission have that effect upon our minds, as to make us with His Majestie's usuall mercy and clemency any wayes contracted with you; And therefore that we may satisfie all good men, not onely of the justice and equity of our proceedings, but also of that charity, and compassion, (of which there scarce can be any accesse in case of blood) These are to require you once more in His Majestie's name (by vertue of our Commission) to lay downe your unlawfull armes, and to conforme your selves to the duties of your allegiance, and to be no more a cause (by your obstinacie) of drawing those calamities upon your country, which even the hearts of strangers bleed to see, and foresee, in case you shall think it fit to accept of your owne safety, and the quiet of your country, at no greater price then your returning to the lawes; These are to assure your city, and every person in it of indempnity for our part, but in case you shall still continue in armes without his Majestie's authority, and against it, These are to call God and man to witnesse, that it is you, which have broken these

lawes, which have hitherto kept this Kingdome in peace, and cannot but expect the bitter fruits of your owne planting.

As for us, so may God blesse us in our proceedings, as we have been farre from giving occasion to this unaturall warre, and as wee are, and ever have been ready to embrace all just wayes, of composing it, in which way wee are ready to approve ourselves

Your very loving Friends,
RALPH HOPTON, W.ASHBURNHAM, JOHN BERKLEY
Alphington, December 30, 1642.

Letter II

The answer of the Maior of EXCETER.

Gentlemen,
You had no answer to your first letter, because your Commission, whereof you sent me a copie, I conceive, had no relation to our city. To the second letter, signed by Collonell Ashburnham, I thought it not fit to give a serious answer, the contents being as farre from my beliefe, as your intention, for I cannot be perswaded to find those friendly in this city, that have invaded the county of Devon with an army, and used the inhabitants as enemies; And besides, this city being committed (under our most gratious soveraigne) to my charge, and government, I should falsifie that trust very much, if I should receive into it numbers of power, to master both it, and me.

For our taking of armes for our defence, even your approach in the manner you came, is a sufficient reason, if there were no more, But the defence of those lawes, and that government by Parliaments which hath so long kept this Kingdome in happy peace, is the cause of our arming, no more doubting of the lawfulnesse of the authority then I do of my humble duty, and faithfull allegiance to his Majesty, the oath whereof I have often taken, and ever will keepe.

To the authors of this unnaturall warre, all evill is wished by all good men; I doe not impute the beginning of it to you, because I know it not, I wish I could acquit you of the prosecution, while we pray for a blessed reconciliation between His Majesty, and this Parliament, and doe our best to defend both; There are some that have most unfaithfully perswaded his Majesty to bend his royall face against that Court [of

Parliament], to the destruction of the fundamentall lawes, and ruine of the Kingdome: That you are a partner in the execution at least of that designe, is my confident beliefe, being manifest by your practise; your discerting this unaturall and destructive warre, and joyning with us of this city in prayers to God, and petitions to his sacred Majesty, to vouchsafe a concurrence with his faithfull Lordes and Commons in Parliament, to give a speedy remedy to these bleeding miseries, would cause me really to signe my selfe,

>Your friend to serve you
>Christopher Clarke
>Maior'

Source: E.84 (45)

Document 12: Instructions for the city's defence

These orders, issued in the wake of the unsuccessful Royalist attack of December 1642 (see chapter 4, pp. 74–75), were intended to strengthen Exeter's defences. Once again, the concern of the Parliamentary authorities to exclude 'malignants' from all positions of trust within the city, and to replace them with 'choice men', 'trusty men', 'faithfull men' and 'men to be confided in'—pro-Parliamentarians, in other words—is made crystal clear. Note, too, the care which was taken to search 'disaffected persons' houses and to prevent the populace at large from conversing with Royalist prisoners. (NB—words placed in parenthesis are taken from a rough draft of the original document.)

'Anno 1642. January. 23th daye.

1. That the Magasin be forthwith viewed & made up as follows:
Powder—80 Barrils
Match—40 C waight
Musket Bullets (of severall sizes)—30 C weight
Carbine Bullets—4 C weight
Cannon Shott—1000 of severall sizes per the gunners direccon.

Two chambers to every stock fowler & 2 or 3 stock fowlers more to be procured.

2. That more gunners be procured, men to be confided in.
3. That a douzen iron rods with wormes & scowrers be made for the musketts, & some to be at each gate & the castle.

4. That 4 or 5 companyes of volunteers of the country be procured.
 5. That 40 inhabitants of the citty, men to be confided in, may be added to the captains & officers of the volunteers to take their turnes to be over the watches at the severall corpe de gards.
 6. That some choice men be consiggered for the castle.
 7. That the dikes (about the) citty be made deeper, & more falling & people summoned by the drum for expedition: & the walls & (houses) removed.
 8. That the Great (Church) be kept continually shut & a guarde ther by night: & a trusty man to keep the keyes.
 9. That flankers (be made, per) Captain Baxter's direction.
10. That turnepikes (be set at) each gate & att the bridge foot.
11. That dikes & drawbridges (be made) at each gate to prevent blowing up the (gate).
12. That Topsham (&) the (river be effectu)ally secured, & that (Powderham) Castle (be demolished) or secured, & Radford house fortifyed.
13. That some fortification be made (at) Cowley Bridge so as to command the way from Stoke.
14. That the remote parts of the suberbs be baricaded &c.
15. That there be a strict restraint of the prisoners & none suffered to speake with them, but by order of the Deputie Lieutenants, & in presence of the corporall of the watch, & (none to preach there but by permission).
16. (That all) malignants & disaffected (persons be secured or dismiste).
17. (That noe women) or children nor (howsehold goods be passed out of the citty without) order of the Deputie (Lieutenants).
18. (That in case) of fire some aldermen (be named with the sheriffe to cleer) the streets by a proclamacion: (that the Comitty may attend it) who are to prepare bucketts & crooks &c. beforehand.
19. That all hay & straw be removed from about the guildhall.
20. That proclamation be made to require every man to make provision of corne, pease, & other needfull thinges & also of fewell.
21. That hand mills be procured from the country &c. there being one in St. Thomas parish.
22. That all disaffected persons be throughly disarmed & their howses dewly searched.
23. That for securing the mills, the cliffs at Head-ware bee made good.
24. That St. Davids hill be secured wher there's most command.

25. That the wall twixt Eastgate & the castle be viewed, & that some common passage be opened & the High Geole & Orchard's howse be carefully looked unto having outlets to the said wall & a hollow tower (in the said wale to be repaired) & a vaut from the Geole.
26. That Doctor Salter, Mr. Rodes, Thomas Orchard and others who came lately in to be secured or put forth of the cittye.
27. That the Winners [i.e. Wynards Almshouses] (be made goode and the) street before itt.
28. That the guildhall (without Eastgate) be secured for the passage from Paris (Street and the) lane going into Southenhay by Crosses the smith (to be) damned up.
29. That the trees in (Southenhay be) cut downe & brought into the cittye & (some of those) in the Bonney.
30. That the trees (in the) old church yard be carryed to every gate some.
31. That more corps (de guard) howses be appointed.
32. That strict (discipline may) be (observed) towards all souldiers that neglect (their) duty.
33. [torn] ... particuler faithfull men to ... [illegible] that a considerable quantitie of match, bullett ... balls, & if you can procure some morter peces, they will be very useful.
34. To order that some turnepikes, flankers, or galleries according to former description be made presently without the walls.
35. To take an exact muster of the men, and their armes which are now within this citty: as well trayners [i.e. members of the trained bands] as volunteers, & also those that are fitt to bare armes & have none, as also that each howse holder present to [blank] within his parish what quantity of armes & what sort of armes he hath within his howse, to the intent that on any extraordinary occasion they may be brought forth, & not otherwise: and if any shall refuse to certify the number of their armes, that those that doe soe shall be severely punished & loose their armes.
36. That this being done Mr. Mayor & the Deputyes expresse how many souldiers they think needfull to be called into the citty and when.
37. That one particuler time be assigned to meete to consult during these times & exactlie observed.
38. That an expresse be sent to the Parliament with desires for armes &c. as above said.

DOCUMENTS

39. That a letter be written to Generall Stamford to desire his care of this place.
40. That a constant courier ... [illegible—'be had'?] for to have intelligences, & scouts settled so that when one ... [illegible —'comes in'?] another may goe out.

[Additional Directives]

[1] [torn] ... round to ... heapes of stones, which may be taken from the battlements, or turrets.
[2] The walls to be exactly searched without and within the walls in all houses & sellers that are adjoyning, specially Orchard's house at Eastgate, & Southgate prison.
[3] No watches to be sent to their courts of gard ... [illegible—'or'?] to any quarter till examined if they have powder, match & bullets.
[4] Let all the centinells be firelocks & snapances.
[5] Let every souldier have 4 bandoleers of powder, 4 bullets, & 2 yards of match worne about his arme, & one to view them every pay daie, & allowe out of their wages for any thing mispent.
[6] No bells to ring for any dead, or clocks to strike, while the citty is beseeged.
[7] A corps de garde to be kept in the old churchyard, & to sit in St. Maries tower and bellfrie with 2 centinells on ye toppe of the tower.
[8] The watch to be set at an exact time at the ringing of guildhall bell which shall ring, about 1/2 a quarter of an howre: and punishment for the absent & for late comers.
[9] All corporalls should be directed in what cases to beat an allarum.'

Source: DRO, DD. 36995.B. (Rough draft = DD.36995.A)

Document 13: The 'Reformation' of the cathedral

This scandalized account of the Parliamentarian desecration of Exeter Cathedral during January 1643 (see chapter 4, pp. 72–73) appeared in a Royalist propaganda tract, Mercurius Rusticus. *The picture may be somewhat overdrawn, but there can be little doubt that it is correct in the essentials; the defaced pictures of Moses and Aaron still survive today, their faces gouged and mutilated by the Roundhead iconoclasts. Rusticus's account is invaluable not only because it gives an idea of the sheer violence of the religious passions which were then raging in Exeter, but also because it positively drips with the sort of disgust and contempt which many city conservatives felt for the sacrilegious activities of the Roundhead mob.*

'Having the [cathedral] church in their possession, in a most puritanical beastly manner they [i.e. the Roundheads] make it a common Jakes for the exonerations of nature, sparing no place, neither the altar, nor the pulpit. Over the communion table, in faire letters of gold, was written the holy and blessed name of *Jesus:* this they expunge as superstitious and execrable. On each side of the commandments the pictures of Moses and Aaron were drawn in full proportion, these they deface. They tear the bookes of common prayer to pieces, and as if this had been too small a contempt . . . [they] burn them at the altar with exceeding great exultations and expressions of joy.

They made the church their storehouse where they kept their ammunition and powder and planted a court of guard to attend it, who used the church with the same reverence they would an alehouse, and defiled it with tippling and taking tobacco. They break and deface all the glass windows in the church, which cannot be replaced for many hundred pounds, and left all those ancient monuments, being painted glass, and containing matter of story only, a miserable spectacle of commiseration to all well-affected hearts that beheld them.

They struck off the heads of all the statues on all monuments in the church, especially they deface the bishops' tombs, leaving one without a head and another without an arm. They pluck down and deface the statue of an ancient queen, the wife of Edward the confessor, *mistaking* it for the statue of the blessed Virgin Mary, the mother of God. They brake down the organs, and, taking two or three hundred pipes with them, in a most scornful, contemptuous manner, went up and down the street, piping with them; and, meeting some of the choristers of the church, whose surplices they had stolen before, scoffingly told them "Boys, we have spoiled your trade; you must go and sing hot pudding pies!".'

Source: E.122 (13)

Document 14: Information presented to the City Sessions Court, 1643

These depositions were made against a pair of humble Exeter men, a weaver and a barber, who had mocked the Parliamentary cause: the first by shouting

DOCUMENTS

'hange the Parliament', the second by exulting in Stamford's defeat at the Battle of Stratton (see chapter 4, p. 77). It is perhaps significant that the inn in which the second man was drinking when he made his outburst belonged to Mark Browning, later a Royalist captain. Several of Exeter's inns seem to have served as unofficial centres for the King's supporters at this time, most notably the Bear, in South Street (see chapter 3, pp. 60–61, and document 8, extract I).

Extract I—21 February
[Roger Boaman of St Mary Major, weaver, was bound over because, in speaking of] 'the present troubles [he] saide that he knewe that the Array side would be the strongest syde, for which he being reprehended ... for that he would dare to speake such words, the said Boaman said againe, God blesse the Kinge and hange the Parliament.'

Extract II—18 May
'Robert Grynkyn of this Cittie watchmaker informeth that yesterday being the 17th of [May] this informant being in the company of John Bond of this Cittie Barber in the house of Marke Browning of this Cittie Innkeeper about XII of the Clocke att noone, and this informant speaking then with one Jeremy Hancocke the Tapster of the said house, and expressinge some sorrowe of the disaster that had fallen the day before in the West partes, and that soe manie men had byn slayne there, the said Bond said Pishe, what needs thee to ... sorrowe, I am nothing sorrowe at all, It is no matter if they had all suffered.'

Source: EQSOB, 64, ff.34, 42

Document 15: Treatment of a suspected spy

This document (written by a Royalist sympathiser) gives an account of the sufferings of Dr William Coxe, one of the Cathedral Canons, whom Hopton had sent to Exeter with peace proposals in June 1643. The harsh treatment meted out to Coxe upon his arrival was surely indicative of Parliamentarian panic following the recent defeat at Stratton (see chapter 4, p. 77). The Roundhead 'Lieutenant Down' who accused Coxe of being a 'Jesuit', or catholic priest, was probably a relative of Mark Down, one of Exeter's puritan ministers.

'After the victory obtained over the rebels ... it was the fortune of ...

[Dr. Cox] to be despatched ... with some proposals of peace, to the garrison of Exeter. When the Doctor arrived at the first guard, he was blind-folded, and in that manner conducted to the quarters of the Earl of Stamford, who received him in a manner very unbecoming ... For he gave him all the reproachful names he could imagine, and sware he would hang him instantly. But first, to extort a confession from him, he offers a knife or dagger to his breast, demanding an answer to some questions which he then asked him.

The Doctor ... replied that he was ordered to deliver some letters from the Army in Cornwall, but had no commission to answer any questions. Upon which the Earl renews his reproaches, and makes offers to stab him; but, finding he could not terrifie the Doctor into a compliance, he then demands of him the letters that he had brought. The handkerchief wherewith the Doctor was hoodwinked had been fastened with a pin, which he had to that time held in his hand, after he had pulled the handkerchief off; and going to take the letters out of his pocket, he put the pin into his mouth; upon which one Major Baxter cried out, What doth the rogue eat there? He swallows papers of intelligence!

Thereupon the Earl, forgetting his peerage, began, in a ridiculous manner, to leap, and skip, and frisk, and cried out Treason! and that he [Cox] was come to betray the city. And presently, clapping his dagger to the Doctor's breast, demanded what it was that he had put into his mouth. The Doctor mildly told him it was the pin, and shewed it him. But the Major, not being satisfied with that answer, presently flies at him, takes him by the throat, and gripped him so hard that he had almost strangled him; whilst the Earl himself cries out, Cut the villain's throat, cut it, and offered to do it with his own hands, putting his knife to it thrice for that purpose; but the Doctor, struggling, still put it by. After this, others that were in the room beat him about the head with their fists. Others scratched his face. Some search his ears, others his mouth (stretching them to such a degree that they put him to great torture) to find out papers. Nor was this all, for they tore his hair from his head; and one forced his fingers down his very throat, insomuch that, at last, he fainted away under their barbarous usage, and was very like to have expired upon the place.

The Doctor had a trumpeter sent with him when he came upon the message, whom they treated in a barbarous manner also, but not to that degree they did the Doctor himself. After this they were both ordered into an outer room, where the same insolencies are again renewed, and the very dreggs of the people animated to be executioners of those barbarities upon the Doctor. From hence they are committed to prison, where they are both stripped naked, and their cloaths narrowly searched; but, no papers yet appearing, they were resolved to search within as well as without, and in a manner to turn them inside outside, and for this purpose prepared two vomits, which they forced them to take, and ply the Doctor more especially with posset drink, and an infusion in it to promote the operation. And, tho' they saw that what came from him was with great difficulty and torment, yet they kept him all night upon this rack, till at last it drew the blood from him.

This inhuman usage brought the Doctor so low that in three days he was not able to receive any subsistence; and, during this extremity and weakness, many of the townspeople came to see him, as if he had been a publick shew, who, instead of pitying, revile and reproach him. And, among the rest, one Lieutenant Down, rushing one night into the chamber, asked for the Jesuit, and, calling him rogue and all those other vile names which himself deserved, offered to have murdered him, had not a soldier then present interposed.

After the Doctor had recovered strength enough ... he was brought before the council of war, where he complained of his usage. But I do not find that he had any satisfaction made him; instead ... he was sent to be imprisoned on board the ships (a very common way of dealing with the clergy in those times) at Topsham, where the stench and noysome smell had almost poisoned him. The Doctor's lady, hearing of her husband's barbarous usage, hastened to him at Exeter, and with much entreaty obtained leave to go on shipboard to see him, but at her return was herself imprisoned, till the ship in which her husband was confined sailed out of the river for London, where the Doctor was long detained a prisoner.'

Source: F.C. Hingeston Randolph (ed.), *Dr Walker's 'Sufferings of the Clergy' in the Diocese of Exeter during the Great Rebellion* (Plymouth, 1908), pp. 54–55

Document 16: The sufferings of Doctor Whynell

The document reproduced below tells the story of Dr John Whynell, minister of St John's parish, who refused to take the Parliamentarian oath, or Covenant (see document 10), and was punished by the Roundhead authorities as a result. What makes the account particularly interesting is the fact that it reproduces, apparently verbatim, the words of a relatively humble Exeter woman who had witnessed the events described.

'When My Lord Stanford was sent with a percell of Gray Cots to govern that Ceety [i.e. Exeter], Doctor Weynell had a house opposite to St Johns Church and on a Sunday afternoon as he and his wife ware going to Church comes one Mr Brookeing [a Parliamentarian member of the Committee for Safety] and another to him with a paper and tould him hee must take that Oth which hee refused telling them hee could not but they prest him though hee still denighed. Then hee was tould by them hee must reed it in the Church: and after much ado hee said that hee might do, which affter sermon hee did [marginal note: 'Brooking and others stayd to heare it reed'] and turned to a place of Scriptur: that an Oth must be taken in truth, richusness and judgement and desired them [i.e. his parishioners] to looke on a table which hung up in ye Church in which was the protistation [see document 2] and a greate many of thar hands ware to it, and then was going out of the Church att the littell door under the Bow, but then some of his parishiones cot hold of him and desired to know how they must do it when hee set an exampell to the contrary: att which he tould them they might better then hee for hee in all ye degrees hee had taken [had] swore to ye King:

So Mr Brooking and the other, never leting him step home, car[ri]ed him before My Lord Stanford: and aleaged against him his refusing to take the Oth and of what an ill consequens it was that it hindred his parish likeways: for which My Lord gave him sharp reperamands and ordred hee shud be hanged [marginal note: 'ther was a galos on Estgate on purpose to hang such as they disliked'] which the Doctor desired might not be till hee had been tryed to which My Lord answred hee had had Tryall enough; but how ever My Lord said hee shud be banashed and it shud be death [to] whoever shud releve him or take him in and hee was not to go further than thare own gards with out the gats: so out att Estgate hee was put and orders given to plunder his house: which some of his naighbors heareing secured all that was valeable over gardens backwards for him. The first night hee was walking before Mr Mathew's dore without Southgate not knowing whare to rest and old Mrs Mathews, Mrs Burnell's grand mother, said to him shee knew how twas with him but hee shud not ly in the streets but shee wood entertaine him: hee was very unwilling shee shud rune such a hasard but shee said shee did not care and made him come in that night: and from thens he went to his house att St Lenards which was lett to tenents: but filled with Roundheads: amongst which was on Corll [i.e. 'Colonel'?] Semor who was extreme sevell [i.e. 'civil'] to ye Doctor.

Till now his pore wife knew not whare to find him and so went thether to see him: and on her returne Southgat by reson of the seegs was shut up only the wickett [was open] but as shee was steping throw it one Bagster, an ingeneare, tould her she shud not come in for shee had car[ri]ed intelegenes to the King's Army which lay in Hevetree: [marginal note: 'shee was big with child'] and held a muskett to her brest telling her shee shud be shot if shee atemted to come in and had given the same orders att all the gates: on which she returned to St Lenerds and found Corll Semor walking with the Doctor to whome shee complined of this fellow: so the Corll said what had hee [i.e. Bagster] to do to act as he did, it was not his plais to do so but advised the Doctor to draw up a pitision to My Lord for the Doctor and shee to be att thare house in town or to be in the Country and he would go with her: but when that was done they let the Corll in but wood have keipt her out till My Lorde [sic: slip for 'Semor'?] said he wood throw up his comition: so they let her in but Bagster was not tharein but left such ordus [i.e. orders to let her in]: hee was att My Lords and when hee saw her wispred 'My Lord': however shee gave her pitision which very complysantly hee refused to answer telling her hee could not grant it for it might occation him a delle of displesuer: but by her impertunety: after a long delebration hee tould her shee shud go to the Mayor and he shud do what hee wood: which shee desired him to insert under her pettision: My Lord was loth to do it but att last did.

One Mr Clarke was Mayor, an honist king's man and her frend, who was willing to grant it and was seconded by Alderman Crosing: but Alderman White stood up and protested if it was so hee wood never more apeare thare: on which Mrs Weynell desired to know why hee was agaynst the Doctor that had been old frends: and hee said hee was a man that did more mischife than a littell armey and besides hee was against the Cause: so the Mayor called her aside [and told her] hee durst not press it for twas in thare power to serve him as they had the doctor but shee shud come another day on which My Lord Stanford wood be thare, which shee did but hee was not in Court but sent his secretery who sayed Doctor Weynell was a limb of Anty-Christ for hee preached up sedition and was for popery and refused the oth, Ergo, hee was a limb of the Anty-Christ and Mrs Weynell tould him if that was all the proufe hee could bring, Ergo, hee was a fooll: this set the whole Court in to such a laughter as made him rune out.

After this shee went and remained att St Lenerds till the seegs grew so warme that the bullets came throw the curtens and was like to have murdred them, so the maid tooke up as meny as shee could car[ri]e in her apron and went to My Lord Stanford, who forsaw the Ceety could not hold long, so hee tould the maid her Maister and Mistress might go whare they wood for secuerety: then they went to Heveytree to the King's Army whare they ware treted well and the Doctor who had formally practised phisick was made Phisition Generall to all the Western Army: and in a littell time the Ceety was taken and they returned to thare house.'

Source: Bod., J. Walker MSS, C.2, ff.252-252r.

Document 17: *Death of a bystander*

This extract from the burial register of St Edmunds parish is dated 7 July 1643 and records the accidental death by shooting of the parish clerk's teenage son during the Royalist occupation of St Thomas (see chapter 4, p. 80). The document shows how ordinary people could become caught up in the struggle between King and Parliament, with tragic results. It also contains a somewhat confusing contemporary assessment of just what the two sides were fighting over.

[The burial is recorded of] 'Hoyle, William, son of James, and the daye beeffore hee was stricken ded with a bollett through the hed and thatt day theare was an Exterordenary fight beetweene the Cittey and those which came against them in this year Anno: 1643, which was called by the name of Cavaleeres, which came for the Kinges Right; and to fight for the Parliament's Right to deceve the Kinge of his Right if possibell, per mee, James Hoyle, parish clarke.'

Source: WCSL, J. Nesbitt (ed.), 'St Edmond's Parish Register', (DCRS, 1932), p. 54

DOCUMENTS

Document 18: Letter from one of the besieged

This letter, sent out of Exeter in August 1643 and later reprinted in a Roundhead news-pamphlet, gives a good idea of the situation in the city towards the end of the first siege. Particularly interesting is the author's assertion that, after having heard rumours of the disorder which had accompanied the recent capture of Bristol by the King's forces, the Exeter Royalists had been frightened into contributing towards their own city's defence. This was precisely the sort of reaction which Civil War propagandists hoped to obtain by peddling exaggerated stories of the other side's 'atrocities' (see chapter 5, p. 87 and document 22)

'The
COPIE OF A LETTER
sent from
EXETER
By a gentleman of quality, to a worthy
friend of his dwelling in London . . .

Sir, The miserable estate and condition of our city I conceive is sufficiently known, yet there hath not any wayes, or meanes, beene neglected by our Maior, Aldermen, and the rest of those worthy citizens, who have been both vigilant and watchfull for prevention of danger; and although some part of this our citie is surrounded (and by those bloodthirsty people which seek to destroy us, our lives, liberty, and religion) yet we hope in due time to asswage their malice, and confound their devices.

There was lately a hot fight between us and our enemy, and cannons plaid on both sides, but little or no hurt done, onely we took eighty or thereabouts of them prisoners. Since which time, Sir William Courtney commander in chief, Collonel Actland, Collonel Fulford, and the rest of the Kings partie, have laid at ease, eating and drinking up the sweat of poore men's labours. The Cavalleres with their numbers amounting neere upon three thousand horse and foot, lyeth at Apsom, Saint Thomas his parish, Affington, and the passage betweene Kirton and Exeter. As for the east and southerne part we have free passage, and have daily great supplies of provision from Tiverton, Silferton, Collompton, and Bradninch, but for how long this will so continue, God knowes, we feare not long, but suspect that a greater force will shortly environ us from

Bristol, and so besiege all parts. Wee stand onely upon our guard, and thinke it not fit to sally out to raise the siege, for feare of being put to retreat and disorder we should not have sufficient to manage our workes; as our enemy lyeth upon advantage, so we expect aide from Plimouth and Dartmouth, till which time here can be no issue of the businesse . . .'

'The malignant prisoners, both gentlemen and clergy now in durance, were, upon the Cavaliers besieging our city, very deboist [i.e. debauched], and mutinous, swearing they would burne and fire the houses over their heads, and although I call them prisoners, yet they had too much liberty, going and comming when and where they pleased, such ingrateful persons are worthy of restraint, and are rewarded since accordingly. At Ratford house, where the late Judge Dodderidge lived, we have mounted 3 peeces of ordnance, and fifty or sixty musketiers, to keepe the enemy from comming over the river, yet such is their desperatenesse, that they attempt it daily, and come over robbing and stealing our horse, sheep, and cattle, and make much spoil, that neither they nor their commanders have any feare of God, or rule of good manners. Sir John Barkely, a great commander of the Cavaliers, hath done very great spoil amongst us, posting to and fro with 150 horse, imposing upon the subject such heavie taxations, that the subject cannot bear; their horses and goods plundered, their persons threatned, and imprisoned, and I think it is no newes to the world, that this county hath . . . its share of troubles.'

'Yet God is all sufficient, and wee doubt not but hee will strengthen us, as daily he doth; for since the surrendring of Bristol, where within 24 houres after we heard the truth thereof, how the matter was caried, and upon what terms the souldiers and inhabitants should depart, as in the articles of agreement is largely expressed, none of which being performed, but the city rifled, yea, and all both friend and foe, though the Malignants to be known from others stucke greene boughes at their doores, and wore them in their hats; yet being all pillaged, the Malignants amongst us knowing that they shall taste of the same sauce, if the like occasion happen to us as in Bristol, begin to be well affected, and encourageth the rest, and at this present doe voluntarily as hard duty as a common souldier; so that those Malignants amongst us that are of strength and ability, I am perswaded, will shew themselves more forward in this wrong cause, as they terme it, for the love of their goods, then any other man amongst us. Therefore if any assistance come to us speedily, we doubt not but to remove those ill neighbours about us, and be at liberty. I cannot certifie you with more then I have said of the proceedings amongst us, but wee have had lately intelligence from Bristol, that there is a regiment or two upon the march, or ready to march at Dorchester and Waymouth, I see not how, or who should resist them; neither is it expected that there can be prevention given, unlesse some considerable force be sent downe to joyne with the country, and to resist and make head . . .

Thus praying to God to deliver us out of the hands of our oppressors, I rest,

Your affectionate friend, I.S. Exeter, Aug.3. 1643.'

Source: E.65 (2)

Document 19: The siege of 1643, a Parliamentarian account

This account of the second siege was clearly written by someone who wished to clear the Earl of Stamford of the charges of cowardice and incompetence which had been levelled at him following the defeat at Stratton. Note the writer's attribution of Exeter's eventual surrender to the apathy of the townsfolk.

[Stamford's defeat at Stratton is first described] '. . . and so to Exeter, where he [Stamford] was besieged by young Chidleigh . . . and continued besieged three monthes and nineteene dayes; during which time, we heare it was laboured in the city of London on the behalfe of the Earle that there might be 2,000 of their new auxiliaries sent thither by sea, with the Earle of Warwick, who otherwise attempted the raising of the siege, but either for want of that strength or else by the treachery of Sir Alexander Cary . . . could not effect it, though he lost three ships in attempting it . . .

But no supply coming from the city of London or elsewhere, nor intelligence passing, the siege was so streight, and the citizens of Exeter not well stomaching their souldiers, nor paying them, nor quartering them like men, suffering hundreds of them to lye upon [market] stalls, whereby above a thousand of them ran away, and most probably to the enemy: they urged the Earle to their conditions, although the enemy himselfe had but two dayes before offered fifteen dayes time to send to the Parliament for aid, or else to render upon honourable conditions, which was then refused, but these are plausible enough to those that hope only to be quiet in this world, and wish for peace and pardon at any rate, which I beleeve they shall as well enjoy as their apple trees.

Sir, I shall adde one thing more, to tell you the generosity of the city of Exeter, and their affections to the Parliament's armes, that although the 500 men left in the town had indured so many assaults, watcht constantly every second night, and sometimes foure or five together, and in one of many sallyes had slaine, and taken 200 men, and brought away three pieces of ordnance, and withall they had not lost one inch of ground, would not pay the souldiers nor commanders in the towne, nor give them one farthing at their going out of it.'

Source: DRO, ECA, Press XI, Vol.390 B, 'Articles of Agreement'

Document 20: The siege of 1643, a Royalist account

[This is an extract from the narrative of Colonel Joseph Bamfield, one of the two Royalist Colonels who led the final assault upon the city (see chapter 4, p. 84)

'In the month of June . . . [1643], his Majestie sent Prince Maurits . . . with an army into the west, whereof my regiment was part; to joyne with my Lord Hopton, and Lord Berkeley; who had beaten the Parlement's forces, commanded by the Earle of Stamford, not long before . . . : the conjunction was made . . . [and] the body of the army marched, towards Generall Waller, haveing first despatched my Lord Berkelay, with foure regiments of foote, and some few troupes of horse, to blocque up Exeter, to prevent the Earl of Stamford's raising of forces in Devonshire, who was Generall in the West for the Parlament; but after the Battaile of Stratton reduced to the gouvernment of that citty.

The first day, wee came before it; the enemy despising our small number; sallied out, with a very considerable party; but was vigorously repulsed, beaten, and some of their out worcks, and the south subburbs possessed; which by reason of our want of amunition; and our few forces wee quitted of our own accord, very many of their men where killed, and taken prisoners. The siege continued about twoe months: the Parlament endeavoured twice to succour it, once by land, from Plimouth, and

Dartmouth; which were suprised in their march, beaten and totally dissipated.

Secondly by sea, with the Parlament's fleet, commanded by the Earl of Warwich, having two thowsand souldiers aboarde, which he designed to land at Apsom [Topsham], under the favour of his cannon; but was prevented by our sinking (the night before) divers vessels with stones in the channel. He endeavoured to land at other places on the strand, in his long botes; but was always repulsed with loss, one of his ships was fired by us; another so raked through, by our cannon; that they were constrayned to fire it themselves, not able to bring it of[f].

About this time Bristol was taken by the King's forces. Prince Maurits arrived before Exeter, with about 3,000 Cornish foote, and some horse; having viewed all the quarters, and approches; resolved on an attaque, by the South Gate; which was committed to Colonel Chudly, and mee; with 2,000 men, the manner left to ourselves, at the place where wee intended to fall on; the enemy had twoe out guards, advanced from the Southgate, the distance of musquet shot, of about 3 or 400 men; with a line of communications from the port to the outworks, which, wee could perceive was but slightly mand; wee resolved with firelocks, and pikemen, with pistols by their sydes; that lighted matches should not discover our designe; to march silently an hower before break of day, to assault the line jointly, by way of suprise: he on the left hand near the outguarde, I on the right, neer the port; hopeing therby (if successfull) to cut of[f] the retreat of the enemy, which wee did; by this meanes all in the out works, were either killed, or taken. Whereupon wee lodged ourselves under the wall, reasnably wel couvered; soe neer the port that they durst not attempt a sally: in this condition and consternation; they beat a parley, desired a treaty, sent out hostages; Sir Richard Cave and I, were employed to treat, and had the place rendered even on our owne tearmes.'

Source: J. Bamfield, *Colonel Joseph Bamfield's Apologie*, (The Hague, 1685)

Document 21: Attack and surrender, September 1643

This account of the final attack on Exeter and the city's subsequent surrender is taken from the Royalist newspamphlet, Mercurius Aulicus, *a publication which customarily adopted an arch, somewhat sarcastic, style. Note the ridicule directed at the Earl of Stamford.*

'And now, reader, I must give thee a sad relation which (if you either love the King or his enemies) will certainly much affect thee; which (in a word) is, that on Monday last Prince Maurice took possession of the city of Exceter for His Majesty. For Biddeford, Appleford [i.e. Appledore], and Barnstaple being all delivered up to the King's Forces, the rebellious city of Exceter was the chiefe place stood out in the West; Prince Maurice therefore being desirous to make a short worke of the war in those parts gave a very hot assault upon the city upon Sunday last, and did not onlye shake the wals in severall places, but by shooting granadoes into the towne, had fired a good part of the suburbs: the souldiers and others in the towne, seeing the greatnesse of their danger, desired a parley, in which the Prince offered them such conditions as had beene given before to Bristol; which being rejected by the Rebells (who would needes stand it out a little longer upon point of honour) His Majestie's forces pursued the assault so eagerly the next day after, that they made themselves masters of the great sconce or bulwark, and turned the ordnance thereof on the towne itselfe. Which being perceived by the Rebels and finding that there was no hope of life and safety, but in the seasonablenesse of their submission, they humbly craved to be admitted unto those conditions which before they rejected, and (above their deservings) did obtaine the same.

According to which conditions the towne and castle was delivered to the Prince his Highnesse with all the ordnance, armes and ammunition which was left therin, the city absolutely left to the gracious disposall of His Majesty, the commanders and officers of the Rebells dismissed in safety with their swords by their sides and the common souldiers with cudgels in their hands (which with a little printing will perhaps grow to be swordes next weeke) and they were suffered to take away such goods as were properly and truly theirs. And so this proud city which had so long bid defiance to their native and gracious soveraigne was at last reduced into the power of His Sacred Majesty, and that noble and valiant gentleman Sir John Berkley, who had deserved so much in the whole course of this service, was declared governour therof. It was observed, that when the officers and souldiers issued out of the towne, the Earle of Stamford was found missing, and no word as yet what had become of the man . . . he durst not trust himselfe unto this agreement, but privately slipt out of the towne in some poore disguise. And so the noble, valiant, chaste Earl of Stamford, full of vertue and honour, crept out of

Exceter after he had begged his life, who not two dayes agoe told the Prince, that "not want of courage or sufficient meanes for his subsistence in the citie, but an earnest desire to come and die in His Majestie's favour had made him doe what he did".'

Source: Bod., 4.M.68.Art, *Mercurius Aulicus*, 3–10 September 1643

Document 22: Articles for the surrender of Exeter, 1643

These are the surrender terms which were agreed upon by Stamford and Prince Maurice shortly after the final Royalist attack. The articles show that the defenders were anxious to preserve their consciences, as well as their lives and 'liberties', when the Royalists finally marched in. The fear of 'popery' which obsessed so many of the citizens is hinted at in articles 6 and 9, while article 11 (which the Royalists later chose to ignore, see chapter 5, pp. 93–94 and document 26) provides further evidence of the contemporary dread of being forced to take a 'false oath'.

'ARTICLES OF AGREEMENT
Betweene His EXCELLENCY
PRINCE MAURICE,
and the EARLE of
STAMFORD
Upon the delivery of the City of
EXCESTER, The
fifth of September 1643 . . .

1. It is concluded and agreed on, that the city and castle of Exon be surrendred into the hands of his Highnesse Prince Maurice, with all armes, ensignes, ordnance, ammunition, and all other warlike provisions whatsoever within the said city and castle.

2. That the right honourable Henry Earle of Stanford together with all officers above the degree of lieutenants, both of horse and foote, now within and about this city and castle, do march out of this city and castle, on Thursday the 7 of this moneth, by nine of the clock in the morning, with their troopes of horse, full armes, bagg and baggage, provided it be their owne goods, and that the lieutenants and ensignes march out with their swords at the East Gate, and that the foot souldiers march out at the same time leaving their armes at the Guildhall, all having a safe

convoy to Winsor or to goe elsewere if they please, and such as will stay shall have pay in the King's army.

3. That there be carriages allowed and provided to carry away their bagg and baggage, and sick and hurt souldiers, and that an especiall care be taken of such officers and souldiers as (being sick and wounded) shall be by the Earl of Stanford left behind in the said city, and that upon their recovery they shall have passes to depart to their owne homes respectively.

4. That the King's forces march not into the city till the Parliament's forces are marched out, except 100 musketteeres at the East part through which they passe.

5. That his Highnesse shall forthwith procure a free and generall pardon unto Henry Earle of Stanford, Sir George Chudleigh, Sir John Bampfield, Sir John Northcot, Baronets, Sir Samuel Roberts [sic, error for Rolle], and Sir Nicholas Martin, knights, and unto the Maior, Bailifs and Cominalty of the city of Exon, and to all other persons of what degree, condition, or quality soever, now being within the said city of Exon, for all treasons and other offences whatsoever committed by them, or any of them since the beginning of this present Parliament relating to these unhappy differences between His Majesty and the two houses of Parliament, and that all or any of them shall have his particular pardon for the foresaid offences or treasons if he shall sue forth the same.

6. That the true Protestant religion now established by law shall be preserved and exercised in the city.

7. That all persons, citizens and inhabitants may at any time depart with their families, goods and estates, unto any part of this Kingdome, and that they and every of them shall have power to dispose, sell or alien either by themselves or others, whatsoever goods or parts of their estates, they shall not convey or carry with them.

8. That all persons now in this city may have free liberty to repaire to their houses in the countrey or elsewhere, and there to remaine in safety, and enjoy their estates, lands, rents, and goods without plundering, fine or imprisonment, or any other molestation, and may travell to and fro without any interruption, hindrance or deniall.

9. That all ministers and preachers of God's word now within this city

shall have free liberty either to stay here or go to their own houses, cures or charges, or elsewhere within his Majestie's dominions, with their wives, children, families and goods, there to abide peaceably and to exercise their ministeriall functions, and to enjoy their estates according to the laws of the land.

10. That all the charters, liberties, priviledges and franchises, lands, estates, goods and debts of the said city shall be preserved and confirmed, and that the ancient government thereof, the present governours and officers may remaine and continue in their former condition.

11. That no new oath or protestation be enforced upon any, nor any compelled to take up arms against the Parliament.

12. That for avoiding inconveniences and distractions the quartering of souldiers be referred to the Maior and Governour of the city for the time being.

13. That all these articles which are now agreed upon shall be ratified and confirmed by His Majesty under the great seal of England.

14. That the officers and souldiers in their marching out shall not be reproached, or have any disgracefull speeches or affronts offered or given unto them by any officer or souldier of the King's, and that the convoy appointed to march with them may goe and returne safely without any violence or wrong offered unto them by any force of the adverse party.'

Source: DRO, ECA, Press XI, vol. 390 B

Document 23: Extract from a Parliamentarian newsbook, September 1643

This vivid description of alleged Royalist atrocities in Exeter circulated widely during the closing months of 1643. But, despite the author's claims that he himself was a Devonshire man and had been present at the city's surrender, the account is suspiciously short of local detail. Moreover, it is flatly contradicted by several other sources (see ch. 5, p. 87). Bearing this in mind, it is tempting to conclude that the piece was not an accurate report of events but rather a work of black propaganda, of the type which was so common during the 1640s. Note the author's assumption that his pamphlet would be heard as well as read; Civil War newsbooks were commonly read out aloud to the illiterate by their better educated neighbours.

'Exeter, that famous city in the West, having most nobly for the space of 3 moneths defended itself . . . [has surrendered]. The articles agreed upon I could here relate, but that I have greater matters to insist upon . . . and besides there hath been something already printed concerning the said articles [see document 20]. Now therefore, I hold it a fit and convenient time to relate unto you the cruell and unlawfull dealings of the Cavaliers, after they had entered into the city.

Whereby all that reads, or heares this book read, may the better understand how farre the destroying Enemies are from keeping their promises, and how little conscience they make of their wayes: for it is too well known in all the western part, that they which are called Prince Ruperts and Prince Maurice his Cavaliers are most of them addicted to such cruelties, that they shew themselves more like Tigers, or Savage Beares, then humane men, and so they may gain wealth they care not who they have it from, nor how they come by it; as shall appear in this following discourse, wherein shall be exprest nothing but what I the Author of this Newes was an eye-witnesse of, and will maintain it against all objections.

The Cavaliers having entered the forenamed city of Exceter used the people most cruelly and did all the violence they could do to them, onely sparing their lives; whereby we may perceive how farre they are from keeping their promises which they make. The rude souldiers would not forbeare upon the least discontent given to them to draw their rapiers upon the citizens and wound them, but especially when they are in their cups, they swagger, roare, sweare and domineere, plundering, pillaging or doing any other kind of wrong. To break shops and houses, they count it as nothing, taking away boots, shoes, stockings, hats or any other commodities they can lay their hands on, and no Justice dares to resist them, and by this meanes the city is in such a miserable condition that they are even terrified to the death.

The Majestrates of the city are fined at extraordinary rates, and when they have payed what the Cavaliers demand, they will force them, as they doe in other places, to repay it again. Sir John Berkly by his Majesties authority was made Governour of the city . . . who is a member of such vile disposition that he favours their wicked designes, whereby they become the more audacious. I, being a native in that county, am in very sad and sorrowful condition, for my friends and neighbours, who are

Devonshire men born and bred. O that I could weep tears of bloud for them, which by treachery are brought to everlasting slavery!'

Source: E.70 (13)

Document 24: List of the city ordnance

This document, which lists all the cannon mounted around the defensive perimeter at Exeter, was almost certainly compiled in the immediate aftermath of the city's surrender. Very similar lists were drawn up for Dartmouth and Weymouth—two other west country towns captured by Prince Maurice in summer 1643—and were subsequently despatched to the main Royalist Ordnance Office at Oxford, presumably so that the Royalist High Command could gain an accurate picture of the resources which were available to them in the West (see I. Roy, (ed.) The Royalist Ordnance Papers: Part 1, (Oxfordshire Record Society, 1963-64), pp. 295, 303-04). The 'Exeter list' seems to have become detached from the main body of Royalist Ordnance Papers, and is printed below for the first time.

'A list of all such guns as are now on the Castle Walles and about the Citty of Exeter on batteries

In the south east of the Castle
2 high sacars all of iron, neare in weight—2200 1/3
1 sacar cut weigheth neere—2100 1/3

In the north west of the Castle
1 Demy culverin of iron neere—3200
1 high sacar in weight neere—2200
1 low sacar cut, neere—2100

In Eastgate below
1 murtherer gros
1 iron drake in the blockhouse & a base with her chambers

On the other side on the toppe of the gate
2 mynyons of iron neere each—1306

On the walles neere East gate on the first and second batteries
2 low sacars neere in weight each—1123

On the next battery
1 high sacar neere in weight—1324

On the same walles neere Southgate
2 iron guns, one sacar, neere—1520
1 mynyon neere in weight—1125

In Southgate below
1 broken sacar

On the toppe of the gate
2 mynyons neere each—1255

On the battery neere Southgate
1 mynion of iron neere of weight—1283

On the Key Battery
2 mynyons of iron neere—1211

On Reeds Battery
1 sacar yt was crack't but amended neere—2231

Under Westgate
1 murtherer gros

At Horse Poole without the gate
2 iron guns, one high sacar, neere—2522
1 long mynyon crack't, weight—935

On the Bridge
2 broken iron guns, one sacar & a faulcon

On the Snaile Tower battery
3 iron guns, one high sacar, neere—2323
2 low sacars, weighing each—1313

On the new battery near Northgate
1 high mynyon—910

On the toppe of Northgate
2 mynyons neere each—1110

Under the gate
1 grosse murtherer

On Brodnidge battery on the walles neere the Castle
1 mynyon neere—1124

All these are iron.

Below in the Castle
1 whole culverin of bras[s] whose mussell is broken away being on his field carriadge and wheeles

On the Maine Guard
1 drake of bras[s]

The store in the Magazeene in Exeter of powder 2500

Match	10,000
Demyculverin shot	40
Sacar shot	90
Mynyon shot	60
Faulcon shot	40
Faulconet shot	20
Ravenet shot	[Blank]

Peeces of all kinds = 41.'

Source: BL, Add.MSS, 27402, f.81

Document 25: Information presented to the City Sessions Court, 1644

These depositions were all made against Parliamentary sympathizers, reflecting the fact that the Exeter sessions court was now staffed by pro-Royalist judges. All of the accused were women, and quite humble ones at that, the first being described as a maid servant, the second as a spinster and the third as a tanner's wife. These outspoken female supporters of Parliament had their Royalist counterparts (see, for example, chapter 6, p. 132) and it is quite clear that, in Exeter at least, women as well as men had become politicized by the national conflict.

Extract I—8 January
'Edward Cleincke and Owen Davye, Barrelbearers, depose that this present day, they comyng into the house of one Andrewe Quashe of this cittie, and being in the shoppe and speaking with the children of the said Quashe there of the report that was then in the said cittie of the routing of Sir William Waller and his forces . . . Marie Morris a servant of the said Quashes being then in one other roome in the said house, came

neare to the said shoppe and called to the said Quashes children, and sayde to them Whie do you talke with those Cavallier Rogues (meaning the said Barrlebearers). And said further to the said Barrlebearers that though the day were theirs nowe yet the longest day would have an end, which words tending to sedition and disheartening of the souldiers in his Majesties service in this Cittie, it is ordered that some of the Constables shall apprehend the said Marie Morris, and bring her before one of the Justices to be examined thereuppon.'

Extract II—20 February
'[Rebecca Fox, of Exeter, spinster, bound over] uppon the informacon of Marie Hayne of this cittie spinster, who deposed 19 instantis the last weeke att a Bakehouse in this Cittie the said Rebecca said that Sir William Waller had manie good prayers to come hither. And if he came he would take a course with all the Cavallier roagues and turne them all out of Towne &c.'

Extract III—1 March
'Margaret Archepole of the parishe of Alphington in the Countie of Devon widowe deposeth that this present Friday in the markett she heard Margaret Way, the wife of John Way of this Cittie leather taner, to speake of the siege that was latelie made by the Kings Majesties Forces against this Cittie and of the Cavalliers, and said that the Roundheadds were better than the Cavaliers. And that she did hope to see the tymes againe.'

Source: EQSOB, 64, ff.48, 50, 52

Document 26: The Oath of Association

The Royalists imposed this oath upon all adult males in Exeter, Devon and Cornwall during early 1644. On a superficial reading, the initial section of the oath seems very similar to the Parliament's Protestation of 1642 (see document 10); both documents swore to uphold the rights of King and Parliament and to protect the 'true reformed Protestant Religion'. The Royalist oath not only swore to protect the Church from 'popery', however, but also from 'innovations of Sectaries and Schismatiques'—from puritanism, in other words. Moreover, it went on to cast doubt upon the 'pretended' authority of Parliament, and to enjoin resistance to the Scots and to the Roundhead garrison of Plymouth. No supporter of Parliament could have taken this oath with a clear conscience, and it is easy to see why the document aroused such widespread opposition in Devon and Exeter (see chapter 5, pp. 93–94).

'I, A.B., doe in the presence of Almighty God promise, vow and protest with my utmost power to maintaine and defend the true reformed Protestant Religion established by Law in this Kingdome against all Popery, Popish and other Innovations of Sectaries and Schismatiques, as also his Majesties person and rights against all forces whatsoever, and in like manner the Laws, liberties and priviledges of Parliament and of this Kingdome.

And I shall to the utmost of my power preserve and defend the peace of the two counties of Cornewall and Devon, and all persons that shall unite themselves by this protestation in the due performancie thereof, and to my power assist His Majesties Armies for reducing the Towne of Plymmouth, and resistance of all forces of Scots invaders and others, leavyed under pretence of any authority of [the] two House of Parliament, or otherwise, without his Majesties personall consent.'

Source: E.30 (1)

Document 27: Petition of Honor Crutchett

Honor Crutchett was the widow of John Crutchett, blacksmith, a man who had worked on the city fortifications during the period of Parliamentary control. Following John's death, Honor wrote this petition in an effort to recover some of the money which he was owed by the Chamber. Unfortunately for her, the Parliamentarian town councillors who had initially ordered the work had now been replaced by pro-Royalist ones, so it seems unlikely that her plea was successful. Her petition illustrates the difficulties which a sudden upheaval in civic government could cause for ordinary people.

'To the right worshippful the maior of the cittie of Exon, the Aldermen his Brethren, and the rest of the common counsell of the said cittie.

The humble peticon of Honor Crutchett, widdowe.

Shewinge: that your poore peticioner hath six children whereof 3 of them can gett somewhat towards their mayntenance, but the other[s] cannot. And a while since your peticioners late husband did worke for the cittie being forced thereunto, and had little or noe other worke of them, but that which she had never any moneyes for, for which there is due to her from the cittie about the sume of £22, Mr Christopher Clarkes worshipp beinge then Maior with Mr John Hackwell & Mr Adam Bennetts worshipps did set their hands to a note of 40s of itt, and Mr Jasper Ratcliffe signed the other note for the rest, which severall notes are ready to be shewen, your peticioner beinge in extreame distresse for want of money, shee owinge an honest debt unto Mr John Elwill [of] about £17, which hath caused her to keepe house these 6 monethes for feare of arrestinge, by which meanes she hath lost her customers soe that she is almost undone.

Wherefore her most humble desire is that your worshipps wilbe pleased to comiserate her cause and to use some speedy meanes that she may be payd her money whereby to pay her debts that she may be att libertie to followe her callinge.

And she shall ever pray for your worshipps prosperitie, & happie government &c.'

Source: DRO, Petitions for Relief, File 3, No.3

Document 28: *The Exeter Oath*

This oath was imposed upon the people of Exeter by the Royalists during summer 1645, in anticipation of a Parliamentary attack. It was the fourth such oath which the inhabitants had been forced to take since 1641, and followed on the heels of the Parliament's Protestation of 1641 (see document 2), the Exeter Covenant of 1642 (see document 9) and the Royalist Oath of Association of 1644 (see document 26).

'I, A.B., do freely and from my heart swear, vow and protest in the presence of Almighty God, that I will use my best endeavour to maintain and defend this city of Exeter against all forces raised or to be raised without his Majesties consent upon any pretence whatsoever, and particularly against the forces now under the command of Sir Thomas Fairfax or any other that shall command them, or any other forces against this city, and all forces which do or shall adhere to them or their party, & I will neither directly nor indirectly give or (so far as in me lieth) suffer to be given any intelligence, advice, or information to the Army or to any of those forces now under the command of Sir Thomas Fairfax, nor to any other forces (not raised by the King's consent) which that now, or at any time hereafter, come against, lie before, or attempt the taking, besieging, or blocking up of this city of Exeter.

But will from time to time discover to the Governor or Lieutenant Governor of this City, any one, and all such as I shal know or probably suspect to give any such intelligence or information. As likewise that I will discover to the Governour or his Lieutenant Governour, all treacheries, plots, designes, conspiracies and attempts, which I shall know, hear of or probably suspect to be intended or plotted against his Majesties Person, or the said city, or any of his Majesties armies, towns, or forces. Neither will I, or shall any other by my procurement, directly, or indirectly, by words or otherwise, disswade or discourage any of the souldiers or the inhabitants of this city from ingaging themselves, or persisting in his Majesties service, or the defence of this city against the forces aforesaid.

And this I vow and protest according to the usuall sense and meaning of the words hereof, without any equivocation or mentall reservation whatsoever, and shall to the utmost of my power observe and perform the same; so help me God.'

Source: E.297 (3)

Document 29: Summons and response, 1646

These documents trace the course of the correspondence between Fairfax and Berkley in January 1646 (see chapter 6, p. 124). Note the reference in Fairfax's second letter to the hardships which were being endured by the civilian population.

Letter I—27 January

'SIR, Being come with my Army into these parts, I thought fit to send you this summons, for the delivery of the City of Exeter, with the Forts, Ordnance, Arms and Ammunition belonging unto the same, unto my hands, for the use of the Parliament. As I do not doubt when I shall attempt the place to carry it, trusting onely in the goodnesse of God, whereof we have had so large experience; so I am not ignorant, but there may be much effusion of bloud on both sides, and of ruine to the Inhabitants of the City, who have suffered so much already, and putting both the Officers and Gentlemen upon extremities, which will make their condition more desparate, then they are at present. To avoyd which, I think good to offer both you and them as followeth:

To your self, and all the Officers, Lords and Gentlemen (not excepted by Parliament) liberty to go home with all your goods to your houses, there to live peaceably, or passes to go beyond sea (if desired) and to give you Letters reccomendatory for the obtaining moderate compositions for your estates in giving yourselves by promise never to beare Armes against the Parliament, nor to do any thing to the prejudice of their affaires. To the Citizens and Townesmen, a free enjoyment of their liberties, and estates upon the aforementioned considerations. To the Common Souldiers, liberty to go home peaceably to their habitations, upon like promise, never to beare Armes against the Parliament, nor to do anything to the prejudice of their affaires.

If your honour be inclined to accept of this offer, I shall be glad, if you refuse it (as I thinke you cannot reasonably and possibly expect relief) Sir, the extremity which (by your refusall) will come upon upon the Inhabitants and Common Souldiers will lye upon your accompt; and truly Sir, the Artifice (to say no more of it) whereby those poore people have been deluded by feeding them with the hopes of the Kings coming with an Army out of the East to their rescue, and the Prince his coming out of the West, will not answer the misery, and ruine you will bring upon them, which to avoid is the cause of this my offer to you, and to which I expect your speedy answer, and rest

Your Servant, Thomas Fairfax.'

Source: E.320 (18)

Letter II—28 January

'SIR, I have received your summons for the delivery of this place for the use of the Parliament, this trust was derived unto me from his Majesty, which I shall endeavour to discharge to the best of my power through God's assistance, had I other inclinations they would have bin diverted by your propositions, the most important being not cleere, for we known not who are excepted, how far your recommendations will prevaile, what Compositions will be thought moderate, or if they be beyond our abilities; with what rigour they will be exacted, if all the actions of our lives whatsoever were but as innocent as our hands are of the bloud that shall bee shed in the defence of our most righteous Cause, we should in all events rest in perfect peace of mind, however we have no reason to despaire of God's blessings who is able to deliver us, and may at present without a miracle, his highness having so considerable a force at so neere distance to us, we are the farther off, yet my honour and duty is still neere unto me who am,

Your Servant, John Berkley.'

Source: E.320 (21)

Letter III—29 January

'SIR, To your refusall (to maintain the City of Exeter) upon the obligations of honour and duty mentioned in your Answer to your Summons, I shall not have thought fit to have made any Reply, those rules being as you say neerest to your self, and therefore as to your self, are to be judged of by you; but because I conceive you set too low an esteem upon those Propositions which are made to the Officers and Gentlemen, and do a little reflect on the Honour of the Parliament and my own: I think myself bound to say somewhat in vindication thereof, they that have hitherto tasted of their favour upon a voluntary submission (who are not a few) are sufficient witnesses of the Mercy and Moderation of the Parliament in the Fines imposed on them, and for exacting with rigour what hath been so imposed; I believe that one instance can be given thereof in all the Kingdome, I can with contentment give way to your low opinion of the prevalency of my recommendation, upon the smallnesse of my merit, to which I say no more; however in that I undertake to be Master of my Honour and Word to them that trust me, and perhaps it would not be so fruitlesse as you imagine. Who are personally excepted by the Parliament, I am not able to give you a present accompt, neither can I say there are any such within your Garrison. As I had power to give you a summons, so I believe it lyes also in my power to give souldiers souldierly conditions, and thus you have a Reply to all, Because (as I said before) you mentioned Duty and Conscience, and forgot in your Answer (that which seemes to me as incumbent upon both, as any thing you have said) to wit, a due care of the Inhabitants of that poor and miserable place you are in, made so by fireing of so many of their Habitations, and those heavy pressures wherewith they have been so long burthened, and now the exposing them to the deprivation of their lives, and that little estate that is left them, that I say you should speak of conscience, and forget; this seemes very strange to mee. That your eyes may be opened, and they beste provided for, is the wishe of,

Your Servant, Fairfax.'

Source: E.320 (22)

Document 30: Treaty of surrender, 1646

These are the surrender terms which were eventually agreed on by Fairfax and Berkeley in April 1646, following the protracted negotiations at Poltimore House (see chapter 6, pp. 133–34). As had been the case in 1643, the defenders sought to ensure that no new oaths would be imposed upon the inhabitants, while particular care was taken to preserve the city churches from the sort of devastation which had occurred during the initial period of Parliamentary control (see articles 5 and 21).

'Articles of agreement concluded on by Thomas Hammond, Lieutenant-general of the ordnance, Colonel Sir Hardress Waller, Colonel Edward Harley, Colonel Lambert, Commissary-general Stane, and Major Watson, Scoutmaster-general, commissioners on the behalf of the right honourable his Excellency Sir Thomas Fairfax, General of the Parliament's forces, on the one party; and Sir Henry Berkeley, Sir George Cary, Colonel Ashburnham, Colonel Godolphin, Captain Fitz-Gerald, Master Jo. Weare, Master Robert Walker, and Master Thomas Knight [sic, error for 'Knott'], commissioners on the behalf of Sir John Berkeley knight, governor of the city of Excester, on the other party, touching and concerning the rendition of the said city and garrison, as followeth:

I. That the city and garrison of Excester, together with the castle, and all forts and mounts, places of defence, of or belonging to the same, with all ordnance, arms, and ammunition, provisions and furniture of war belonging to the garrison, (excepting what shall be excepted in the ensuing articles), shall be delivered unto Sir Thomas Fairfax, general of the parliament's forces, or to any whom he shall appoint to receive them, for the use of the parliament, on Monday next after the date hereof, being the thirteenth of this instant April, by twelve of the clock at noon.

II. That if any officer, soldier, or any person included in these articles, wrong or plunder in person or goods (in their march away or before) any citizen or countryman, or any person whatsoever, he shall, as far as he is able, give satisfaction to the persons so injured at the judgment of his excellency Sir Thomas Fairfax.

III. That if any officer, soldier, or any person (included in these articles) shall, after the date hereof, wilfully break, deface, spoil, or embezzle any arms, or other provisions of war whatsoever, by the precedent articles to be surrendered as aforesaid, he shall lose the benefit of the ensuing articles.

IV. That the princess Henrietta and her governess, with her household, shall have full liberty to pass with their plate, moneys, and goods, within twenty days after the conclusion of this treaty, (when she shall desire,) to any place within the continent of England or dominion of Wales, at the election of the governess . . . and that fit and convenient carriages be provided for their passage, at reasonable rates.

V. That the cathedral church, nor any other church within the city shall be defaced, or any thing belonging thereunto spoiled or taken away by any soldier or person of either side whatsoever.

VI. That the governor, together with all lords, clergymen, gentlemen, captains, officers, troopers, and common soldiers, shall march out of the city on Monday next, the 13th of April, by twelve of the clock at noon, with their horses, full arms, bag and baggage, and their goods, colours flying, drums beating, matches lighted, bullets, full bandaliers, with sufficient convoys unto Oxford, or unto Helston in Cornwall, at their several elections, and in case the governor of Oxford shall refuse to receive the common soldiers that shall march thither, they are there to deliver up their arms to the convoy, and have passes to repair to their several homes, and those that march unto Helston are there to be disbanded, and to have passes to their several homes. That all troopers and common soldiers which march not as aforesaid shall deliver up their arms, except their swords, and have liberty to go to their own homes with bag and baggage, and shall not be compelled to take up arms against the king.

VII. That all those which shall march to the garrisons aforesaid shall have free quarter in their march, and not be obliged to march above ten miles a day, and that such other soldiers as are inhabitants in the city shall receive free liberty to march out or remain therein, without being compelled to take up arms against the king; and if any soldiers fall sick upon their march, that convenient carriages and accommodations shall be provided for them.

VIII. That all lords, gentlemen, clergymen, chaplains, and officers, that shall choose to go beyond the seas, shall march away with their full arms for their own use; and that all common soldiers shall march away with their full arms, with a sufficient convoy unto the port which they shall choose for their transportation; which arms they shall there lay down and deliver unto the governor of the next garrison belonging to the parliament.

IX. That neither the officers, soldiers, nor any person whatsoever, in their going out of the city, shall be reproached, or have any disgraceful speeches or affront offered to them, or any of their persons wronged, rifled, searched, or their goods seized, or taken away from them by any person whatsoever.

X. That the governors, lords, gentlemen, clergymen, chaplains, commanders, oficers and soldiers, comprised in these articles, shall be allowed and assisted in providing of sufficient carriages at reasonable rates to carry away their bag, baggage, and goods; and that care be taken, by the future governor of the said city, for the curing of such sick or wounded officers and soldiers as shall be left in the city, and that upon recovery they shall have passes to repair to their own houses respectively.

XI. That the parliament forces come not into the city until the king's forces be marched out, except 150 foot, and one troop of horse, with their officers.

XII. That no lords, knights, gentlemen, clergymen, chaplains, (excepting those who are by name excepted by parliament from pardon and composition), officers, citizens, and soldiers, and all other persons comprised within these articles, shall be questioned or accountable for any act past by them done, (or by any other by their procurement), relating unto the unhappy differences betwixt his majesty and parliament, they submitting themselves to reasonable and moderate composition for their estates, which the general, Sir Thomas Fairfax, shall really endeavour with the parliament, that it shall not exceed two years' value of any man's real estate respectively, and for personal, according to the ordinary rule, not exceeding the proportion aforesaid; which composition being made, they shall have indemnity for their persons, and enjoy their estates and all other immunities, without payment of any fifth or twentieth part, or any other taxes or impositions, except what shall be hereafter charged upon them in common with other subjects of this kingdom, by authority of parliament.

XIII. That all lords, knights, gentlemen, clergy, and chaplains, (excepted in the precedent articles), shall have liberty to go unto any of the king's garrisons, and to have a safe-conduct for themselves and servants, to go unto the parliament to obtain their composition for their estates, and indemnity for their persons.

XIV. That all horses, arms, money, and other goods whatsoever, taken as lawful prizes of war, before or during the siege, now in the city, be continued in the possession of the present possessors.

XV. That all officers, gentlemen, citizens, inhabitants, clergymen, chaplains, soldiers, and all other persons within the city, during the time of their making their composition, shall have free liberty either to inhabit within the same city, or shall have free liberty at any time to depart with their families, goods, and estates, unto any part of this kingdom in the parliament's quarters.

XVI. That all charters, customs, privileges, franchises, liberties, lands, estates, goods, and debts, of the mayor, aldermen, bailiff, commonalty, as a corporation, and all other corporations of the said city, shall be enjoyed by them, and that the ancient government thereof remain as formerly.

XVII. That if any persons or inhabitants which are comprised within these articles shall break any of them, that such breach shall only touch and concern such persons, and they to make such satisfaction for the same as the cause doth require.

XVIII. That all persons comprised within these articles shall have a certificate under the hand of his excellency Sir Thomas Fairfax, or the future governor of the city, that such persons were in the city at that time of the surrendering thereof, and are to have the benefit of these articles.

XIX. That his excellency Sir Thomas Fairfax give asssurance, that all officers and soldiers in the parliament's army, and all others under his command, shall duly and exactly observe all articles aforesaid; and that if they or any of them shall directly or indirectly violate or infringe the same, upon complaint thereof, justice may be done, and reparation made.

XX. That the inhabitants of the city shall be eased and freed from all free quarter or billet of soldiers, except in cases of urgent necessity, other than for lodging, and that to be ordered and disposed by the advice of the mayor or his deputy.

XXI. That no oath, covenant, protestation, or subscription (relating thereunto) shall be imposed upon any person whatsoever comprised within these articles, but only such as shall bind all persons aforesaid not to bear arms against the parliament of England now sitting at Westminster, nor wilfully do any act prejudicial unto their affairs.

XXII. That for the further and clearer understanding of the precedent articles, it is hereby declared that the true meaning of them is, that all persons comprised within these articles shall quietly and peaceably enjoy all their goods, debts, and movables during the space of four months next ensuing.

XXIII. That Mount Radford, and the ward in St Thomas parish, with the provisions of war thereunto belonging, be delivered unto His Excellency Sir Thomas Fairfax, or whom he shall appoint to receive them, in assurance of the performance of the precedent articles, to morrow by six of the clock in the afternoon, being the 7th of April; and that four such gentlemen or officers as his excellency shall approve of shall be delivered at the same time as hostages for the performance of the foregoing articles on the one part, and two hostages, such as Sir John Berkeley, knight, governor of the city of Excester shall approve of, and appoint to be received for performance on the other part.

XXIV. Lastly, that these articles be ratified and confirmed mutually by his excellency Sir Thomas Fairfax on the one part, and Sir John Berkeley, knight, governor of the city, on the other part.

I do hereby ratify and confirm the articles abovesaid, agreed on by the commissioners on my part.

THO. FAIRFAX. April 9, 1647.'

Source: J. Sprigg, *Anglia Rediviva*, (Oxford, 1854 edn), pp. 244–49

DOCUMENTS

Document 31: Description of Exeter's defences

This account was sent to London by a Parliamentary correspondent in April 1646. It is the fullest contemporary description of the city defences.

'Exeter is a verie strong place, and therefore the work is so much the greater, and the more praise to be given to God, for taking it without bloudshed. On the West side, Ex river runs all along without the wall, and compasseth in the Bonhayes and the Shelley like two Islands, and Crolditch is on the South-West, and workes and deep ditches made round about the City, which is walled round; on the West side is the South gate [sic, the writer clearly means *West* Gate], in the middle of the wall, made very strong, by which stands Alhallowes in the wall, and neere to Cliffe side (North of the West gate, or Mary Steps) is a mount in the wall, and two Towers on the South end of it. The North gate is a strong place like a little castle in the wall, and betweene that and the East gate is the castle which is also in the wall, in which is severall towers, and a deep moat about it, neere unto which is the East gate, and on the South thereof two mounts, neere to one of which is Bedford-house within the wall. The South gate is also verie strong, large, and high, which hath one tower upon the wall, and another within the City; and on the East of the gate are two mounts both in the wall which together with other strengths being considered we may wonder that the enemy were so easily perswaded to surrender.'

Source: WCSL, SB/EXE/1646/FAI, 'The Agreement for the Surrender of the City of Exeter'

Document 32: Provision for wounded Roundhead veterans, 1657–59

For many years after 1646, former soldiers who had been crippled during the Civil War remained a common sight on the streets of Exeter. During the Interregnum those who had been seriously wounded while fighting for the Parliament were entitled to a small pension. Sometimes the pensions proved inadequate, however, and impecunious veterans were forced to beg the county quarter sessions court for an increment, or, at the very least, an extraordinary, one-off payment (a 'special hardship grant' as it might be termed today). These documents illustrate the court's response to three such requests during the 1650s.

[1] 'Whereas it appeareth that Arthur Tucker of St Davids in Exon hath been active in the service of the Commonwealth under the command of Major Thomas Saundry, Captain James Richards and others, in which service he was wounded in his arm and [made] decrepit in his lyms . . . the [County] Treasurer [is] ordered to pay him 50s for his present releife.'

[2] 'Whereas Thomas Pearce of St Davids, a maymed souldier . . . hath 40s yearly for his maintenance allowed him, being very poor in misery & distres by reason of the severall wounds he received in the service of the State, which 40s is noe way able to relieve him, [it is] ordered that he shall have from henceforth 40s more, which the Treas[urer] . . . is to pay.'

[3] 'Whereas it appeareth that Richard Bettey of St Davids was a souldier in Lyme [Regis] under the comand of Collonell Thomas Ceely, Governour thereof, who in the tyme of his service received many dangerous wounds and is now impotent . . . the Treasurer [is] to forthwith pay 20s for his present maintenance.'

Source: WCSL, O.M. Moger (ed.), 'Devonshire Quarter Sessions Civil War Petitions', vol. 2, pp. 372, 377

Document 33: Petition of Jeffrey Downing, 1664–65

The Restoration of 1660 prompted a revolution in civic affairs at Exeter; as the old 'rebel' Chamber men were purged and a new set of ultra-Royalist councillors chosen to replace them. Prominent among this latter group was Allan Penny, who had served as a captain under Charles I and had been one of the mainstays of the Royalist cause in Exeter throughout the 1640s and 1650s. Penny was later elected mayor and during the year of his mayoralty several poverty-stricken former Royalist soldiers wrote to him begging for charity. One such plea is reproduced below; it helps to show the terrible condition to which many of the Civil War's victims were eventually reduced.

'To the right Worshippfull Allin Penney, Maior of the cittie of Exon.

The humble peticion of Jeffery Downing of the parish of St Lawrence.

Sheweth: That your poore peticioner have alwaies bine faithfully [sic] unto his Majesties service, and was a souldier under Captain Webber against the Seige of Lyme under your worshipps command, and in the tyme of warr have sufferd much imprisonment, soe that your peticioner with his famally is brought very low and in a sade and deplored condicion, have[ing] nothing for himselfe and famally to ly one but a bed of straw, and all that your peticioner can gett is but sufficient to provide meate and drinke, soe that without your worshipp be moved with compasion towards these obijects of pittye, his wife being a sickly woman and lame soe that she is not able to doe anything towards the maintenance of our famally [gap, 'we will perish'?], beseeching your worshipp if there be any money for pious uses in your worshipps custetie it may be extended to the releefe of your poore peticioners famally.

And as in all dutie ever bound to pray for your worshipps health heare and blest with eternall happines heareafter.'

Source: DRO, Petitions for Relief, File 4, No. 31

Document 34: Petition of Christopher Boast, 1664–65

Another petition to Mayor Penny from a former Royalist soldier who had fallen on hard times.

'To the Right Worshipfull Mr Alan Penye Esquire, Mayor of the Citty of Exon, with the Worshipfull the Aldermen of the same.

The humble peticon of Christopher Boast, weaver, of St Sidwells.

Sheweth: That your peticoner hath bin a laborious man in his vocation and hath had fyve children, and did serve most his tyme in the Armye of King Charles the first and now the times are soe hard and dead that your peticioner cannott gett any work to sett his hand to on his trade. Now the most humble request of your peticioner is that your worshipps wilbe pleased to commisserate his sad condicon and to extend your known and bountifull charity unto him that he may in some manner passe over this hard time and hee shalbe ever bound to pray for your worshipps wellfare & happines &c.'

Source: DRO, Petitions for Relief, File 4, No. 38.

Document 35: Petition of Valentine Bishop, (nd)

This concluding document, an undated petition to the Exeter Chamber, shows that the Civil War had proved ruinous even for many of those who had taken no part in the fighting. It is clear that poor Valentine Bishop never really recovered from the war-time demolition of his properties near the Magdalen Almshouses (in the city's southern suburbs). Reduced to gathering 'dung' in the streets, Bishop may perhaps stand as a symbol for all the many hundreds of humble Exeter men and women whose lives were shattered by the 'fiery trialls' of the Great Civil War.

'To the right Worshippfuls the Maior of this Cittye and the Aldermen, his Brethren.

The humble peticon of Vallentine Bishop of the parrish of Trinitye.

Sheweth your worshipps that your poore peticoner is a most misserable poore creature being of the Age of threescore yeeres & upwards, hath a long tyme gathered the Dung in the streets, hee being a weak creature and not able to doe as hee would, haveing a poore sickly woman to his wife, doth desire your worshipps that you would bee pleased to give him the graunt of one of those howses that is now building att Maudling. And your poore peticioner shall ever bee bound to pray for your worshipps long life here and everlasting in the world to come.

Your poore peticioner had two howses burnt hard by the Maudling when the cittye was beseeged, as he can prove by divers of the parrishners.'

Source: DRO, Petitions For Relief, File 3, No. 51

Tables

Table 1

Attendance at Pre-War Chamber Meetings
5 January 1636 to 16 August 1642

	1	2	3	4
Ignatius Jurdain	176	182	97%	[Died, 1640]
James Gould	232	245	95%	[Parliamentarian]
John Hakewill	230	245	94%	[Parliamentarian]
Thomas Crossing	227	245	93%	[Neutral?]
Richard Yeo	114	125	91%	[Neutral?]
Richard Saunders	206	245	84%	[Parliamentarian]
James White	281	538	4%	[Parliamentarian]
Joseph Trobridge	204	245	83%	[Parliamentarian?]
John Acland	95	117	81%	[Died, 1639]
Walter White	201	245	80%	[Parliamentarian]
Richard Crossing	55	70	79%	[Parliamentarian]
Adam Bennet	191	245	78%	[Parliamentarian]
John Cupper	186	245	76%	[Neutral/Royalist]
Phillip Crossing	36	48	75%	[Parliamentarian]
James Tucker	184	245	75%	[Parliamentarian]
Christopher Clerk	181	245	74%	[Parliamentarian]
John Martin	67	91	74%	[Royalist]
John Lynn	179	245	73%	[Royalist]
Roger Mallack	177	245	72%	[Neutral/Royalist]
Robert Walker	149	245	60%	[Royalist]
Hugh Crocker	141	245	58%	[Royalist]
Nicholas Spicer	119	245	49%	[Royalist]
John Colleton	19	48	40%	[Royalist]

KEY

Column 1: Total number of meetings which each councillor attended between 5 January 1636 and 16 August 1642.

Column 2: Maximum number of meetings which each councillor *could* have attended between 5 January 1636 and 16 August 1642 (taking into account appointments after 1636 and deaths before 1642).

Column 3: Figure in column one expressed as a percentage of the figure in column two (i.e. overall attendance record).

Column 4: Eventual wartime allegiance.

(NB. One member of the Chamber, Simon Snow, has not been included in the table. This is because he spent much of the period 1636-42 in London.)

Table 2

Attendance at 'Parliamentarian' Chamber Meetings 25 August 1642 to 28 August 1643

	1	2	3	4
Christopher Clerk	32	32	100%	[Parliamentarian]
Richard Crossing	32	32	100%	[Parliamentarian]
James Gould	32	32	100%	[Parliamentarian]
John Hakewill	31	32	97%	[Parliamentarian]
Walter White	31	32	97%	[Parliamentarian]
Richard Yeo	30	32	94%	[Neutral?]
Thomas Crossing	29	32	91%	[Neutral?]
James Tucker	29	32	91%	[Parliamentarian]
James White	29	32	91%	[Parliamentarian]
Richard Saunders	28	32	88%	[Parliamentarian]
Adam Bennet	27	32	84%	[Parliamentarian]
Phillip Crossing	26	32	81%	[Parliamentarian]
Joseph Trobridge	14	20	70%	[Parliamentarian?]
Roger Mallack	22	32	69%	[Neutral/Royalist]

TABLES

James Marshall	21	32	66%	[Parliamentarian]
John Cupper	21	32	66%	[Neutral/Royalist]
John Lovering	8	13	61%	[Parliamentarian]
Hugh Crocker	14	32	44%	[Royalist]
Nicholas Spicer	7	32	22%	[Royalist]
John Colleton	5	32	16%	[Royalist]
Robert Walker	2	32	6%	[Royalist]
John Martin	0	32	0%	(Royalist]

KEY
Column 1: Total number of meetings which each councillor attended between 25 August 1642 and 28 August 1643.

Column 2: Maximum number of meetings which each councillor *could* have attended between 25 August 1642 and 28 August 1643 (taking into account late appointments and deaths).

Column 3: Figure in column one expressed as a percentage of the figure in column two (i.e. overall attendance record).

Column 4: Wartime allegiance.

(NB. Two members of the Chamber, John Lynn and Simon Snow, have not been included in the table. This is because they spent much of the period 1642–43 in London.)

Table 3

Attendance at 'Royalist' Chamber Meetings 21 September 1643 to 1 April 1646

	1	2	3	4
John Cupper	68	68	100%	[Neutral/Royalist]
Thomas Crossing	27	27	100%	[Neutral?]
Roger Mallack	65	68	96%	[Neutral/Royalist]
Hugh Crocker	64	68	94%	[Royalist]

FROM DELIVERANCE TO DESTRUCTION

Robert Walker	61	68	90%	[Royalist]
Nicholas Spicer	58	68	85%	[Royalist]
Richard Yeo	56	68	82%	[Neutral?]
John Martin	53	68	78%	[Royalist]
John Colleton	43	68	63%	[Royalist]
Richard Crossing	13	68	19%	[Parliamentarian]
Phillip Crossing	12	68	18%	[Parliamentarian]
James Marshall	12	68	18%	[Parliamentarian]
Christopher Clerk	12	68	18%	[Parliamentarian]
John Hakewill	10	68	15%	[Parliamentarian]
Richard Saunders	8	68	12%	[Parliamentarian]
Walter White	4	68	6%	[Parliamentarian]
James Gould	3	68	4%	[Parliamentarian]
John Lovering	2	68	3%	[Parliamentarian]
Adam Bennet	1	68	1%	[Parliamentarian]

KEY

Column 1: Total number of meetings which each councillor attended between 21 September 1643 and 1 April 1646.

Column 2: Maximum number of meetings which each councillor *could* have attended between 21 September 1643 and 1 April 1646.

Column 3: Figure in column one expressed as a percentage of the figure in column two (i.e. overall attendance record.)

Column 4: Wartime allegiance.

(NB. Four long-established members of the Chamber—John Lynn, Simon Snow, James Tucker and James White—have not been included in the table. This is because the first two spent the entire period 1643–46 in London, and the last two died almost immediately after the Royalist take-over. The eight new Chamber men elected after September 1643—Christopher Broadridge, John Butler, Ralph Herman, Thomas Knott, John Lavers, John Parr, Alan Penny and Thomas Pitt—have also been excluded. As one might expect, all were regular attenders at council meetings, with the significant exception of Thomas Knott.)

Index

Aaron, brother of Moses, 187-88
Abbot, George, archbishop, 27
Acland, John, colonel, 195
Acland, John, councillor, 63
Alphington (Devon), 69, 84, 109, 111, 123-25, 128, 183, 195, 208
  Peamore House, 124, 128
Anabaptists, 165
'Anti-deliverancers', 50, 169-70
Antwerp (Netherlands), 32
Appledore (Devon), 200
Archepole, Margaret, widow, 208
arminianism, 31, 34-35, 45, 49-50, 51, 170
Array, commission of, 171, 177, 189
Ashburnham, Sir William, 181-83, 214
Axe, Matthew, dyer, 101
Axminster (Devon), 107

Bagster, Peter, captain, 64, 87, 180, 185, 190, 193
Baker, Alexander, priest, 30
Baker, Thomas, clergyman, 53-54, 57-58
Ball, Sir Peter, 89, 96, 123
Bamfield, Joseph, colonel, 84, 98, 198-99
Bampfield, Sir John, 202
Baramore, Lord, 171
Barnstaple (Devon), 93, 125, 200
Bartlet, John, clergyman, 18
Baskerville, Elizabeth, 19
Bastard, Otho, apprentice, 57
Bath (Somerset), 100
Bennett, Adam, alderman, 52, 63, 73, 88-89, 96, 140, 178, 180, 210
Berkeley, Sir Henry, 214
Berkeley, Sir John, 78, 91-92, 97-99, 101, 103-108, ch. 6 *passim*, 181-83, 196, 198, 200, 204, 211- 14, 218
Berwick (Northumberland), 165
Bettey, Richard, ex-soldier, 220
Bideford (Devon), 200

billeting, 16, 91, 102, 104, 112, 116
Billinge, Thomas, soldier, 16
Bishop, Valentine, scavenger, 221-22
Bishop's Clyst (Devon), 111-12
Bishop's Nympton (Devon), 177
Blight, William, gentleman, 64-65
Boaman, Roger, weaver, 189
Boast, Christopher, weaver, 221
Bond, John, barber, 189
Bond, John, preacher, 4, 43, 49-50, 53, 75, 86, 93-95, 168-69
Bourchier, Henry, fifth Earl of Bath, 59-62, 92, 173-74
Bovey Tracey (Devon), 120
Bradninch (Devon), 112, 195
Bridgwater (Somerset), 97, 102-103
Bristol (Somerset), 1-2, 67, 82, 99, 103, 105, 195, 196-97, 199-200
Broadclyst, (Devon), 51, 112, 115
  Culm John House, 131-33
Broadridge, Christopher, merchant, 102
Browning, Mark, innkeeper, 189
Brownscombe, Elizabeth, 26
Buller, John, colonel, 133
Buncombe, Robert, 103-104
Burnell, Lawrence, doctor, 73
Burnell, John, cleric, 54-55
Burnell, Margaret, 26
Burnell, —, Mrs, 193
Butler, John, councillor, 174

Carew, Sir Alexander, 197
Carey, Sir George, 214
Carey, Valentine, bishop, 31, 34
Carpenter, Giles, captain, 32
Carter, Robert, yeoman, 51
Carwithen, Nicholas, grocer, 55-58, 62
catholics and catholicism, 17-18, 20, 27-33, 51, 55-57, 60, 95, 166-68, 181, 189, 201, 208-09

227

Cave, Sir Richard, 84, 199
Ceely, Thomas, colonel, 111-12, 129, 220
Chambers, William, soldier, 138
Charles I, 16, 29-36, 38-40, 42-47, 56, 58-60, 96, 98-99, 102, 125, 165, 167, 170-71, 178, 212
Charles, Prince of Wales, 104-07, 119-20, 126-27, 129, 212
Cholwill, Mary, housewife, 132
Chudleigh (Devon), 119
Chudleigh, Sir George, 202
Chudleigh, James, colonel, 84, 197-98
Cleinck, Edward, barrel-bearer, 207
Clerk, Christopher, councillor, 66, 87-89, 182-84, 193-94, 210
Clerk, Samuel, committee-man, 96
cloth industry, 11-12, 45
Clyst, river, 111-12
Colebrooke (Devon), 57
Colleton, John, councillor, 62, 87-88, 140, 173-74
'Committee for Exeter', 96
'Committee for Safetie', 64-65, 85, 95-96, 170, 173-75, 185, 192
Comyns, Richard, porter, 39-42, 67, 71
Comyns, Elizabeth, housewife, 40-42
constables, 22, 24-25, 28-29, 35-36, 40-42, 52, 66-67, 90, 174
Coombe, William, fuller, 101
Cooze, John, committee-man, 174
Cooze, Ralph, gaoler, 90
Cornwall and the Cornish, 29, 68-70, 74, 76-77, 93, 97, 102, 117, 119-20, 123, 129, 134-35, 138, 177-78, 180, 190, 199
Cotton, Edward, archdeacon, 41
Cotton, William, bishop, 34
Couch, Anna, widow, 101
councillors, 14, 27, 35, 40, 44, 46-47, 49, 58, 60, 62-63, 72, 87-90, 96, 100, 131, 140-41, 172, 209
court, high commission, 165
court, sessions, 22-23, 25, 36, 42, 51, 54-55, 57-58, 65, 89, 100-101, 177-78, 188-89, 207-08
Courtney, Maria, spinster, 95
Courtney, Sir William, 195
Coventry, John, colonel, 129
Cowley (Devon), 70, 77, 98, 114, 185
Coxe, William, canon, 77, 189-91
Crediton (Devon), 70, 98, 109, 114-16, 118, 120, 130, 195
Crewkerne (Somerset), 168
Crocker, Sir Hugh, 62, 87-88, 92, 95, 98-99, 101, 131, 134, 140-41

Crocker, Samuel, captain, 95, 174
Cromwell, Oliver, 135
Cropredy Bridge, battle of, 101
Crosse, John, apprentice, 55-57
Crosses, —, smith, 186
Crossing, Philip, councillor, 88, 96, 140
Crossing, Richard, councillor, 47, 63, 73, 88, 96, 140, 174
Crossing, Thomas, alderman, 43, 63, 88-89
Crutchett, Honor, widow, 209-10
Crutchett, John, blacksmith, 210
Cullompton (Devon), 82, 112, 195
Culm, river, 111
Cupper, John, councillor, 88-89, 131, 180.

Dark, Johan, servant, 139
Darke, John, 42
Dartmouth (Devon), 56, 93, 115, 120-21, 196, 198, 205
Davye, Owen, barrel-bearer, 207
Dawlish (Devon), 123
Dean Prior (Devon), 16
Deane, —, captain, 117
demolition, 3, 77, 82, 108-09, 111, 136-39, 213, 222
Denmark, 170
disease, 3, 11, 15, 23-24, 30-31, 90, 111-12, 116
Dodderidge, —, judge, 196
Dorchester (Dorset), 197
Down, Mark, minister, 189
Down, —, lieutenant, 189, 191
Downing, Jeffrey, ex-soldier, 220
Drake, Sir Francis, 19

Edward the Confessor, 188
Edwards, Philip, watchman, 64
elections, 14, 25, 44, 46, 48, 52, 58, 66, 174, 180
Eles, Thomas, merchant, 95
Elizabeth I, 18
Elwill, John, 210
Essex, Earl of, 97-99, 171
Evans, J.T., 2
Evans, Richard, captain, 65, 96, 174
Exe, river, 7, 11-12, 15, 52, 69, 80-82, 109, 111-12, 116-17, 125, 127, 137, 185, 191, 196, 198, 219
Exeter, *passim*
  All-Hallows Goldsmith Street parish, 9, 12
  All-Hallows on the Wall parish, 11, 219
  Anchor Inn, 17
  St Anne's Chapel, 123, 136
  Bear Inn, 17, 61, 177, 189

INDEX

Bedford House, 91, 97, 99, 101, 131, 137, 219
Bell Inn, 17
Bishops' Palace, 137
Bonhay, 52, 102, 186, 219
Bradninch Battery, 206
Broad Gate, 9, 39-41, 84
Butcher Row, 11
Carfax, 9, 11-12
Castle, 7, 14, 32, 65, 132, 177-78, 185-86, 205, 207
Cathedral, 9, 14, 35-36, 43, 47, 53-57, 71, 74, 96, 171, 185, 187-88, 215
Cathedral Close, 9, 14-15, 27, 35, 39-41, 51, 63, 84, 186-87
Chamber, 14-15, 18-19, 21, 27, 29, 33-37, 42-44, 46, 49, 51-52, 56-61, ch. 4 *passim*, 86-92, 94, 96-98, 100, 102-04, 108, 116, 129, 131-32, 137-41, 165, 172-73, 176- 79, 181, 209, 220
City walls, 7, 11-12, 56, 64-65, 72, 74-75, 78, 83, 92, 128, 175-76, 179, 186-87, 219
Crolditch, 219
St Davids parish, 12, 83, 134, 136, 185, 220
Dean and Chapter, 14-15, 33-37, 40, 42-47, 49, 53, 55, 63, 65, 71, 74, 90, 92, 97, 99, 179
Duryard Wood, 175
East Gate, 7, 9, 11-12, 17, 65-66, 77, 83, 178-79, 186-87, 192, 201, 205, 219
St Edmonds parish, 12, 136-37, 194
Exebridge, 80, 82, 92, 118, 126, 129, 136, 185, 206
Fore Street, 11
Friernhay, 11
Great Conduit, 9, 11
Guildhall, 9, 14-16, 40-41, 64, 124, 137, 180, 185, 201
Head-weir, 185
High Street, 9, 11, 19, 84
Holy Trinity parish, 12, 136
Horsepool, 81, 206
St John's Bow parish, 11, 17, 192
St John's hospital, 103
St Kerrian parish, 12
King's Arms Inn, 17
St Lawrence parish, 9, 58, 220
Little Conduit, 9
Longbrook Valley, 7
Magdalen almshouses, 222
St Martins parish, 12
St Mary Arches parish, 12, 18-19, 25, 34, 47, 53, 57-58, 167-68
St Mary Major parish, 53-54, 57, 187, 189
St Mary Steps parish, 12, 97, 102, 136, 219
Mount Radford, 83, 109, 129, 134, 185, 196, 218
New Inn, 59, 76
North Gate, 7, 12, 178, 206, 219
North Street, 9, 11
Northernhay, 175
St Olaves parish, 12
Paris Street, 186
St Petrocks parish, 12, 18, 97, 102
Quay Battery, 206
Quay Gate, 7, 137
Quay Lane, 180
Rock Lane, 16
Shilhay, 219
St Sidwells fee, 14
St Sidwells parish, 9, 12, 35-36, 47, 77, 123, 136, 169, 186, 221
Snail Tower, 206
South Gate, 7, 9, 11-12, 65, 137, 179, 187, 193, 199, 206, 219
South Street, 9, 16-17, 189
Southernhay, 83, 92, 102, 186
Stepcote Hill, 11, 82
St Stephens fee, 14
St Stephens parish, 9, 12
'Underground passages', 9, 65, 77, 179, 186
West Gate, 7, 11, 16-17, 64, 81-82, 84, 137, 178, 206, 219
Workhouse, 15
Wynards almshouses, 186
Exminster (Devon), 118
Exmouth (Devon), 81, 123, 128-29

Fairfax, Sir Thomas, 102, 108, ch. 6 *passim*, 210-18
Fitzgerald, —, captain, 214
Flanders, 106
Ford, Thomas, committee-man, 174
Forde, William, preacher, 18
Fox, Rebecca, spinster, 208
France, 16, 30-31, 106, 115, 170, 173
freemen, 14, 46, 48
Frowde, Philip, colonel, 99, 101
Fulford, Thomas, colonel, 195

Gibbons, Edward, 73-74
Gilbert, Francis, clerk, 41-42
Gill, John, committee-man, 174
Glyde, William, chandler, 67
Godolphin, —, colonel, 214

Goring, Lord George, 104-108, 114-15
Gould, James, councillor, 63, 88, 96, 140, 173-74, 180
Grenville, Sir Richard, 114
Grynkyn, Robert, watchmaker, 189
Gunpowder Plot, 27
Guernsey, 19-20
Gyles, Francis, gentleman, 177-78

Hague, the (Netherlands), 173
Hakewill, John, councillor, 63, 75, 88-89, 173-74, 210
Hall, George, archdeacon, 65, 178-79
Hall, Jane, vagrant, 23
Hall, Joseph, bishop, 34, 36, 165-66
Hammond, Thomas, colonel, 111-12, 121, 123-24, 135, 214
Hampshire, 91
Hampton Court, 56
Hance, Hugh, brewer, 50
Hancocke, Jeremy, tapster, 189
Harley, Edward, colonel, 214
Hastings, Mr Henry, 171
Hawkyns, Jonathan, cutler, 66-67, 179
Hayne, Marie, spinster, 208
Hazard, John, preacher, 18
Heavitree (Devon), 16, 82, 130, 193-94
Helliar, Nicholas, gentleman, 30
Helston (Cornwall), 134, 215
Helyer, William, archdeacon, 43, 73-74
Henrietta, princess, 215
Henrietta Maria, queen consort to Charles I, 30, 96-97
Herbert, —, colonel, 129
Herrick, Robert, poet, 16-17
Hill, Thomas, husbandman, 177-78
Hogenberg, Remegius, 7
Holland, 106, 173
Holmes, William, committee-man, 174
Honiton (Devon), 107, 112
Hooper, Able, weaver, 178
Hoppyn, John, bailiff, 35
Hopton, Sir Ralph, 68-72, 74, 78, 114, 127, 180-83, 189, 198
Hore, Robert, watchman, 64
Hotham, Sir John, 171
Howell, Roger, 1
Hoyle, James, clerk, 194
Hoyle, William, son of above, 194
Hughes, George, preacher, 75, 86
Hull (Yorkshire), 40, 171
Hunks, Sir Fulk, 129
Hutchinson, William, canon, 72-74
Hyward, Able, lieutenant, 70

iconoclasm, 47, 49, 51, 53, 72, 166-67, 187-88
Ide (Devon), 69
Inwardleigh (Devon), 75
Ireland and the Irish, 53, 57, 60, 168, 170-71
Isaac, Samuel, town-clerk, 74, 96, 174

Jagoe, Nicholas, tailor, 57
James I, 27-30, 50, 178
Jeffries, Ursula, 95
Jynkyns, Richard, soldier, 16
Jurdain, Ignatius, alderman, ch. 2 *passim*, 38-43, 47, 50, 55-56, 59, 62, 86, 141, 172
justices of the peace, 22-23, 25-28, 36, 39, 48, 50, 51-58, 60-61, 89, 93-95, 139, 172, 177, 204, 207

Kellye, Richard, innkeeper, 178
Kelway, Thomas, soldier, 139
Kennycott, Nicholas, weaver, 93
Knott, Thomas, councillor, 131-32, 174, 214

Lambert, —, colonel, 214
Langport, battle of, 102, 104
Laud, William, archbishop, 31, 34, 49, 166
Launceston (Cornwall), 104, 177-78
Laurence, Edward, bailiff, 103-104
Lancashire, 28, 170
Leach, George, brewer, 136-37
lectures, 18, 52, 58, 168-69
Leicestershire, 171
Lenthall, William, speaker of the House of Commons, 165
St Leonards (Devon), 193-94
London, 21, 26, 30, 32, 40, 43, 45, 47, 53, 56, 58, 63-64, 72, 74-75, 80, 87-88, 95-96, 105-06, 166, 171, 174, 177, 191, 195, 197, 219
  Goldsmiths' Hall, 74
  St Pauls, 45
  Tower of, 166
Lostwithiel (Cornwall), 99
Lovering, John, councillor, 88, 96, 140, 174
Lyme (Dorset), 19-20, 97, 99, 128, 220
Lynn, John, councillor, 88-89, 174.

MacCaffrey, Wallace, 1, 14
Macey, George, grocer, 57-58
Mallack, Roger, councillor, 88-89, 95, 131
Mamhead (Devon), 123
Manton, John, clergyman, 18
Marshall, James, councillor, 58, 88, 140
Marston Moor, battle of, 97, 101
Martin, John, councillor, 88

INDEX

Martin, Sir Nicholas, 202
Massey, Edward, major-general, 112
Matthews, —, Mr, 193
Matthews, —, Mrs, 193
Maurice, Prince, 82-87, 91, 97-99, 198-201, 204-05
Mico, John, clergyman, 18
militia, 14, 65, 75, 89, 101, 170, 176-77, 186
Minshall, Thomas, gentleman, 53, 55
Moore, Adrian, weaver, 52
Morris, Marie, servant, 207-08
Mortimore, John, constable, 41
Moses, 187-88
Muddyforde, John, councillor, 27
Munster (Ireland), 171
Musgrove, Lord, 171

Naseby, battle of, 102
'neutralism', 1-3, 59, 61, 67, 83-84, 87-89
New Model Army, 102-03, 107-08, ch. 6 *passim*
Newark (Nottinghamshire), 101
Newcastle (Northumberland), 1, 47, 100
Newton St Cyres (Devon), 109, 120, 130
Nichols, Ferdinando, cleric, 25-26
Northcott, Sir John, 80, 202
Norwich (Norfolk), 1-2
Nutwell House (Devon), 116-17

oaths, , 57, 71, 93-95, 103, 166-69, 180-81, 192-94, 201, 203, 208-09, 210-11, 215
Okehampton (Devon), 97-98, 108, 117
Orchard, Thomas, gentleman, 186-87
Ottery St Mary (Devon), 112, 114-16
Oxford, 90, 92, 96, 99, 101, 107, 123, 134, 205, 215

Pafford, Henry, servant, 41
Painter, Henry, preacher, 18, 52-53, 57-58, 75-76, 86
Paris (France), 173
Parliament, members of, 14, 19, 25, 46, 48-49, 61, 76, 88, 96
Pearce, Thomas, ex-soldier, 220
Peck, —, Mr, 26
Pennington, Donald, 3
Penny, Alan, councillor, 103, 220-21
Penny, John, alderman, 47-48, 51-52, 57, 165
Peterson, William, Dean, 35-36
petitions, 56-59, 77, 170
Phipps, Robert, Mr, 102
Pince, John, fuller, 51
Piper, —, lieutenant colonel, 119

Plymouth (Devon), 56, 69, 76, 103, 196, 198, 208-09
Poltimore (Devon), 107, 111-12, 115, 133, 214
Porter, Agnes, 25
Porter, Stephen, 3
Potter, George, merchant, 106
poverty and the poor, 11-14, 21, 24, 45-46, 92, 180, 219-22
Powderham (Devon), 81, 116-18, 123, 128, 185
preaching, 5, 9, 18, 20, 30-31, 43, 49-50, 59, 75, 168-70, 171-73, 185, 192, 202
Prigge, Henry, draper, 84-85, 87, 95, 174
propaganda, 60-61, 68, 70, 87, 106, 171, 177-78, 187, 195-97, 203-05
prostitution, 17, 25, 48
Prowse, John, councillor, 27
punishments, 15-16, 22, 48-49, 187
puritans and puritanism, 18, ch. 2 *passim*, 38-39, 42-44, 46-52, 54-55, 57, 58, 62-63, 66-67, 75-77, 86, 94, 135, 141, 165, 167, 172, 208-09
Pym, Alexander, captain, 66-67, 70
Pym, John, MP, 56

Quashe, Andrew, 207-08

Rainsborough, Thomas, colonel, 112
Raleigh, Sir Walter, 19
Ratcliffe, Jasper, 210
Rewe (Devon), 112
Reymes, Bullen, colonel, 129
Rhe, Isle de, 16
Richards, James, captain, 220
riots, 12, 40-42, 51, 66-67, 166
Robertes, Rebecca, 25
Robyns, Elizabeth, 101
Rodes, —, Mr, 186
Rolle, Sir Samuel, 202
Rose-Troup, Frances, 25
Rosser, Richard, yeoman, 177-78
Rowcliffe, Henry, notary, 55
Roy, Ian, 3
Rupert, Prince, 82, 97, 101, 204
Ruthen, William, colonel, 69, 71-72

Salt Ash (Cornwall), 178
Salter, Anthony, doctor, 186
Saunders, Richard, councillor, 42, 52, 63-64, 73, 76, 88-89, 140, 166
Saundry, Thomas, major, 220
Scotland and the Scots, 38-40, 43-45, 47, 49-50, 69, 97, 165-66, 168, 208-09
Semor, —, colonel, 193

231

Shapcott, —, colonel, 130
Sherwood, Robert, surveyor, 7, 9, 17
Silverton (Devon), 109, 195
Smyth, George, 41
Snape, Edmund, preacher, 18
Snowe, Simon, councillor, 48, 88
Somerset, 66, 171
Sowden, John, 51
Spain and the Spanish, 29, 32
Spanish Match, the, 34
Spicer, Nicholas, councillor, 62, 87-89, 99-102, 140
Sports, book of, 28-29, 33
sports and games, 17, 22-23, 25, 28-29, 52
Sprague, John, constable, 52
Stamford, Earl of, ch. 4, *passim*, 90, 187, 189-90, 192-94, 197-202
Stane, —, commissary, 214
Stannaries, the, 44
Stapeldon, Lewis, weaver, 58
Star Chamber, court of, 27, 43
Starcross (Devon), 81
Stoke Canon (Devon), 108, 111-12, 185
Stone, —, widow, 16
Stratton, battle of, 77, 189, 197-98
Sussex, 16
Sutcliffe, Matthew, Dean, 34-35

Taunton (Somerset), 26, 99, 102
Tavistock (Devon), 56, 68, 75, 120
taxation, 3, 68, 72-74, 91-92, 102, 196
Tayler, William, cordwainer, 57
St Thomas (Devon), 12, 18, 76, 80-82, 108, 118, 120, 125, 128, 136, 185, 194-95
   Barley House, 124-25, 128
   Bowhill House, 125
   Bridewell, 125-26, 136
   Cowick Street, 125-26
   Exwick Mills, 125
   Hayes Barton, 82
   'Hunkses Fort', 126, 134, 218
   Marsh House, 125
   West Indies Inn, 76, 80
Tiverton (Devon), 82, 97, 112, 116, 195
Topsham (Devon), 69, 73, 78, 81, 96, 109, 111, 125, 185, 191, 195, 199
Tothill House (Devon), 124
Totnes (Devon), 56, 121
Trescott, Thomas, preacher, 59-60, 75, 172
Trivett, John, skinner, 138
Trivett, Julian, 138
Trobridge, Joseph, councillor, 63

Tucker, Arthur, ex-soldier, 220
Tucker, James, alderman, 43-44, 46, 48, 88-89, 173-74, 180
Tucker, John, clerk, 53-54

Underdown, David, 2-3

Vaughan, Nicholas, captain, 15, 175
Vigures, John, cordwainer, 51, 53.

Wagstaffe, Joseph, major-general, 117
Walker, Robert, councillor, 44-46, 48, 50, 59, 62, 87-88, 95-96, 101, 131-32, 140-41, 165, 214
Walker, Thomas, councillor, 27, 50
Waller, Sir Hardress, 116, 118, 128-30, 214
Waller, Sir William, 198, 207-08
Walplate, Susanna, Mrs, 95
Warwick, Earl of, 80-82, 197-98
watchmen, 39, 56, 59, 63-64, 66-67, 173-76, 179-80, 185, 187
Watson, —, major, 214
Way, John, tanner, 208
Way, Margaret, wife of above, 208
Webber, —, captain, 220
Welden, —, colonel, 129
Wentworth, Thomas, Earl of Strafford, 166
Were, John, counsellor 132, 214
Westminster, 49
Wexford (Ireland), 171
Weymouth (Dorset), 197, 205
White, James, councillor, 49, 63, 88, 165-66, 170, 174
White, Walter, councillor, 63, 66, 88, 140, 180, 194
Whitestone (Devon), 120
Whynell, John, clergyman, 90, 192-94
Willes, —, Mr, 178
Wilson, Aaron, doctor, 74
Windsor (Berkshire), 202
witchcraft, 16
Wix, —, captain, 127
women, 9, 11, 15-16, 23, 25-26, 40-42, 77, 95, 101, 121, 132, 134, 138-39, 185, 192-94, 207-08

Yeo, Richard, councillor, 63, 88-89, 174
York, 1, 58, 170-71

Zeager, Simon, fuller, 60
Zion, 169

Milton Keynes UK
Ingram Content Group UK Ltd.
UKHW021447141223
434365UK00034B/523